a publication of

think Outside the SOX

PUBLISHER Alexis Yiorgos Xenakis

EDITOR Elaine Rowley

MANAGING EDITOR Karen Bright

TECHNICAL EDITOR Rick Mondragon

INSTRUCTION EDITOR Sandi Rosner

INSTRUCTION PROOFERS Ginger Smith, Karen Weiberg

EDITORIAL COORDINATORS Kristi Miller, Sue Nelson

ART DIRECTOR Natalie Sorenson

PHOTOGRAPHER Alexis Yiorgos Xenakis

STYLIST Natalie Sorenson

ASSISTANT TO THE PUBLISHER Lisa Mannes

CHIEF EXECUTIVE OFFICER Benjamin Levisay

DIRECTOR, PUBLISHING SERVICES David Xenakis

TECHNICAL ILLUSTRATOR Carol Skallerud

PRODUCTION DIRECTOR & COLOR SPECIALIST Dennis Pearson

BOOK PRODUCTION MANAGER Greg Hoogeveen

MARKETING MANAGER Lisa Mannes

BOOKS DISTRIBUTION Mavis Smith

MIS Jason Bittner

ISBN 13: 9781933064185

Produced in Sioux Falls,
South Dakota by XRX, Inc.
PO Box 965
Sioux Falls, SD
57101-0965
USA

605.338.2450

Visit us online — knittinguniverse.com

# think Outside the SOX

Photography by Alexis Xenakis

# the sox

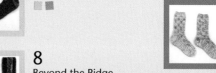

classic

holes in my socks

playing with color

outside the box

twist & turn

gallery

 **4** Forgettable Socks

 **6** Dreamin' of Tulips

 **8** Beyond the Ridge

 **10** Salt Water Taffy

 **12** Split Reed

 **14** Outside Sox

 **16** Classy Crochet

 **20** Hopscotch

 **22** Hester's Socks

 **24** Branched Fern

 **26** Button-up Socks

 **28** Girl's Best Friend

 **31** In the Peaceful Forest

 **34** Lace Me Up Kilt Hose

 **36** Rough Weather

 **38** Apple of My Eyelet

 **40** High Country Sunrise

 **42** Wandering Vine

 **46** Interlochen Cables

 **48** Luck O' the Irish

 **50** Ruby Slippers

 **52** Celtic Pride Kilt Hose

 **55** Shylo Socks

 **58** Bees & Blossoms

 **61** Sea Foam & Shells

 **64** Find Your Way Home

 **66** Twisted Mosaic

## Gallery 162

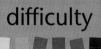

# Welcome

"*We were completely smitten when someone veered off in a direction no one had ever gone before. Initially, they started from something we recognized, but then took it in many directions. We were like detectives tracking it: so they did this, ...and then they had to figure that out...*"
— Cat Bordhi

think outside the **SOX**

"There were exquisite socks that did
not win prizes, but won our hearts."
— Lucy Neatby

"Some socks are like people—you walk into a room, and there
are some people that immediately catch your attention, they
are the stars of the show. And there are others that you really
need to sit next to, spend some time with, because their
charms are a little more subtle."
— Sandi Rosner

Contest judges Cat Bordhi, Lucy Neatby, and Sandi Rosner with all 296 pairs of socks at STITCHES West.

# Anatomy & Construction of SOX

When **SocksSocksSocks** was published in 1999, nearly all of the socks were knit from the cuff down on double-pointed needles. Anything else was an aberration. Well, things have changed. Nearly a third of the socks featured in this book are knit from the toe up. Almost half are worked with either one or two circular needles. Each approach has its benefits and a loyal cadre of practitioners.

Throughout this book, the designer's choice of needle technique and direction of knitting have been respected. As you use these patterns, or embark on your own sock adventure, it is helpful to have a working knowledge of all the options.

## Working with 3 double-pointed needles (DPNS)

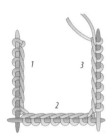 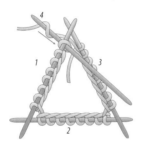

Cast stitches onto 1 dpn.
**1** Rearrange stitches on 3 dpns. Check carefully that stitches are not twisted around a dpn or between dpns before beginning to work in rounds.

**2** With a 4th dpn, work all stitches from first dpn. Use that empty dpn to work the stitches from the 2nd dpn. Use that empty dpn to work the stitches from the 3rd dpn— one round completed. Notice that you work with only 2 dpns at a time. As you work the first few rounds, be careful that the stitches do not twist between the needles.

## Working with 4 double-pointed needles (DPNS)

Arrange the stitches on 4 needles and knit with the fifth.

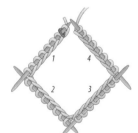 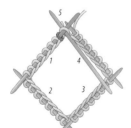 

### Toe up or Top down?
While some ethnic knitting traditions feature socks worked from the toe up, British and American knitters have usually started at the cuff and worked their way down to the toe. Why reverse this tried and true method? In a word, frugality. Avid sock knitters tend to have lots of little bits and pieces left over when the socks are done. Working from the toe up lets you use every yard of yarn, because the length of the leg is determined by how much yarn you have. You can keep knitting until you have just enough left for the cuff.

While you may prefer one direction over the other, try both. Stitch patterns can look dramatically different when viewed upside down, and you may find that working in the reverse direction gives you just the look you want.

### One, Two, Four, or Five?
Socks and other small tubular shapes can be knit with one or two circular needles, or four or five double-pointed needles. In most cases, you can easily convert a pattern from one needle style to another. Try them all and choose your favorite.

### Double-pointed needles
Before technology enabled the mass production of high quality circular needles, double-pointed needles were the standard. They come in varying materials and lengths and in sets of 4 or 5 needles. To work with double-pointed needles, cast your stitches onto 1 needle. Distribute the stitches over 3 or 4 needles as described in your pattern.

Join to work in the round, taking care that stitches do not twist around or between needles. You will only work with 2 needles at a time; the others hold the stitches until you are ready for them. Use the empty fourth or fifth needle to work the stitches from the first needle, then use the now empty-needle to work the stitches from the second needle, and so on.

## Two circular needles

When working with two circular needles, remember that each needle holds a specific portion of stitches and only that needle is used to work those stitches. It's helpful to use needles with different colored tips, say gold and silver. You will work stitches from gold point to the other gold point and work stitches from silver point to the other silver point; unless directed otherwise. The gold needle holds the instep and front leg stitches, and will be used to knit those stitches, while the silver needle dangles from the heel and back leg stitches. A complete round includes working the stitches from both needles, so you would do the same with the silver needle to knit the sole, heel, and back leg stitches while the gold needle is at rest. The patterns refer to the needles as Needle 1 and Needle 2. While many authors recommend 24" long needles be used for this technique, your needles can be of any length.

## One circular needle – The Magic Loop

The technique of using one long circular needle to work a small tube was dubbed "The Magic Loop" when a booklet by that name was written by Bev Galeskas and Sarah Hauschka in 2002.

The Magic Loop requires a long circular needle, 36" or longer, with a flexible cable connecting the points. After casting on the required number of stitches, the stitches are divided in half, and a loop of needle cable is pulled out between the groups. The first group of stitches is moved to the nearest needle point and worked with the other point. This group is now moved to the needle

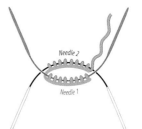 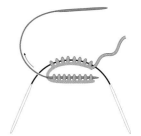

*1* Cast on the total number of stitches onto Needle 1, then separate them evenly onto 2 needles.

*2* Slide the first needle to the left, placing stitches onto point of needle.

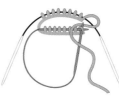 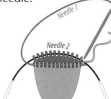

*3* With other end of same needle, work across (being careful not to twist first row).

*4* Repeat Steps 2 and 3 for 2nd needle to finish round. Repeat Steps 2 through 4 for all rounds.

cable, the second group is moved to the point and is worked. If you stop in the middle of working a group, you'll have a large loop sticking out on either side of your knitting.

Patterns designed for the Magic Loop technique will use Needle 1 and Needle 2 to refer to the groups of stitches, even though only one circular needle is in use.

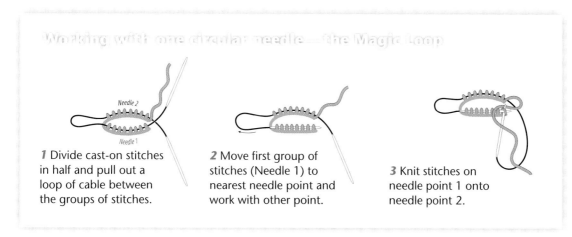

*1* Divide cast-on stitches in half and pull out a loop of cable between the groups of stitches.

*2* Move first group of stitches (Needle 1) to nearest needle point and work with other point.

*3* Knit stitches on needle point 1 onto needle point 2.

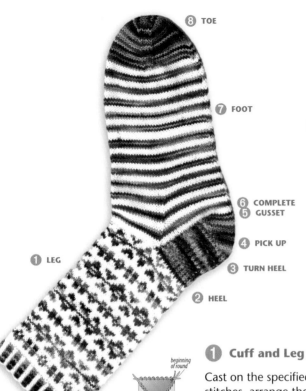

① LEG

② HEEL

③ TURN HEEL

④ PICK UP

⑤ GUSSET

⑥ COMPLETE

⑦ FOOT

⑧ TOE

# 8 Steps to Sock Success

Most socks are simply tubes with shaped heels and toes. Our overview of a basic sock takes you through the process step by step. While you'll find many variations and embellishments on this basic framework throughout this book, spend a moment to familiarize yourself with these steps to help you get the lay of the land.

## ① Cuff and Leg

Cast on the specified number of stitches, arrange them on double-pointed or circular needles, and join to work in the round. You may find that the yarn tail from your cast-on is a sufficient indication of the beginning of the round, but if you want to use a marker, use a removable marker attached to the knitting. Work the cuff and leg of your sock as directed.

*beginning of round*

## ② Heel Flap

The flap for the back of the heel is worked back and forth in rows, usually over half the original number of stitches. The remaining stitches will become the instep and top of the foot —they wait on needles or on a holder while the heel is worked.

## ③ Turn Heel

Continuing on the heel stitches, work back and forth in short rows to form the triangular or semi-circular piece which curves the flap around the back of your heel and puts the bend in your sock. Each short row goes only part way across a row, then turns back, leaving some unworked stitches. Each short row gets a little longer, until all the stitches have been worked.

## ④ Pick up Gusset Stitches

Pick up and knit stitches down the side of your heel flap (usually 1 stitch for every 2 rows). Knit across the instep stitches. Pick up and knit stitches up the other side of the heel flap.

## ⑤ Resume Working in the Round

*beginning of round*

Your beginning of round is usually at the center of the heel, but your pattern may vary.

## ⑥ Shape Gussets

Begin working down the foot, decreasing before and after the instep stitches, usually every other row, until you are back to your original stitch count.

## ⑦ Foot

Work even until the sock is long enough to reach the base of the big toe—usually 2" less than the finished length.

## ⑧ Toe

Decrease stitches to shape the toe, usually 4 stitches every other round, though your pattern may vary. Finish and close the toe as directed in your pattern.

# Other Considerations

**Yarns** A wide variety of yarns were used in these socks—a few were spun or dyed by the knitters, others are commercial yarns, and a few may no longer be available. In the instructions, yarns are described by yardage and weight: Super Fine, Fine, Light, or Medium. See page 179 for helpful information on yarn substitution if needed and desired.

**Techniques and abbreviations** See pages 168–179 for an explanation of techniques and abbreviations used.

**Sizing** The main adjustment required for most socks is the foot length. Most toe shapings add approximately 2" to the length of the foot, so adjust the foot length of the sock accordingly. A few patterns are written for several sizes or give suggestions for sizing.

**Stitch patterns** Once you understand the construction of a sock, you can begin to consider stitch or color patterns. Often the patterning is interrupted by the heel and continues only on the top of the foot. Comfort and wear is a consideration for the heel, bottom of foot, and toe—smooth, uniform stitch patterns are best. Socks give many people an opportunity to work pattern stitches in the round—even things they may not have thought possible, such as entrelac and intarsia.

**Heel stitch** Most heels are worked with a chain-stitch selvage (slipping the first stitch of every row) to make picking up the gusset stitches easier. Many heels are also worked in a slip stitch pattern that adds padding and durability.

# Adapting Patterns to Your Preference

Most patterns can easily be worked on the needle style of your choice.

| If the pattern calls for... | And you want to work with... | Do this... |
| --- | --- | --- |
| Double-pointed needles | 2 circular needles | Use one needle for the back of leg/heel/sole stitches and the other for the top of foot/front of leg stitches. |
| Double-pointed needles | The Magic Loop | Arrange the back of leg/heel/sole stitches together in one group and the top of foot/front of leg stitches together in the other group. |
| 2 Circular needles | The Magic Loop | Place the Needle 1 stitches in one group and the Needle 2 stitches in the other group. |
| 2 Circular needles | Double-pointed needles | Divide the back of leg/heel/sole stitches over 2 needles. The top of foot/front of leg stitches can be grouped on 1 needle or divided over 2 needles. |
| The Magic Loop | 2 circular needles | No change needed—place the Needle 1 stitches on one needle and the Needle 2 stitches on the other. |
| The Magic Loop | Double-pointed needles | Divide the back of leg/heel/sole stitches over 2 needles. The top of foot/front of leg stitches can be grouped on 1 or 2 needles. |

Classic

easy+

Adult M
**A** 8"
**B** 9½"

10cm/4"

32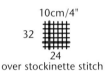

24

over stockinette stitch

1 2 **3** 4 5 6

Light weight
**A** 125 yds
**B** 125 yds

Five 3.5mm/US 4
or size to obtain gauge

**&**

cable needle (cn)

Shown in
*COLINETTE* Cadenza in
color Whirley Fig (A) and
Elephants Daydream (B)

Leena Siikaniemi     Ilmajoki, Finland

## PINK SOCK

### Leg
Using tubular cast-on and A, cast on 48 stitches. Arrange 12 stitches on each of 4 needles. Join to work in the round. Work in k1, p1 rib for 4".
Maintain rib on Needles 1 & 4 and work Needles 2 & 3 as follows: *Rounds 1 & 3* **Needle 2** Rib 7, k5; **Needle 3** k4, rib 8. *Rounds 2 & 4* **Needle 2** Rib 7, p5; **Needle 3** p4, rib 8. *Rounds 5 & 7* **Needle 2** Rib 3, k9; **Needle 3** k8, rib 4. *Rounds 6 & 8* **Needle 2** Rib 3, p9; **Needle 3** p8, rib 4. *Rounds 9 & 11* Knit. *Rounds 10 & 12* Purl.

### Heel flap
*Next row* K12, turn. *Next row* P24. Work back and forth on these 24 stitches for heel. Place remaining 24 stitches (Needles 2 & 3) on hold for instep. *Row 1* (RS) Sl 1, knit to end. *Row 2* (WS) Sl 1, purl to end. *Row 3* *Sl 1, k1; repeat from*. *Row 4* Sl 1, purl to end. Repeat last 4 rows 4 more times, then work Rows 1 & 2 once.

### Turn heel
*Row 1* (RS) K15, SSK, k1, turn. *Row 2* Sl 1, p**7**, p2tog, p1, turn. *Row 3* Sl 1, k**8**, SSK, k1, turn. *Row 4* Sl 1, p**9**, p2tog, p1, turn. *Row 5* Sl 1, k**10**, SSK, turn. *Row 6* Sl 1, p**10**, p2tog, turn. Repeat last 2 rows 3 more times—12 stitches. *Row 13* Sl 1, k11.

### Gussets
*Set-up* Pick up and k12 along left side of heel flap. Replace instep stitches on 2 needles and k24. With another needle, pick up and k12 along right side of heel flap, then knit 6 heel stitches—

60 stitches. Slip remaining 6 heel stitches to next needle; beginning of round is at center of heel. *Round 1* **Needle 1** K6, p10, p2tog; **Needles 2 & 3** purl; **Needle 4** p2tog, p10, k6. *Rounds 2 & 4* Knit. *Round 3* **Needle 1** K6, p11; **Needles 2 & 3** purl; **Needle 4** p11, k6. On following rounds, knit stitches on Needles 1 & 4 and work Needles 2 & 3 as follows: * *Round 5* **Needle 2** P2tog, purl to end; **Needle 3** purl to last 2 stitches, p2tog. *Rounds 6 & 8* Knit. *Round 7* **Needles 2 & 3** Purl. Repeat from* 4 more times—48 stitches. Arrange 12 stitches each on Needles 1 & 3 and 24 stitches on Needle 2, with beginning of round at center of sole.

### Foot
Knit stitches on Needles 1 & 3 and work Needle 2 as follows: *Round 1* K7, p10, k7. *Rounds 2 & 4* Knit. *Round 3* K9, p6, k9. *Round 5* K9, p1, k4, p1, k9. *Rounds 6, 8, 10, 12* Knit. *Round 7* K9, p1, sl 2 sts to cn and hold to back, k2, k2 from cn, p1, k9. *Round 9* K9, p1, k4, p1, k9. *Round 11* K9, p6, k9. Work even in stockinette stitch for 1½", or until foot is 2" less than desired length.

### Toe
*Next round* [K4, k2tog] 8 times—40 stitches. Work 4 rounds even. *Next round* [K3, k2tog] 8 times—32 stitches. Work 3 rounds even. *Next round* [K2, k2tog] 8 times—24 stitches. Work 2 rounds even. *Next round* [K1, k2tog] 8 times—16 stitches. Knit 1 round. *Next round* [K2tog] 8 times—8 stitches. Cut yarn, draw through remaining stitches, pull tight and fasten off.

## NOTES
*1 See page 168 for any unfamiliar techniques. **2** Sock is worked cuff down on double-pointed needles.*

## GREEN SOCK

### Leg

Using tubular cast-on and B, cast on 48 stitches. Arrange 12 stitches on each of 4 needles and join to work in the round. Work in k2, p2 rib for 4". Maintaining rib on Needles 1 & 4, work Needles 2 & 3 as follows:

*Next 2 rounds* **Needle 2** Rib 6, p6; **Needle 3** p6, rib 6. *Next 2 rounds* **Needle 2** Rib 6, k6; **Needle 3** k6, rib 6. *Next 2 rounds* **Needle 2** Rib 2, p10; **Needle 3** p10, rib 2. *Next 2 rounds* **Needle 2** Rib 2, k10; **Needle 3** k10, rib 2. *Next 2 rounds* **Needles 2 & 3** Purl.

### Heel flap & turn heel

Work as Pink Sock EXCEPT on heel flap, do not work Rows 3 & 4, repeat Rows 1 & 2 eleven more times.

### Gussets

Set up as for Pink Sock. Knit 1 round. * *Next 2 rounds* Work Rounds 1 & 3 of Pink Sock. *Next 2 rounds* Knit. *Next round* **Needle 1** Knit; **Needle 2** p2tog, purl to end; **Needle 3** purl to last 2 stitches, p2tog; **Needle 4** knit. *Next round* **Needle 1** Knit; **Needles 2 & 3** purl; **Needle 4** knit. Repeat from * 4 more times—48 stitches. Rearrange on 3 needles as for Pink Sock.

### Foot

Knit stitches on Needles 1 & 3 and work Needle 2 as follows: *Next 2 rounds* K7, p10, k7. *Next 2 rounds* Knit. *Next 2 rounds* K9, p6, k9. Work even in stockinette stitch for 2¼" or until foot is about 2" less than desired length.

### Toe

Work as for Pink Sock.

*easy +*

Adult S
**A** 7"
**B** 8"

10cm/4"

48
34

over stockinette stitch

 2 3 4 5 6

Super Fine weight

**A** 50 yds
**B–G** 25 yds each
**H** 150 yds

Four 2.5mm/US 1½,
or size to obtain gauge

Shown in
*DREAM IN COLOR* Smooshy
in Blue Lagoon (A), Cool Fire
(B), Giant Peach (C), Strange
Harvest (D), Spring Tickle
(E), Happy Forest (F), Some
Summer Sky (G), and Visual
Purple (H)

# Dreamin' of Tulips

*Lynn Bunjevcevic*   Newmarket, Ontario, Canada

## Cuff

With A, cast on 60 stitches. Arrange 18 stitches on Needle 1, 24 stitches on Needle 2, and 18 stitches on Needle 3. Join to work in the round. Knit 4 rounds. Change to B and work in k1, p1 rib for 8 rounds.

## Leg

*Next round* With C, *p1, k1; repeat from*. Knit 7 rounds. Repeat last 8 rounds with D, then with E, F, G, and H.

## Heel flap

Slip last 2 stitches on Needle 1 to Needle 2. Slip first 2 stitches on Needle 3 to Needle 2. Divide the 28 stitches from Needle 2 onto 2 needles for instep. With Needle 3, knit stitches from Needle 1—32 stitches for heel. Cut yarn. Work back and forth on Needle 3 as follows: *Row 1* (WS) With A, k1, p14, p2tog, p14, k1—31 stitches. *Row 2* (RS) [K1, sl 1] to last stitch, k1. *Row 3* K1, purl to last stitch, k1. *Row 4* K1, [k1, sl 1] to last 2 stitches, k2. *Row 5* Repeat Row 3. Repeat Rows 2–5 until flap measures 2½", end with RS row.

## Turn heel

*Row 1* (WS) P15, p2tog, p1, turn. *Row 2* K3, SSK, k1, turn. *Row 3* P**4**, p2tog, p1, turn. *Row 4* K**5**, SSK, k1, turn. *Row 5* P**6**, p2tog, p1, turn. Continue to work 1 more stitch before decrease every row, end k**15**, SSK, turn—16 stitches. Cut yarn.

## Gussets

Move instep stitches to one needle. With RS facing, join H to heel stitches and with spare dpn, k8. With Needle 1, k8, then pick up and k20 along side of heel flap; with Needle 2, knit 28 instep stitches; with Needle 3, pick up and k20 along side of heel flap, then k8 from spare needle—84 stitches; beginning of round is at center of heel. *Round 1* **Needle 1** Knit to last 3 stitches, k2tog, k1; **Needle 2** knit; **Needle 3** k1, SSK, knit to end of round. *Round 2* Knit. Repeat last 2 rounds 11 more times—60 stitches.

## Foot

Work even in stockinette stitch until foot measures 6½" from back of heel, or 1½" less than desired length. Cut yarn.

## Toe

*Round 1* **Needle 1** With A, knit to last 3 sts, k2tog, k1; **Needle 2** k1, SSK, knit to last 3 stitches, k2tog, k1; **Needle 3** k1, SSK, knit to end of round. *Round 2* Knit. Repeat last 2 rounds 8 times more—24 stitches.

## Finishing

With Needle 3, knit stitches from Needle 1. Graft toe.

## NOTES

*1 See page 168 for any unfamiliar techniques. 2 Sock is worked cuff down on double-pointed needles. 3 These socks were designed to use yarn left over from making a baby sweater. Since only small amounts of most colors are needed, this project is a great stash buster. Arrange your leftover sock yarns in a sequence that pleases you.*

**easy +**

Adult M
**A** 8"
**B** 8"

10cm/4"

52

36

over stockinette stitch

 **1** 2 3 4 5 6

Super Fine weight
**MC** 350 yds
**CC** 125 yds

Five 2.25mm/US 1,
or size to obtain gauge

**&**

Yarn needle

Shown in
*CHERRY TREE HILL YARN*
Supersock Solids in Cherry
(MC) and *CLAUDIA HAND
PAINTED YARN* Fingering in
Tropicana (CC)

# Beyond the Ridge

*Rebecca Aldrich Bowen*    *Saint Augustine, Florida*

## RIGHT SOCK

### Leg

With CC, cast on 42 stitches, leaving an 18" tail. *Next 3 rows* *K2, p1; repeat from*. *Begin Chart A* Work Rows 1–12, then work Rows 1–7. With MC, work Chart B until there are 31 ridges on RS. Cut yarn. Using the tail from the cast-on, graft the live stitches from the needle to the WS of the first row of Chart B.

With MC, beginning under the flap of rib, pick up and knit 72 stitches around leg (approximately 3 stitch for every 2 rows)—18 stitches on each of 4 dpn. Leave the flap free. Work 6 rounds in stockinette stitch.

### Heel flap

*1st row* K4, turn. *Next row* P30. Work back and forth on these 30 stitches for heel. Arrange remaining 42 stitches on 2 dpn for instep. Join CC, but do not cut MC. With CC, knit 4 rows. Cut CC. With MC, work 28 rows in stockinette stitch.

### Heel turn

*Row 1* With MC, k15; cut MC; join CC and k2, k2tog, k1, turn. *Row 2* Sl 1, p5, SSP, p1, turn. Note that there are gaps where the work is turned. *Row 3* Sl 1, knit to 1 stitch before the gap, k2tog, k1, turn. *Row 4* Sl 1, purl to 1 stitch before the gap, SSP, p1, turn. Repeat last 2 rows until all heel flap stitches have been worked—18 stitches remain. Cut CC; join MC.

### Gussets and instep

With MC, k9. With a free dpn, k9, then pick up and k17 down side of heel flap and 1 in corner before instep (Needle 1). Knit the 42 instep stitches (Needles 2 & 3). With a free dpn, pick up and k1 in corner after instep stitches, and k17 up side of heel flap, then knit 9 heel stitches (Needle 4)—96 stitches.

*Round 1* Knit. *Round 2* **Needle 1** Knit to last 3 stitches, k2tog, k1; **Needles 2 & 3** knit; **Needle 4** k1, SSK, knit to end. Repeat last 2 rounds 11 more times—72 stitches remain.

**Chart A**

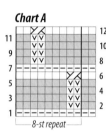

8-st repeat

**Chart B**

4 sts

### Color key

□ CC
▨ MC

### Stitch key

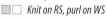

▨□ *Knit on RS, purl on WS*

– *Purl on RS, knit on WS*

V *Sl 1 purlwise with yarn on WS*

✕ *1/1 RT K2tog, leaving stitches on needle; insert right needle between stitches just worked and knit first stitch again; slip both stitches off needle.*

## NOTES

*1 See page 168 for any unfamiliar techniques. 2 The leg of the sock is worked from side to side as a flat piece then joined into a tube. Stitches are picked up from one end of the tube for the heel and foot of the sock.*

## Foot

Work even in stockinette stitch until foot measures 5¾" from back of heel, or 2¼" shorter than desired length. With CC, knit 1 round, purl 1 round. *Next 2 rounds* With MC, [k3, sl 1] to end. With CC, knit 1 round, purl 1 round.

## Toe

*Decrease round* [K10, k2tog] around. Working 1 fewer stitch before k2tog every time, work decrease round every 3rd round 3 times, every other round 3 times, then every round 3 times. *Next round* [K2tog] around—6 stitches. Cut yarn, draw through remaining stitches, pull tight and fasten off.

## LEFT SOCK

Work same as right sock EXCEPT:

## Leg

Do not cut yarn after working Chart B AND use it to pick up the 72 stitches.

## Heel flap

*1st row* K26, turn.

Adult M
**A** 7"
**B** 9"

10cm/4"

52  
36
over stockinette stitch

 2 3 4 5 6

Super Fine weight
**A & B** 200 yds each

Five 2.25mm/US 1,
or size to obtain gauge

**&**

Waste yarn, spare dpn,
yarn needle

Shown in
*SWTC* Tofutsies in Two Step
(A) and Four Leaf Toever (B)

**Color key**
▨ A (RS)   ▢ A (WS)
▢ B

⁗⁗⁗ *live stitches*
〰〰 *picked-up stitches*
── *joined edge*
→ *direction of work*

# Salt Water Taffy

*Mary Tanti   Saltspring Island, British Columbia, Canada*

Divide A and B each into 2 balls (A1 and A2, B1 and B2).

## Cuff
Using a temporary cast-on and waste yarn, cast on 48 stitches. With A, knit 1 row. Turn and work base triangles as follows:
*Row 1* (RS) K2, turn. *Row 2* Sl 1, p**1**, turn.
*Row 3* Sl 1, k**2**, turn. *Row 4* Sl 1, p**2**, turn.
*Row 5* Sl 1, k**3**, turn. *Row 6* Sl 1, p**3**, turn.
*Row 7* Sl 1, k**4**, turn. *Row 8* Sl 1, p**4**, turn.
*Row 9* Sl 1, k**5**, turn. *Row 10* Sl 1, p**5**, turn.
*Row 11* Sl 1, k**7**, turn. *Row 12* Sl 1, p**1**, turn.
Repeat Rows 3–12 six more times, then repeat Rows 3–10 once. *Last row* Sl 1, k5 —
8 triangles. Arrange stitches to work in the round with 2 triangles on each of 4 needles.

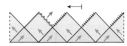

*Tier 2* Work rectangles with WS facing, joining to live stitches of same Tier 2 rectangles.

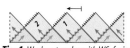

*Tier 1* Work rectangles with WS facing

Work Base Triangles

*TIER 1* With WS facing, join B to tip of any triangle. *Pick up and p5 down free edge of triangle. Pick up 1 more stitch and knit it together with first stitch from adjoining triangle. Turn. *Rows 1, 3, 5, 7, & 9* Sl 1, k5, turn. *Rows 2, 4, 6, & 8* Sl 1, p4, p2tog (last stitch with next stitch of triangle). *Row 10* Sl 1, p4, p2tog, do not turn. Repeat from* 7 more times—8 rectangles. Cut B.

*TIER 2* With WS facing, join A to bottom of any rectangle. *Pick up and p5 up free edge of rectangle. Purl first stitch from top of same rectangle. Turn. *Rows 1, 3, 5, 7, & 9* Sl 1, k5, turn. *Rows 2, 4, 6, & 8* Sl 1, p4, p2tog (last stitch with next stitch at top of same rectangle). *Row 10* Sl 1, p4, p2tog, do not turn. Repeat from* 7 more times. Cut A.

*TIER 3* With B, work same as Tier 2 EXCEPT do not cut B.

## NOTES
*1 See page 168 for any unfamiliar techniques. 2 Socks are worked cuff down on double-pointed needles.*
*3 Wind a small ball of yarn (about 20 grams, or 100 yds) from each skein. You will work the cuff with the skeins only, and work the leg and foot with both the skein and the separate ball of yarn.*

Remove waste yarn and place stitches from cast-on on a spare needle; hold behind work. Knit 1 round, knitting each stitch from final row of rectangles together with corresponding cast-on stitch. AT SAME TIME, increase 16 stitches evenly around—64 stitches. Purl 1 round.

## Leg

Arrange 16 stitches on each of 4 needles. *Set up spiral stripe* **Needle 1** (N1) K16 with B1; **Needle 2** (N2) k16 with B2 ; **Needle 3** (N3) k16 with A1; **Needle 4** (N4) k16 with A2. Return to N4; using A1 from end of N3, k14, sl 2. Return to N3; using B2 from end of N2, k16. Continue on to N4 and k12, sl 4. Return to N2; using B1 from end of N1, k16. Continue on to N3 and k16. Continue on to N4 and k10, sl 6.

*Spiral stripe* Beginning with N1 and A2, k56, sl 6. Pick up the leading strand of yarn and k56, sl 6. Continue as established, being careful not to twist yarns, until 44 rounds are complete (11 stripes of each color), or desired length to top of heel. End with yarns between N3 and N4, working final round with skein B.

## Heel flap

*Set up* Slip first stitch of N2 to N1. Heel flap is worked back and forth on 33 stitches on N4 and N1 with A2 and B2; leave A1 and B1 attached and place 31 stitches on N2 and N3 on hold for instep. *Row 1* K33 A, turn. *Row 2* Sl 1, k31 A, p1 B. *Row 3* Sl 1, k32 B. *Row 4* Sl 1, k31 B, p1 A. For rest of heel on RS rows, weave color not in use along WS for additional reinforcement. *Row 5* (RS) With A, sl 1, k2, [sl 1, k1] 13 times, sl 1, k3. *Row 6* Sl 1, k2 A, [p1 B, p1 A] 13 times, p1 B, k2 A, p1 B. *Row 7* With B, sl 1, k3, [sl 1, k1] 13 times, k3. *Row 8* Sl 1, k2 B, [p1 B, p1 A] 13 times, p1 B, k2 B, p1 A. Repeat Rows 5–8 seven more times, then repeat Rows 5 and 6 once.

## Turn heel

*Row 1* (RS) With B, sl 1, k20, SSK, k1, turn. *Row 2* Sl 1, p**10**, p2tog, p1 A, turn. *Row 3* With A, sl 1, k**11**, SSK, k1, turn. *Row 4* Sl 1, p**12**, p2tog, p1 B, turn. *Row 5* With B, sl 1, k**13**, SSK, k1, turn. Continue as established, alternating 2 rows B and 2 rows A, and working 1 more stitch before decreases every row until *Row 12* Sl 1, p**19**, p2tog, turn. Cut both yarns.

## Gussets

Return to beginning of heel flap. With B, pick up and k1 in corner, then 20 stitches up side of heel flap; knit 21 heel stitches, marking center stitch for center of sole; pick up and k21 down side of heel flap and 1 stitch in corner, wrap next stitch and turn work. With yarn to WS, slip first instep stitch. Bring yarn to RS and slip instep stitch back to its original needle. Turn work.

*Next row* (WS) P1 and move this stitch to instep needle, p2tog, purl to last 2 stitches before instep, p2tog—93 stitches, 32 on instep, 61 on heel. Turn. Resume working in the round and continue Spiral stripe. *Round 1 and all odd-numbered rounds* Knit. *Rounds 2–26* **Heel** K1, SSK, knit to last 3, k2tog, k1; **Instep** knit—67 stitches after Round 26. *Round 28* K1, SSK, k14, SSK, k13, k2tog, k1—64 stitches. Knit 3 rounds. Work even in Spiral pattern until foot measures 8" from back of heel, or 1½" less than desired length. End with A1 and A2 at beginning of heel/sole stitches and B1 and B2 at beginning of instep stitches. Place markers at beginning of instep stitches and beginning of sole stitches.

## Toe

*Decrease round* K1, SSK, knit to 3 before marker, k2tog, k1, slip marker, k1, SSK, knit to 3 before marker, k2tog, k1. Work Decrease round every other round until 36 stitches remain, end with A1 and A2 at beginning of instep stitches, and B1 and B2 at beginning of sole stitches. Decreasing as established, work 2 rows of A across instep and 1 row of B across sole—32 stitches. Arrange 16 instep stitches on one needle and 16 sole stitches on another. With B, graft toe.

*easy+*

Adult M
**A** 8"
**B** 10"

10cm/4"

48 / 36

over stockinette stitch

1 2 **3** 4 5 6

Light weight
400 yds

Five 2.25mm/US 1,
or size to obtain gauge

Shown in
*MOUNTAIN COLORS*
Bearfoot in Mountain
Twilight

# Split Reed

Joseph L. Rogers    Casper, Wyoming

## Cuff
Use Twisted Long-tail Cast-on to cast on 64 stitches. Arrange 16 stitches on each of 4 needles. Join to work in the round. Work in k2, p2 rib for 2½". *Next round* [K2, p2, k1, knit in front and back of stitch (kf&b), p2, k2, p2, k1, kf&b, p2] 4 times—72 stitches. *Next round* [K2, p2, k2, p3] 8 times. Purl 1 round.

## Leg
*Begin Chart A* Work Rounds 1–12 four times, then Rounds 1–7 once.

## Heel flap
Knit 36. Work back and forth on these stitches for heel. Leave remaining 36 stitches on hold for instep. Purl 1 row. Work 4 rows of Chart B 9 times.

## Turn heel
*Note* Slip first stitch of rows knitwise on RS rows and purlwise on WS rows. *Row 1*(RS) K22, turn. *Row 2* (WS) Sl 1, p**7**, turn. *Row 3* Sl 1, k**8**, turn. *Row 4* Sl 1, p**9**, turn. *Row 5* Sl 1, k**10**, turn. Continue to work 1 more stitch before turning on every row, until *Row 12* Sl 1, p**17**, turn. *Row 13* Sl 1, k14, SSK, k2, turn. *Row 14* Sl 1, p14, p2tog, p2, turn. Repeat last 2 rows 8 times more—18 stitches.

## Gussets
*Next row* With a spare needle, k9; **Needle 1** k9, then pick up and k20 along side of heel flap; **Needles 2 & 3** knit across instep stitches; **Needle 4** pick up and k20 along side of heel flap, then k9 from spare needle—94 sts; beginning of round is at center of heel.

*Round 1* **Needle 1** Knit; **Needles 2 & 3** continue in chart pattern as established; **Needle 4** knit. *Round 2* **Needle 1** Knit to last 3 stitches, k2tog, k1; **Needles 2 & 3** continue chart pattern; **Needle 4** k1, SSK, knit to end of round. Repeat last 2 rounds until 72 stitches remain.

## Foot
Work even in stockinette stitch and chart pattern as established until foot measures approximately 8" from back of heel, or 2" less than desired length, end with Round 2 or 8 of chart.

## Toe
*Round 1, decrease round* **Needle 1** Knit to last 4 stitches, SSK, k2; **Needle 2** k2, k2tog, knit to end of needle; **Needle 3** knit to last 4 stitches, SSK, k2; **Needle 4** k2, k2tog, knit to end of round. *Rounds 2–4* Knit. *Round 5* Repeat decrease round. *Rounds 6 & 7* Knit. *Rounds 8–10* Repeat Rounds 5–7. *Round 11* Repeat decrease round. *Round 12* Knit. *Rounds 13–16* Repeat Rounds 11 & 12 twice more. Work decrease round every round until 16 stitches remain. *Next round* K2tog around—8 stitches.

Cut yarn, draw through remaining stitches, pull tight, and fasten off.

## NOTES
*1 See page 168 for any unfamiliar techniques. 2 Sock is worked cuff down on double-pointed needles.*

12

**Chart A**

12
11
10
9
8
7
6
5
4
3
2
1

└─6-st repeat─┘

**Chart B**

4
2

3
1

14x

**Stitch key**

☐ Knit on RS, purl on WS
▨ Purl RS, knit on WS
Ⓥ Sl as if to knit with yarn to WS
Ⓥ Sl as if to purl with yarn to RS
Ⓥ Sl as if to purl with yarn to WS

Adult M
**A** 7"
**B** 8½"

10cm/4"

28 ▦

24

over k2, p2 rib with A
and larger needles

10cm/4"

44 ▦

32

over stockinette stitch with
B and smaller needles

1 2 3 **4** 5 6

Medium weight
**A** 180 yds

**1** 2 3 4 5 6

Super Fine weight
**B** 300 yds

✕

4.5mm/US 7 or size to
obtain gauge

✕✕

Four 4.5mm/US 7

Four 2.75mm/US 2 or size to
obtain gauge

**&**

2 sport zippers 7"/18cm long

Sewing thread to match,
yarn needle

Shown in
*BERROCO* Jasper in Mochica
Blue (A) and *ARAUCANIA*
Ranco in Denim (B)

# Outside Sox

*Julie Gaddy*    San Antonio, Texas

## Cuff
With A and straight needles, loosely cast on 48 stitches. *Row 1* (RS) K1, [p2, k2] to last 3 stitches, p2, slip 1 purlwise with yarn in front (sl 1 wyif). *Row 2* K3, [p2, k2] to last stitch, sl 1 wyif. Continue in k2, p2 rib for 6½", end with Row 2, purling the last stitch instead of slipping it.

## Leg
With RS facing, change to larger double-pointed needles (dpn) and join to work in the round as follows: **Needle 1** K1, p2, [k2, p2] 3 times; **Needle 2** [k2, p2] 4 times; **Needle 3** [k2, p2] 4 times, k1; slip last stitch from Needle 3 to Needle 1 — 16 stitches on each needle. Work in k2, p2 rib until 13" from cast-on. *Next round* With smaller dpn and B, [k1, kf&b, k2] to end — 60 stitches. Knit for 1½".

## Divide for heel
**Right sock** K30 and place on hold for instep; knit remaining stitches onto one dpn for heel; turn.
**Left sock** K30 onto one dpn for heel; place remaining stitches on hold for instep; turn.

## Heel
Work back and forth on heel stitches: *Row 1* (WS) Slip 1 with yarn to WS (sl 1), purl to end of row. *Row 2* [Sl 1, k1] around. Repeat last 2 rows 14 more times.

## Turn heel
*Row 1* Sl 1, p**16**, p2tog, p1, turn. *Row 2* Sl 1, k**5**, k2tog, k1, turn. *Row 3* Sl 1, p**6**, p2tog, p1, turn. *Row 4* Sl 1, k**7**, k2tog, k1, turn. *Row 5* Sl 1, p**8**, p2tog, p1, turn. Continue working 1 stitch more before decrease every row; end sl 1, k**15**, k2tog, k1 — 18 stitches remain.

## Gussets
With a free dpn, pick up and k19 down side of heel. Move instep stitches to 1 dpn and, with a free dpn, knit across. With a free dpn, pick up and k19 up side of heel, then knit 9 heel stitches. Slide remaining 9 heel stitches to beginning of 1st dpn — 86 stitches, beginning of round is at center heel. *Round 1* Knit. *Round 2* **Needle 1** Knit to last 3 stitches, k2tog, k1; **Needle 2** knit; **Needle 3** k1, SSK, knit to end. Repeat last 2 rounds 12 more times — 60 stitches.

## Foot
Work even until foot measures 6½" from back of heel, or 2" less than desired length.

## NOTES
*1 See page 168 for any unfamiliar techniques. 2 Sock is worked cuff down, first back and forth on straight needles, then around on double-pointed needles.* *3 See inserting zipper on page 179.*

## Toe

*Round 1* **Needle 1** Knit to last 3 stitches, k2tog, k1; **Needle 2** k1, SSK, knit to last 3 stitches, k2tog, k1; *Needle 3* k1, SSK, knit to end. *Round 2* Knit. Repeat last 2 rounds 7 more times, then work Round 1 twice—20 stitches remain. Knit the stitches on Needle 1 and move them to Needle 3. Cut yarn, leaving an 18" tail. Graft toe.

## Zippers

Wash zippers to pre-shrink. With RS of sock facing, pin zipper into position with teeth exposed between open edges of cuff. Use sewing thread to sew zipper in place by hand or machine. When cuff is turned down, tape is concealed.

*easy +*

Adult S
**A** 7"
**B** 8"

10cm/4"

40
32

over stockinette stitch

1 2 **3** 4 5 6

Light weight
300 yds

Five 2.25mm/US 1,
or size to obtain gauge

3.25mm/US D-3

**&**

2 buttons ¾"
(18mm) square

Shown in
*MOUNTAIN COLORS*
Bearfoot Granite Peak

**Chart**          **Stitch key**

|   | ⌄ | 4 |          ☐ *Knit*
|   | ⌄ | 3 |          ▨ *Purl*
|   |   | 2 |          ☑ *Sl 1 wyib*
|   |   | 1 |          ☒ *Sl 1 wyif*

*2-st repeat*

# Classy Crochet

*Pamela J. Whyte*     *Beaverton, Oregon*

## Cuff
Cast on 60 stitches. Work back and forth in garter stitch (knit every row) for 24 rows (12 ridges).

## Leg
Arrange 14 stitches on Needle 1, 16 stitches on Needles 2 and 3, and 14 stitches on Needle 4. Join to work in the round. *Round 1* Purl. *Begin Chart.* Work Chart pattern until piece measures approximately 3½" from beginning, end with Row 4.

## Heel Flap
Knit stitches on Needle 1 and slip them to Needle 4. Needle 4 now holds 28 heel stitches; Needles 2 & 3 each hold 16 instep stitches. Work back and forth on heel stitches. *Row 1* (WS) Sl 1, purl to end. *Row 2* [Sl 1, k1] around. Repeat last 2 rows 13 more times.

## Turn Heel
*Row 1* (WS) Sl 1, p14, p2tog, p1, turn. *Row 2* Sl 1, k4, SSK, k1, turn. *Row 3* Sl 1, p5, p2tog, p1, turn. *Row 4* Sl 1, k**6**, SSK, k1, turn. *Row 5* Sl 1, p**7**, p2tog, p1, turn. Continue working 1 more stitch before decrease every row until *Row 12* Sl 1, k**14**, SSK, k1—16 stitches.

## Gussets
Continuing with heel needle, pick up and k14 along left side of heel flap. With another needle, knit instep stitches (Row 1 of Chart pattern). With another needle, pick up and k14 along right side of heel flap, then k8—76 stitches; beginning of round is at center of heel. Arrange stitches with 22 stitches on Needle 1, 16 stitches each on Needles 2 & 3, and 22 stitches on Needle 4. *Round 1* **Needle 1** Knit to last 3 stitches, k2tog, k1 **Needles 2 & 3** continue Chart pattern; **Needle 4** k1, SSK, knit to end. *Round 2* **Needle 1** Knit; **Needles 2 & 3** Chart pattern; **Needle 4** knit. Repeat last 2 rounds 7 more times—60 stitches.

## Foot
Work even in stockinette stitch and Chart pattern as established until foot measures 6" from back of heel, or 2" less than desired length.

## Toe
Move first stitch from Needle 2 to end of Needle 1; move last stitch from Needle 3 to beginning of Needle 4—15 stitches on each needle. *Round 1* [Knit to last 3 stitches on needle, k2tog, k1; k1, SSK, knit to end of needle] 2 times. *Round 2* Knit. Repeat last 2 rounds 6 more times, then Round 1 six times—8 stitches remain. Move stitches from Needle 2 to Needle 1 and from Needle 4 to Needle 3. Graft toe.

## NOTES
*1 See page 168 for any unfamiliar techniques. 2 Sock is worked cuff down on double-pointed needles.*

## Finishing
### Shell edging

With RS facing and crochet hook, join yarn to base of cuff V-opening. Work 6 double crochet (dc) into edge stitch 4 ridges above side of V; single crochet (sc) into edge stitch 4 ridges above. Work 9 dc into corner stitch. *Skip 2 stitches and sc in next stitch, skip 2 stitches and 6 dc in next stitch; repeat from* to next corner. Work 9 dc in corner. Work sc into edge stitch 4 ridges below, work 6 dc into edge stitch 4 ridges below, work slip stitch at bottom of V. Fasten off. Sew button to cuff 1½" from edge.

# Holes

**intermediate**

Adult M
**A** 8"
**B** 9"

10cm/4"

50  34

over stockinette stitch

**1** 2 3 4 5 6

Super Fine weight
400 yds

Five 2.25mm/US 1,
or size to obtain gauge

Shown in
*PAGEWOOD FARM*
Chugiak in Lilac

# Hopscotch

*Lisa Swanson*   Minneapolis, Minnesota

## Cuff
Cast on 72 stitches. Arrange 18 stitches on each of 4 needles. Join to work in the round. Work in k2, p2 rib for 1".

## Leg
*Begin Chart* *Work Rounds 1–4 three times, then work Rounds 13–16 three times. Repeat from* twice more.

## Heel flap
With Needle 4, knit stitches on Needle 1. Work back and forth on these 36 stitches for heel flap. *Row 1* (WS) P36. *Row 2* (RS) [Sl 1, k1] around. *Row 3* Sl 1, purl to end of row. Repeat last 2 rows 17 more times.

## Turn heel
*Row 1*(RS) Sl 1, k19, SSK, k1, turn. *Row 2* Sl 1, p5, p2tog, p1, turn. *Row 3* Sl 1, k6, SSK, k1, turn. *Row 4* Sl 1, p7, p2tog, p1, turn. *Row 5* Sl 1, k8, SSK, k1, turn. Continue working 1 more stitch before decrease (SSK or p2tog) every row, end sl 1, p**17**, p2tog, p1, turn—20 stitches.

## Gussets
With a spare needle, k10. With Needle 1, k10, then pick up and k19 stitches along side of heel flap; with Needles 2 & 3 continue chart pattern; with Needle 4, pick up and k19 stitches along side of heel flap, then k10 from spare needle—94 stitches; beginning of round is at center heel.

*Round 1* **Needle 1** Knit to last 3 stitches, k2tog, k1; **Needles 2 & 3** continue chart pattern; **Needle 4** k1, SSK, knit to end. *Round 2* **Needle 1** Knit; **Needles 2 & 3** continue chart pattern; **Needle 4** knit. Repeat last 2 rounds until 72 stitches remain.

## Foot
Work even in stockinette stitch on Needles 1 & 4 and continue chart pattern on Needles 2 & 3 until foot measures approximately 7" from back of heel or 2" less than desired length, end with Round 4 or 16 of chart.

**Chart**

16
15 3x
14
13
4
3
2 3x
1

*18-st repeat*

**Stitch key**
☐ Knit
▧ Purl
◉ Yarn over (yo)
✓ K2tog

## NOTE
*1 See page 168 for any unfamiliar techniques. 2 Sock is worked cuff down on double-pointed needles.*

## Toe

*Round 1* **Needle 1** Knit to last 3 stitches, k2tog, k1; **Needle 2** k1, SSK, k1, *k2tog, yo; repeat from*; **Needle 3** *k2tog, yo; repeat from* to last 4 stitches, k1, k2tog, k1; **Needle 4** k1, SSK, knit to end. *Round 2* Knit. *Rounds 3 & 5* **Needle 1** Knit to last 3 stitches, k2tog, k1; **Needle 2** k1, SSK, knit to end; **Needle 3** knit to last 3 stitches, k2tog, k1; **Needle 4** k1, SSK, knit to end. *Rounds 4 & 6* Knit. Repeat Rounds 1–6 twice more, then repeat Rounds 3 and 6 once—28 stitches.

## Finishing

With Needle 4, knit stitches from Needle 1. Slip stitches from Needle 2 onto Needle 3. Graft toe.

*intermediate*

Adult L
**A** 8½"
**B** 9½"

10cm/4"

38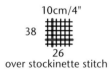

26

over stockinette stitch

1 **2** 3 4 5 6
Fine weight
375 yds

Four 3.75mm/US 5
or size to obtain gauge

**&**

Stitch markers
Small amount smooth
waste yarn

Shown in
Handspun 3-ply Shetland
wool undyed

# Hester's Socks

## Christine Kurk    Red Lion, Pennsylvania

### Twined Knitting
*Knit row* With strand 1, k1; *bring strand 2 over strand 1 and k1; bring strand 1 over strand 2 and knit; repeat from*. *Purl row* With strand 1, p1, *bring strand 2 under strand 1 and p1, bring strand 1 under strand 2 and p1; repeat from*.

### Leg
Using temporary cast-on, cast on 60 stitches. Arrange 20 stitches on each of 3 needles. Join to work in the round. *Round 1* [K8, p2] around. *Begin Chart* Repeat Rounds 1–4 thirteen times, then work Rounds 1 & 2 once more.

### Heel flap
Begin working in Twined Knitting. *Next row* K24; place next 30 stitches on hold for instep. Turn work and work back and forth on remaining 30 stitches for heel. *Row 1* (WS) Sl 1, purl to end. *Row 2* Sl 1, knit to end. Repeat last 2 rows 8 more times, then work Row 1 once.

### Turn heel
*Row 1* (RS) K21, SSK, k1, turn. *Row 2* Sl 1, p11, p2tog, p1, turn. *Row 3* Sl 1, k11, SSK, k1, turn. Repeat last 2 rows 6 more times, then work Row 2 once—14 stitches.

### Gussets
Knit 14 heel stitches. With another needle, pick up and k20 sts along left side of heel flap. With another needle work across instep stitches: k1, place marker (pm), k3, p2, work Row 3 of Chart twice, k4. With another needle, pick up and k20 along right side of heel flap

(Needle 3)—84 stitches. *Next round* Knit to marker, k4, p2, continue chart pattern, k24. *Decrease round* Knit to 2 stitches before marker, k2tog, k3, p2, continue chart pattern, k3, p2, SSK, knit to end. Repeat last 2 rounds 11 more times—60 stitches.

### Foot
Work even in patterns as established until foot measures 7½" from back of heel, or 2" less than desired length, end with Row 2 of Chart.

### Toe
Work toe in Twined Knitting EXCEPT final round, shaping as follows: *Round 1* [K1, SSK, k24, k2tog, k1, pm] twice—56 stitches. *Round 2* Knit. *Round 3* [K1, SSK, knit to 3 stitches before marker, k2tog, k1] twice. Repeat last 2 rounds 5 more times—32 stitches. *Next round* K16 onto each of 2 needles. Graft toe.

### Cuff
Remove waste yarn and recover 60 stitches from cast-on. Arrange on 3 needles and join yarn. *Round 1* [K3, p2] around. The purls in Chart pattern should line up with purls in cuff. Repeat this round 11 more times. *Next round* *[K1, yo] 3 times, [p1, yo] twice; repeat from*. *Bind off round* *Bind off 5 stitches as if to knit, bind off 5 stitches as if to purl; repeat from*.

**Chart**

4
3
2
1

—10-st repeat—

**Stitch key**
☐ Knit
▨ Purl
⟋ K2tog
⟍ SSK
⊙ Yarn over (yo)

### NOTES
*1 See page 168 for any unfamiliar techniques. 2 Sock is worked cuff down on double-pointed needles. 3 The heel and toe are worked in Twined knitting; this technique uses two strands of yarn to produce a thick, sturdy fabric. 4 It is easiest to work Twined knitting using both ends of a center–pull ball. When it is necessary to untangle the 2 strands, stick a needle all the way through the ball and let it hang to untwist.*

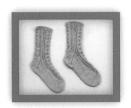

Adult M
**A** 7"
**B** 8"

10cm/4"

44

32

over stockinette stitch

**1** 2 3 4 5 6

Super Fine weight
300 yds

Two 2.25mm/US 1, 50cm
(20") or longer
or size to obtain gauge

Shown in
*LOUET* Gems Fingering
Weight in 55 Willow

# Branched Fern

*Kathleen Williams*    *Barkhamsted, Connecticut*

## Cuff

Cast 40 stitches onto each of 2 needles—80 stitches. Join to work in the round. *Round 1* *K5, slip 2nd, 3rd, 4th and 5th stitches over first stitch, yo; repeat from* to end of round. *Round 2* *K1, [k1, yo, k1 tbl] in next stitch; repeat from* to end of round—64 stitches. *Round 3* K2, *k1tbl, k3; repeat from* to last 2 stitches, k1tbl, k1. *Round 4* P1, *k2, p2; repeat from* to last 3 stitches, k2, p1. *Round 5* Same as Round 4. *Round 6* *P1, [k2, p2] 3 times, k2, p2tog, [k2, p2] 3 times, k2, p1; repeat from* once—62 stitches.

## Leg

*Begin Chart* Work 8 rounds of Chart 7 times.

## Heel flap

Work back and forth on Needle 1 only for heel. *Row 1* (RS) [Sl 1, k1] 7 times, sl 1, k2tog, [sl 1, k1] 7 times—30 stitches. *Row 2* (WS) Sl 1, purl to end of row. *Row 3* [Sl 1, k1] to end of row. Repeat last 2 rows 14 more times.

## Turn heel

*Row 1* (WS) Sl 1, p16, p2tog, p1, turn. *Row 2* Sl 1, k5, SSK, k1, turn. *Row 3* Sl 1, p6, p2tog, p1, turn. *Row 4* Sl 1, k7, SSK, k1, turn. *Row 5* Sl 1, p8, p2tog, p1, turn. Continue working 1 more stitch before decrease every row until *Row 12* Sl 1, k15, SSK, k1, turn—18 stitches.

**Chart**

*31-st repeat*

### Stitch key
- ☐ *Knit*
- ▨ *Purl*
- ⊙ *Yarn over (yo)*
- ⊿ *K2tog*
- ⊾ *SSK*
- ⅗ *K3tog*

## Gussets

With heel needle, pick up and k15 from left edge of heel flap. With instep needle, work Chart across instep stitches. With heel needle, pick up and k15 from right edge of heel flap, then knit to end of needle (new beginning of round). New Needle 1 holds 31 instep stitches; Needle 2 holds 48 heel and gusset stitches. *Next round* **Needle 1** Work in Chart pattern; **Needle 2** k1, SSK, knit to last 3 stitches, k2tog, k1. *Next round* **Needle 1** Chart pattern; **Needle 2** knit. Repeat last 2 rounds 8 more times—31 stitches on Needle 1, 30 stitches on Needle 2.

## NOTES

*1 See page 168 for any unfamiliar techniques. 2 Sock is worked cuff down on 2 circular needles.*

## Foot

Work even in patterns as established until foot measures approximately 6½" from back of heel, or 1½" less than desired length, end with Row 8 of Chart. *Next round* **Needle 1** K14, k2tog, k15; **Needle 2** knit—60 stitches. *Next round* Knit.

## Toe

*Round 1, decrease round* **Needle 1** K1, SSK, knit to last 3 sts, k2tog, k1; **Needle 2** same as Needle 1. *Round 2* Knit. Repeat last 2 rounds 6 more times, then work Round 1 four more times—16 stitches. Graft toe.

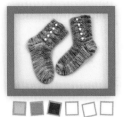

Adult S
**A** 7"
**B** 8"

10cm/4"

48

30

over stockinette stitch using
larger needles

**1** 2 3 4 5 6

Super Fine weight
275 yds

Five 2.25mm/US 1 and
Three 2.75mm/US 2

Ten 9.5mm/³/8"

Shown in
*COLINETTE* Jitterbug
in Monet

Annette Devitt    *Pedricktown, New Jersey*

## Cuff

Using larger needles, cast on 57 stitches.
Work back and forth in rows. *Row 1* (WS) Knit.
*Row 2* (RS) Purl. *Rows 3 & 4* Repeat Rows 1 &
2. *Rows 5 & 6* Knit.

## Leg

Change to smaller needles. *Begin Chart A* Use
appropriate chart for right or left sock. Repeat
Rows 1–12 four times, then work Rows 1–11
once more—58 stitches.

Arrange stitches on 4 double-pointed needles,
with last 6 stitches on side with buttonholes
on a separate needle and remaining stitches
distributed over 3 needles. Form leg into a
tube, placing needle with buttonhole on top of

opposite border. Join first and last 6 stitches of
row by knitting them together. Knit to end of
round, then knit 3 more stitches. Beginning of
round is in center of 6 joining stitches, directly
above buttonhole—52 stitches.

## Divide for heel

*Right sock* **Smaller Needles 1 & 2** Work Round
1 of Chart B, working 13 stitches on each needle
for instep; **Larger Needles 3 & 4** k13 on each
needle for heel and sole.

*Left sock* **Larger Needles 3 & 4** K13 on each
needle for heel and sole; **Smaller Needles 1 & 2**
work Round 1 of Chart B, working 13 stitches on
each needle for instep; **Larger Needles 3 & 4** knit.

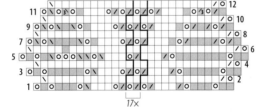

**Chart A, left sock**

17x

**Chart A, right sock**

17x

**Stitch key**
- ☐ *Knit on RS, purl on WS*
- ▨ *Purl on RS, knit on WS*
- ⊙ *Yarn over (yo)*
- ⟋ *K2tog*
- ⟋ *P2tog on RS*
- ⟍ *SSK*
- ⟋₃ *K3tog*
- ⟍₃ *SSSK*

**Chart B, right sock**

9x

**Chart B, left sock**

9x

## NOTES

*1 See page 168 for any unfamiliar techniques. 2 Sock is worked cuff down on double-pointed needles.*
*3 Lace-patterned leg and top of foot is worked on smaller needles; stockinette-stitch heel, sole, and toe*
*are worked on larger needles to compensate for difference in gauge.*

## Heel flap

Work back and forth on Needles 3 & 4 using larger needles. *Rows 1 & 3* (WS) Sl 1, purl to end of row. *Row 2* (RS) [Sl 1, k1] to end. *Row 4* Sl 1, k2, [sl 1, k1] to last stitch, k1. Repeat last 4 rows 6 more times.

## Turn heel

*Row 1* (WS) Sl 1, p13, p2tog, p1, turn. *Row 2* (RS) Sl 1, k**3**, SSK, k1, turn. *Row 3* Sl 1, p**4**, p2tog, p1, turn. *Row 4* Sl 1, k**5**, SSK, k1, turn. *Row 5* Sl 1, p**6**, p2tog, p1, turn. Continue to work 1 more stitch before decrease each row until *Row 11* Sl 1, p**12**, p2tog, turn. *Row 12* Sl 1, k**12**, k2tog—14 stitches.

## Gussets

*Set-up row* With larger needle, pick up and k14 from left side of heel flap. With smaller needles, knit across Needles 1 & 2 (Row 2 of Chart B). **Large Needle 3** Pick up and k14 from right side of heel flap, then k7 from heel. **Large Needle 4** K21—68 stitches; beginning of round is at beginning of instep stitches.

*Next round* **Needles 1 & 2** Work Chart B; **Needle 3** k1, SSK, knit to end; **Needle 4** knit to last 3 stitches, k2tog, k1—2 stitches decreased. *Next round* **Needles 1 & 2** Work Chart B; **Needles 3 & 4** knit. Continue as established, decreasing 2 stitches every other round until 13 stitches remain on each needle.

## Foot

Using smaller needles for instep and larger needles for sole, work even as established, until foot measures approximately 6", or 2" less than desired length, end with Round 2 or 4 of Chart.

## Toe

*Round 1* **Needle 1** K1, SSK, knit to end; **Needle 2** knit to last 3 sts, k2tog, k1; **Needle 3** k1, SSK, knit to end; **Needle 4** knit to last 3 stitches, k2tog, k1. *Round 2* Knit. Repeat Rounds 1 & 2 four more times, then work Round 1 four more times—16 stitches. Cut yarn, leaving a long tail. Graft toe.

## Finishing

Sew buttons to leg to correspond to buttonholes.

*intermediate*

Adult S
**A** 7"
**B** 9"

10cm/4"

46

33

over stockinette stitch

  2 3 4 5 6

Super Fine weight
400 yds

Two 2.25mm/US 1,
or size to obtain gauge

**&**

Unsweetened Kool Aid
drink: mix 2 packets Lemon-
Lime and 1 packet Ice Blue
Raspberry Lemonade
Heavy duty plastic wrap
2 squeeze bottles
Foam brush
Microwave-safe dish
Microwave oven
16 beads Swarovski Crystal
6mm faceted bicone in
crystal AB
Yarn needle

Shown in
*ZITRON* Trekking
Pro Natura undyed

# Girl's Best Friend

*Wendy Gaal*    *Encinitas, California*

## Dyeing the yarn

To achieve the gradation of color in these socks, the yarn was dyed, knit into a "sock blank", then dyed again.

Wind yarn into 2 loose hanks and tie in several places to prevent tangling. Place yarn in a basin of warm water to soak. Mix 1 packet of each flavor separately with a few tablespoons of warm water in squeeze bottles. Squeeze skeins to remove excess water and spread them out on a large piece of plastic wrap. Use squeeze bottles to randomly paint the skeins with both colors, allowing colors to bleed into each other. Be sure all yarn is saturated with dye.

Wrap skein in plastic wrap and place in microwave-safe dish. Microwave on High for 2 minutes. Let sit for 5 minutes. Microwave on High for 2 minutes. Repeat until the water runs nearly clear. Let yarn cool. Unwrap and rinse thoroughly in cool water. Hang skeins to dry.

Knit a "sock blank" with each skein. The blank should be about 60 stitches wide and be worked in stockinette stitch. A knitting machine would make quick work of this.

Place blanks in a basin of warm water to soak. Mix second packet of Lemon-Lime in a small cup. Squeeze excess water from blanks and lay them side by side on a large sheet of plastic wrap. Using foam brush, apply dye to blanks, graduating color from dark at one end to light at the other. Be sure dye soaks through blanks. Wrap blanks in plastic wrap, taking care to preserve gradation of color, and fix dye in microwave oven as before. After rinsing and drying, you can either knit directly from the blanks or wind yarn into balls.

Hang to dry

Knit 2
60 sts wide
rectangles.

mix new color and paint from
dark at one end to pale on the other.

## NOTES

*1 See page 168 for any unfamiliar techniques.*
*2 Sock is worked toe up on 2 circular needles.*
*3 When instructed to "reorient (RYO) mount of yo," slip yo knitwise to right needle, then slip yo purlwise to left needle (see page 65).*

## Working with beads

Pre-string 8 beads when instructed to do so. To place bead, insert right needle into next stitch, move bead into place against work, then knit the stitch. Use your fingers and needle to push bead into place on RS.

## Toe

Using Judy's Magic Cast-on, cast 16 stitches onto each needle.
*Round 1* Knit stitches on Needle 1; knit into back of stitches on Needle 2. *Round 2* [K1, make 1 (M1), knit to 1 stitch before end of needle, M1, k1] twice. *Round 3* Knit. Repeat last 2 rounds 7 more times—64 stitches. On final round, move first stitch from Needle 2 to adjacent end of Needle 1; Needle 1 holds 33 sole stitches and Needle 2 holds 31 instep stitches.

## Foot

Work Needle 1 in stockinette stitch and Needle 2 in Chart A pattern until foot measures 7", or 2" less than desired length. On final round, move first 2 stitches and last 3 stitches from Needle 2 to adjacent ends of Needle 1; Needle 1 holds 38 heel stitches and Needle 2 holds 26 instep stitches.

## Heel

*Note* See page 65 for making yo at beginning of row and reorienting yo (RYO).
Work back and forth on Needle 1. *Row 1* (RS) K**37**, turn. *Row 2* Yo, p**36**, turn. *Row 3* Yo, k**35**, turn. *Row 4* Yo, p**34**, turn. Continue, beginning each row with a yo and working one fewer stitch before turn in each row, until *Row 18* Yo, p**18**, turn. *Row 19* Yo, k**18**, RYO, k2tog, turn. *Row 20* Yo, p**19**, SSP, turn. *Row 21* Yo, k**20**, RYO twice, k3tog, turn. *Row 22* Yo, p**21**, SSSP, turn. Continue, working one more stitch before decrease in each row until all yo's have been worked. Move first 3 stitches and last 2 stitches from Needle 1 to adjacent ends of Needle 2. Needle 1 holds 33 back-of-leg stitches and Needle 2 holds 31 front-of-leg stitches.

## Leg

*Round 1* **Needle 1** K2tog, work Chart B beginning with second stitch—32 stitches on Needle 1; **Needle 2** continue Chart A pattern. Work even in patterns until leg measures approximately 3½", end with Row 28 of Chart A. Break yarn and string 8 beads. Splice yarn and continue in patterns, including beads in Chart A. On final round, M1 at beginning of Needle 2—32 stitches on each needle.

## Cuff

Work k1, p1 rib for 15 rounds. Bind off loosely.

**Chart A**

31 sts

**Chart B**

5x
32 sts

**Stitch key**

- ☐ Knit
- ▨ Purl
- ⟋ K2tog
- ⟍ SSK
- ⋀ S2KP2
- ⊙ Yarn over (yo)
- ■ bead placement (optional)

# In the Peaceful Forest

## Sandy Moore    Minneapolis, Minnesota

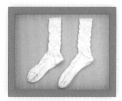

**experienced**

Adult M
**A** 8"
**B** 9½"

10cm/4"

48  36

over stockinette stitch

**1** 2 3 4 5 6

Super fine weight
400 yds

Five 2mm/US 0,
or size to obtain gauge

Shown in
*KNIT PICKS* Bare
Merino Wool Sock Yarn
in undyed natural

## NOTES

*1 See page 168 for any unfamiliar techniques.*
*2 Sock is worked from cuff down on double-pointed needles.*

**Chart A**

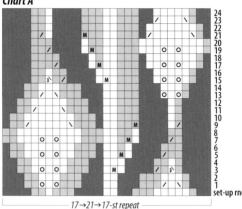

24
23
22
21
20
19
18
17
16
15
14
13
12
11
10
9
8
7
6
5
4
3
2
1
set-up rnd

17→21→17-st repeat

**Chart B**

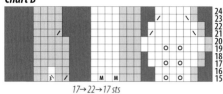

24
23
22
21
20
19
18
17
16
15

17→22→17 sts

**Stitch key**

□ Knit on RS, purl on WS
▨ Purl on RS, knit on WS
◿ K2tog on RS, p2tog on WS
◿ P2tog on RS, k2tog on WS
◺ SSK on RS, SSP on WS
◺ SSP on RS, SSK on WS
O Yarn over (yo)
ᴣ SK2P
M M1 knitwise
M M1 purlwise
■ Stitches do not exist
   in these areas of chart
⅄ Kf&b
P Inc 1 purl
V Sl 1 purlwise with
   yarn at WS of work

## Cuff

Using twisted long-tail cast-on, cast on 69 stitches. Beginning with tail end, distribute stitches as follows: 22 stitches on Needle 1, 22 stitches on Needle 2, and 25 stitches on original needle (Needle 3). With Needle 1 in right hand, Needle 3 in left hand, and yarn to back, slip 1 stitch from Needle 3 to Needle 1. Pass last stitch on Needle 1 over this stitch. Pull both tail yarn and working yarn snug to join the work—68 stitches. Work in k1, p1 rib for 1".

## Leg

Redistribute stitches so 17 stitches are on each of 4 dpn. *Begin Chart A* Work set-up round, Rounds 1–24 twice, work Rounds 1–14 once. *Begin Chart B* Work Chart B on Needle 1; continue Rounds 15–23 of Chart A on Needles 2, 3, and 4.

## Set up for heel flap

*Round 24* Redistribute stitches as follows: Work first 17 stitches in Chart B and next 10 in Chart A (Needle 1). Continue with Chart A as follows: With free needle, work next 17 stitches (Needle 2); with another free needle work next 17 stitches (Needle 3). Slip 7 remaining stitches onto Needle 1—34 stitches on Needle 1. Leave Needles 2 and 3 on hold for instep.

## Heel

Working back and forth in rows on Needle 1, work Rows 1–24 of Chart C. Repeat Rows 23 and 24 five more times.

## Turn heel

*Row 1* (RS) Sl 1, k18, SSK, k1, turn. *Row 2* Sl 1, p5, p2tog, p1, turn. *Row 3* Sl 1, k6, SSK, k1, turn. *Row 4* Sl 1, p7, p2tog, p1, turn. *Row 5* Sl 1, k8, SSK, k1, turn. Continue to work 1 more stitch before decrease every row until *Row 14* Sl 1, p16, p2tog, p1, turn—20 stitches. *Row 15* Sl 1, k9. With free needle, knit remaining 10 stitches.

## Gussets and Instep

Continuing with same needle, pick up and k17 down side of heel flap (Needle 1). Work Round 1 of Chart D across instep stitches (Needle 2). Pick up and k17 up along side of heel flap then k10 from heel (Needle 3)—88 stitches. *Round 2*

**Needle 1** Knit; **Needle 2** work Chart D; **Needle 3** knit. *Round 3*
**Needle 1** Knit to last 3 stitches, k2tog, k1; **Needle 2** work
Chart D; **Needle 3** k1, SSK, knit to end. Repeat these 2 rounds
10 times more. AT SAME TIME, when 20 rounds of Chart D are
complete, begin working Chart E for left foot or Chart F for right
foot as applicable.

### Foot

Continue knitting stitches on Needles 1 & 3, working Needle 2 in
Chart E or F until 68 rounds of chart is complete, then work Needle
2 as follows: K1, purl to last stitch, k1. Continue as established until
foot measures 7½" or 2" less than desired length.

### Toe

*Decrease round* **Needle 1** Knit to last 3 stitches, k2tog, k1;
 **Needle 2** k1, SSK, knit to last 3 stitches, k2tog, k1; **Needle 3** k1,
SSK, knit to end.

Knit 3 rounds. [Work Decrease round. Knit 2 rounds] twice.
[Work Decrease round. Knit 1 round] 3 times. Work Decrease round
until 8 stitches remain. Cut yarn, draw yarn through remaining
stitches, pull tight, and fasten off.

**Chart C**

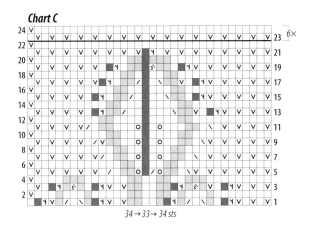

34→33→34 sts

**Chart D**

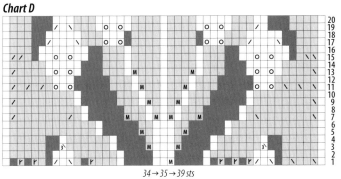

34→35→39 sts

**Chart E**

39→32 sts

**Chart F**

39→32 sts

**intermediate**

Adult M
**A** 7½"
**B** 9"
**C** 16½"

circumference at top of leg 18"

10cm/4"

44
28

over stockinette stitch with 2 strands of yarn held together using smaller needles

 2 3 4 5 6

Super Fine weight
1410 yds

Four 2.5mm/US 1½
or size to obtain gauge

Four 3.25mm/US 3

**&**

Stitch markers

Shown in
*ZITRON* Trekking
Pro Natura Undyed

# Lace Me Up Kilt Hose

*Tanya Thomann*    *Berkley, Michigan*

## Cuff

Using larger needles and 2 strands of yarn held together, cast on 108 stitches. Arrange on 3 needles and join to work in the round. Work 6-round repeat of Chart A 4 times. Knit 1 round, purl 1 round, knit 1 round. Turn work inside out so RS of cuff is on inside. Change to smaller needles. Work k2, p2 rib for 21 rounds.

## Leg

*Next round* [K6, p2] 11 times, k6, place marker (pm), p4, work Chart B over next 6 stitches, p4; panel is at center back. Continue in patterns as established until 6 repeats of Chart B are complete—48 rounds. *Next round* Rib to marker, p2, p2tog, work next row of Chart B, p2tog, p2—106 stitches. *Next round* Rib to marker, p3, work next row of Chart B, p3. *Next round* Rib to marker, p1, p2tog, work next row of Chart B, p2tog, p1—104 stitches. *Next round* Rib to marker, p2, work next row of Chart B, p2. *Next round* [K6, p2tog] 11 times, k6, p2tog, work next row of Chart B, p2tog—91 stitches. Work 11 rounds in k6, p1 rib and chart pattern. *Next round* [SSK, k4, p1] 11 times, SSK, k4, p1, work next row of Chart B, p1— 79 stitches. Work 7 rounds in k5, p1 rib and Chart pattern. *Next round* [SSK, k3, p1] 11 times, SSK, k3, p1, work next row of Chart B, p1—67 stitches. Work even in k4, p1 rib and chart pattern until 18 repeats of Chart B are complete, or desired length to top of heel. *Next round* [SSK, k2, p1] 11 times, SSK, k2, p1, work next row of Chart B, p1—55 stitches.

**Chart A**

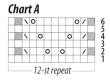

*12-st repeat*

**Chart B**

6 sts

**Stitch key**

☐ Knit
▨ Purl
◉ Yarn over (yo)
╱ K2tog
╲ SSK

## Heel flap

*Next row* K10, turn work. *Next row* (WS) P28. Work back and forth on these 28 stitches for heel flap. Leave remaining 27 stitches on one needle for instep. *Next row* (RS) [Sl 1, k1] to end. *Next row* Sl 1, purl to end. Repeat last 2 rows 15 more times.

## NOTES

*1 See page 168 for any unfamiliar techniques. 2 Sock is worked cuff down on double-pointed needles. 3 Work with 2 strands of yarn held together throughout.*

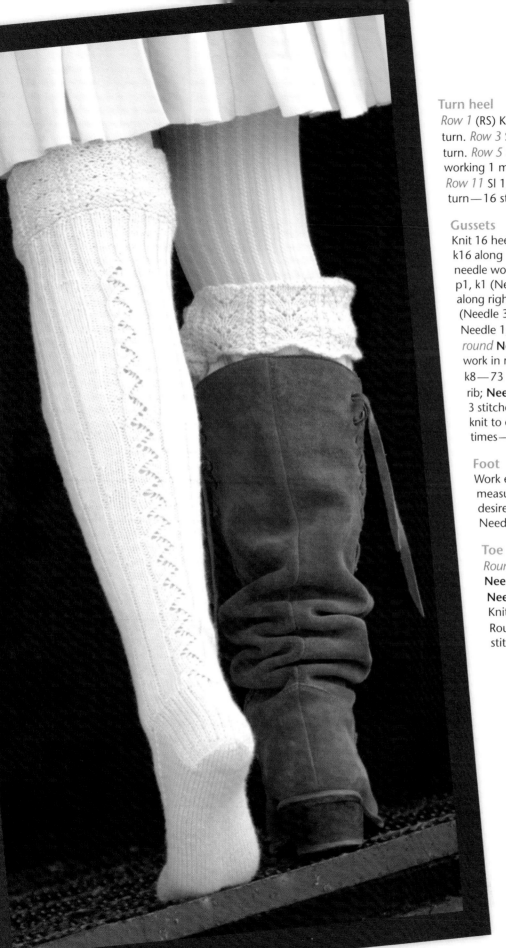

## Turn heel

*Row 1* (RS) K16, SSK, k1, turn. *Row 2* Sl 1, p**5**, p2tog, p1, turn. *Row 3* Sl 1, k**6**, SSK, k1, turn. *Row 4* Sl 1, p**7**, p2tog, p1, turn. *Row 5* Sl 1, k**8**, SSK, k1, turn. Continue as established, working 1 more stitch before p2tog or SSK each row until *Row 11* Sl 1, k**14**, SSK, turn. *Row 12* Sl 1, p**14**, p2tog, turn—16 stitches.

## Gussets

Knit 16 heel stitches. With another needle, pick up and k16 along left side of heel flap (Needle 1). With another needle work across instep stitches: k1, [p1, k3] 6 times, p1, k1 (Needle 2). With another needle, pick up and k16 along right side of heel flap, then knit 8 heel stitches (Needle 3)—75 stitches. Slip remaining 8 heel stitches to Needle 1; beginning of round is at center of heel. *Next round* **Needle 1** K8, k13 tbl, k2tog, k1 tbl; **Needle 2** work in rib as established; **Needle 3** k1 tbl, SSK, k13 tbl, k8—73 stitches. *Next round* **Needle 1** Knit; **Needle 2** rib; **Needle 3** knit. *Next round* **Needle 1** Knit to last 3 stitches, k2tog, k1; **Needle 2** rib; **Needle 3** k1, SSK, knit to end—71 stitches. Repeat last 2 rounds 7 more times—57 stitches.

## Foot

Work even in stockinette stitch and rib until foot measures 7½" from back of heel, or 1½" less than desired length. On last round, decrease 1 stitch on Needle 1—56 stitches.

## Toe

*Round 1* **Needle 1** Knit to last 3 stitches, k2tog, k1; **Needle 2** k1, SSK, knit to last 3 stitches, k2tog, k1; **Needle 3** k1, SSK, knit to end—52 stitches. *Round 2* Knit. Repeat last 2 rounds 6 more times, then work Round 1 three times—16 stitches. *Next round* Knit stitches on Needle 1. Graft toe.

*intermediate*

Adult M
**A** 8"
**B** 8"

10cm/4"

48  

32

over Chart B

 2 3 4 5 6

Super Fine weight
350 yds

Five 2.75mm/US 2
or size to obtain gauge

**&**

Small amount smooth
waste yarn

Shown in
*CHERRY TREE HILL YARN*
Supersock in Tropical Storm

# Rough Weather

## Emily Young    Portland, Maine

### Toe

*Note* See page 65 for making yo at beginning of row and reorienting yo (RYO).
Using a temporary cast-on and waste yarn, cast on 32 stitches. Row 1 (WS) Purl.
*Row 2* K**31**, turn. *Row 3* Yo, p**30**, turn. *Row 4* Yo, k**29**, turn. *Row 5* Yo, p**28**, turn.
Continue as established, beginning each row with a yarn-over and working one fewer
stitch before turn each round, until *Row 21* Yo, p**12**, turn. *Row 22* Yo, k**12**, RYO,
k2tog, turn. *Row 23* Yo, p**13**, SSP, turn. *Row 24* Yo, k**14**, reverse mount of both yo's
one at a time (RYO2), k3tog, turn. *Row 25* Yo, p**15**, SSSP, turn. *Row 26* Yo, k**16**, RYO2,
k3tog, turn. *Row 27* Yo, p**17**, SSSP, turn. Continue as established, beginning each row
with a yo and working one more stitch before the k3tog or SSSP on each round, until
all the yarn-overs have been worked, ending with a WS row. *Next row* Yo, k16. With
a new needle (Needle 2), knit to yo at end of row, slip yo. Recover 32 stitches from
cast-on and place on 2 needles (Needles 3 & 4). Begin working in the round. *Round 1*
Move yo from end of Needle 2 to beginning of Needle 3; k2tog, knit to last stitch on
Needle 4, SSK with yo at beginning of Needle 1—64 stitches.

### Foot

*Begin charts.* Work Chart A 8 times on Needles 1 & 2; work Chart B 4 times on
Needles 3 & 4. Continue as established until piece measures 6½", or about 1½"
less than desired length.

### Heel

Work back and forth on Needles 1 & 2 only for heel. *Row 1* (WS) Purl. *Row 2* K**31**,
turn. *Row 3* Yo, p**30**, turn. *Row 4* Yo, k**29**, turn. *Row 5* Yo, p**28**, turn. Continue as
established, beginning each row with a yo and working one fewer stitch before turn
each round, until *Row 19* Yo, p**14**, turn. *Row 20* Yo, k**14**, RYO, k2tog, turn.
*Row 21* Yo, p**15**, SSP, turn. *Row 22* Yo, k**16**, RYO2, k3tog, turn. *Row 23* Yo, p**17**, SSSP,
turn. *Row 24* Yo, k**18**, RYO2, k3tog, turn. *Row 25* Yo, p**19**, SSSP, turn. Continue as
established, beginning each row with a yo and working one more stitch before k3tog
or SSSP on each round, until all the yo's have been
worked, end with a WS row. *Next row* **Needle 1**
Yo, k16; **Needle 2** knit to yo at end of row, slip yo.
Resume working in round. Move yo from end of
Needle 2 to beginning of Needle 3. K2tog, knit to
last stitch on Needle 4, SSK with yo at beginning of
Needle 1—64 stitches.

**Chart A**

**Chart B**

└ 4-st repeat ┘

└─ 8-st repeat ─┘

### NOTES

*1 See page 168 for any unfamiliar techniques. **2** Sock is worked toe up on double-pointed needles.*

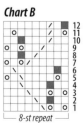

## Chart C

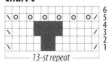

13-st repeat

6
5
4
3
2
1

## Stitch key

☐ Knit

◩ Yarn over (yo)

◩ K2tog

◪ SSK

◼ Stitches do not exist
in these areas of chart

## Leg

Work Chart B 8 times around leg until sock measures 6" above top of the heel, increasing 1 stitch on last round—65 stitches.

## Cuff

Begin working from Chart C. Repeat Chart C 5 times around. Work Rows 1–6 of chart once. Bind off loosely.

Adult M
**A** 8"
**B** 9"

10cm/4"

42

32

over stockinette stitch

2 3 4 5 6

Super Fine weight
340 yds

Two 2.75mm/US 2, 50 cm
(20") or longer

Shown in
*LOUET* Gems in
Fern Green

# Apple of My Eyelet

Karen Marlatt    Burlington, Ontario, Canada

## Cuff

Loosely cast on 32 stitches onto each circular needle—64 stitches. Join to work in the round. *Round 1* Purl. *Round 2* [P1, yo, k1, k2tog, SSK, k1, yo, p1] around. *Round 3* Knit. *Rounds 4–7* Repeat Rounds 2 & 3. *Round 8* Knit. *Rounds 9–12* [P2, k6] around. *Rounds 13–16* K4, [p2, k6] to last 4 stitches, p2, k2. *Rounds 17–24* Repeat Rounds 9–16. *Round 25* Purl. *Round 26* P15, [p2tog, p19] 2 times, p2tog, p5—31 stitches on Needle 1 for front of leg/instep and 30 stitches on Needle 2 for back of leg/heel/sole.

## Leg

**Begin Chart** Work Rounds 1–20 three times, then Rounds 1–2 once. **Next round** Work Round 3 across Needle 1 only.

## Heel flap

Work back and forth on Needle 2 as follows: *Row 1* (RS) K1, [sl 1, k1] to last stitch, k1. *Rows 2 & 4* (WS) K1, purl to end. *Row 3* K2, [sl 1, k1] around. Repeat last 4 rows 5 more times, then work Row 1 once—25 rows total.

## Turn heel

*Row 1* (WS) K1, p14, p2tog, p1, turn. *Row 2* K3, SKP, k1, turn. *Row 3* P4, p2tog, p1, turn. *Row 4* K5, SKP, k1, turn. *Row 5* P6, p2tog, p1, turn. Continue working 1 more stitch before each decrease (p2tog or SKP); end p14, p2tog, p1, turn. *Next row* Knit remaining 16 stitches.

## Gussets

Continuing with Needle 2, pick up and k15 down side of heel flap. *Round 1* **Needle 1** Continue in pattern as established; **Needle 2** pick up and k15 up side of heel flap, knit to end of round—

## NOTE

*1 See page 168 for any unfamiliar techniques. 2 Sock is worked cuff down on 2 circular needles.*

31 stitches on Needle 1, 46 on Needle 2. *Round 2* **Needle 1** Work as established; **Needle 2** k1, SSK, knit to last 3 stitches, k2tog, k1. Repeat last round 7 more times—30 stitches on Needle 2.

## Foot

Work even until foot measures approximately 7", or 2" less than desired length, end with Round 20 of chart.

## Toe

*Round 1* Knit. *Round 2* K15, k2tog, knit to end—60 stitches. *Round 3* [K1, k2tog, knit to last 3 stitches on needle, SSK, k1] twice. *Rounds 4–6* Knit. *Round 7* Repeat Round 3. *Rounds 8 & 9* Knit. *Round 10* Repeat Round 3. *Rounds 11 & 12* Knit. *Rounds 13–20* Repeat Round 3—16 stitches. Cut yarn, leaving a 12" tail. Graft toe.

**Chart**

1×    5×    1×
Needle 2    Needle 1

**Stitch key**

☐ Knit
▨ Purl
⟋ K2tog
⟍ SSK
⊙ Yarn over (yo)
⟋₃ K3tog
Ⓜ Make one (M1)

*intermediate*

Women's M

**A** 8"

**B** 9"

10cm/4"

44

36

over stockinette stitch

**1 2 3 4 5 6**

Fine weight
375 yds

Four 2mm/US 0,
or size to obtain gauge

Shown in
*MOUNTAIN COLORS*
Bearfoot in color Olive

# High Country Sunrise

*Sandy Moore*    *Minneapolis, Minnesota*

## Cuff

Using twisted long-tail cast–on, cast on 60 stitches. Arrange 20 stitches on each of 3 needles and join to work in the round. Work k1, p1 rib for 1".

## Leg

*Rearrange stitches* **Needles 1 & 2** 12 stitches, marker, 12 stitches; **Needle 3** 12 stitches—markers divide pattern repeats. *Begin Chart A.* Work Round 22 once, Rounds 1–22 twice, then Rounds 1–17 once—70 stitches.

## Heel flap

*Next round* **Needles 1 & 2** Work Round 18 of Chart A; **Needle 3** work first 11 stitches in chart pattern, slip 3 remaining stitches to Needle 1; slip first 4 stitches of Needle 2 to Needle 1—35 stitches. Work back and forth on Needle 1 for Heel Flap. *Begin Chart B* Work Rows 1–24 of Chart (removing marker as you work Row 1), then repeat last 2 rows 8 more times—32 stitches.

## Turn heel

*Row 1* (RS) Sl 1, k16, SSK, k1, turn. *Row 2* Sl 1, p4, p2tog, p1, turn. *Row 3* Sl 1, k5, SSK, k1, turn. *Row 4* Sl 1, p6, p2tog, p1, turn. Continue to work 1 more stitch before SSK or p2tog each row until *Row 14* Sl 1, p16, p2tog, turn—18 stitches.

## Gussets

Sl 1, k8 (new beginning of round). With another needle, k9, then pick up and k20 from left edge of heel flap (Needle 1). With another needle, work Round 1 of Chart C across instep stitches (Needle 2). With another needle, pick up and k20 from right edge of heel flap, then knit to end of round (Needle 3). Needles 1 & 3 each hold 29 stitches for heel and gussets; Needle 2 holds 33 stitches for instep. *Next round* **Needle 1** Knit; **Needle 2** work next round of Chart C; **Needle 3** knit. *Next round* **Needle 1** Knit to last 3 stitches, k2tog, k1; **Needle 2** work next round of Chart C; **Needle 3** k1, SSK, knit to end of round. Repeat last 2 rounds 12 more times—16 stitches each on Needles 1 & 3.

### Chart A

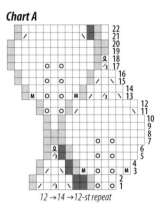

*12 →14 →12-st repeat*

### Chart B

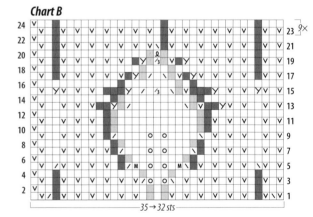

*35 → 32 sts*

## NOTES

*1 See page 168 for any unfamiliar techniques. **2** Sock is worked cuff down on double–pointed needles.*

40

## Stitch key

- ☐ Knit on RS, purl on WS
- ▦ Purl on RS, knit on WS
- ☑ K2tog
- ◰ SSK
- ◿ P2tog
- ◺ SSP
- ◯ Yarn over (yo)
- ⅄ Kf&b
- ⋁ Sl 1 purlwise with yarn at WS of work
- ௐ K1 tbl on RS, p1 tbl on WS
- /3 K3tog on RS, p3tog on WS
- ▮ Stitches do not exist in these areas of chart
- Ⓜ **Open M1** Insert LH needle front front to back and k into front loop - do not twist the stitch
- Ⓜ Make 1 purl

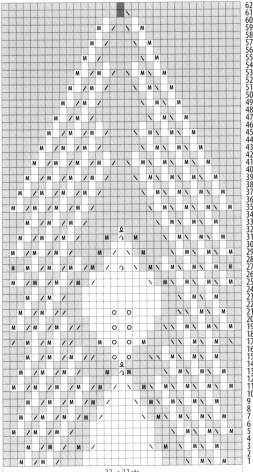

## Chart C

33 → 32 sts

## Foot
Work even in stockinette stitch on Needles 1 & 3 and Chart C on Needle 2. When Chart C is complete, purl all stitches on Needle 2. Continue until foot measures 7" from back of heel, or 2" less than desired length.

## Toe
*Round 1, decrease round* **Needle 1** Knit to last 3 sts, k2tog, k1; **Needle 2** k1, SSK, knit to last 3 sts, k2tog, k1; **Needle 3** k1, SSK, knit to end of round—4 stitches decreased. *Round 2* Knit. Continue in stockinette stitch, working decrease round every 4 rounds once, every 3 rounds twice, every other round 3 times, every round 7 times—8 stitches. Cut yarn, draw through remaining stitches, pull tight and fasten off.

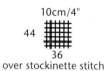

*intermediate*

Adult M
**A** 8"
**B** 9"

10cm/4"

44

36
over stockinette stitch

1 2 **3** 4 5 6

Light weight
350 yds

Four 2.25mm/US 1
or size to obtain gauge

Shown in
*MOUNTAIN COLORS*
Bearfoot in Burgundy

# Wandering Vine

*Mary Stefansen*    *Eugene, Oregon*

## RIGHT SOCK

### Leg

Cast on 71 stitches. Arrange 31 stitches on Needle 1 and 20 stitches each on Needles 2 & 3. Join to work in the round. *Next 2 rounds* [K2, p2] 4 times, k2, place marker (pm), p6, k1, p6, pm, [k2, p2] 10 times. *Begin Chart, set-up round* [K2, p2] 4 times, k2, work Chart A between markers, [k2, p2] 10 times. Continue in k2, p2 rib and Chart pattern until piece measures 6" from cast-on. *Next 8 rounds* Continue Chart pattern and work remaining stitches in stockinette stitch.

### Heel flap

*Next row* K16, turn. Move remaining stitches from Needle 1 to Needle 2. *Next row* P16 from Needle 1 and 19 from Needle 3. Move remaining stitch from Needle 3 to Needle 2. Needle 2 holds instep stitches. Work back and forth on 35 stitches for heel flap. *Row 1* (RS) Sl 1, p2, [sl 1, k1] to last 4 stitches, sl 1, p2, sl 1. *Row 2* Purl. Repeat last 2 rows 12 more times.

### Turn heel

*Row 1* (RS) K21, SSK, k1, turn. *Row 2* Sl 1, p8, p2tog, p1, turn. *Row 3* Sl 1, k9, SSK, k1, turn. *Row 4* Sl 1, p10, p2tog, p1, turn. *Row 5* Sl 1, k11, SSK, k1, turn. Continue as established, working 1 more stitch before decrease each row, until *Row 13* Sl 1, k19, SSK, turn. *Row 14* Sl 1, p19, p2tog—21 stitches. *Row 15* Knit.

### Gussets

With needle holding heel stitches, pick up and p13 along left side of heel flap. With another needle, work 36 instep stitches in patterns as established. With another needle, pick up and p13 along right side of heel flap, then k9, k2tog from heel. Beginning of round is at center of heel; Needles 1 & 3 each hold 23 stitches, Needle 2 holds 36 stitches. *Round 1* **Needle 1** Knit to last 3 stitches, k2tog, k1; **Needle 2** work in patterns as established; **Needle 3** k1, SSK, knit to end. *Round 2* Work even as established. Repeat last 2 rounds 5 more times—70 stitches.

### Foot

Continue in stockinette stitch and Chart A pattern until 14 leaves are complete. Work Rounds 17–34 of Chart between markers. Continue in stockinette stitch only until foot measures 7½", or 1½" less than desired length.

## NOTES

*1 See page 168 for any unfamiliar techniques. **2** Sock is worked from the cuff down on double-pointed needles.*

## Chart A

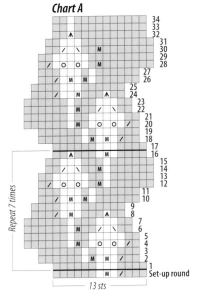

Repeat 7 times

34
33
32
31
30
29
28
27
26
25
24
23
22
21
20
19
18
17
16
15
14
13
12
11
10
9
8
7
6
5
4
3
2
1 Set-up round

13 sts

## Chart B

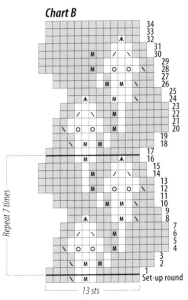

Repeat 7 times

34
33
32
31
30
29
28
27
26
25
24
23
22
21
20
19
18
17
16
15
14
13
12
11
10
9
8
7
6
5
4
3
2
1 Set-up round

13 sts

## Stitch key

- ☐ Knit
- ▨ Purl
- ◿ K2tog
- ◿ P2tog
- ◺ SSK
- Ⓞ Yarn over (yo)
- Ⓜ Make one (M1)
- Ⓜ Make one (M1P)
- ⬣ S2KP2

### Toe

Move last stitch from Needle 2 to Needle 3; Needle 1 now holds 17 stitches, Needle 2 holds 35 stitches, and Needle 3 holds 18 stitches. *Rounds 1–13* **Needle 1** Knit to last 3 stitches, k2tog, k1; **Needle 2** K1, SSK, knit to last 3 stitches, k2tog, k1; **Needle 3** K1, SSK, knit to end—18 stitches. Knit stitches on Needle 1. Graft toe.

### LEFT SOCK
#### Leg

Cast on 71 stitches. Arrange 20 stitches on Needle 1, 16 on Needle 2, and 35 on Needle 3. *Next 2 rounds* [K2, p2] 9 times, k2, place marker (pm), p6, k1, p6, pm, [k2, p2] 5 times. *Set-up round* [K2, p2] 9 times, k2, work Chart B between markers, [k2, p2] 5 times. Continue as for Right Sock to Heel Flap.

### Heel flap

*Next row* K17, turn. Move remaining 3 stitches from Needle 1 to Needle 2. *Next row* P17 from Needle 1 and 18 from Needle 3. Move remaining stitches from Needle 3 to Needle 2. Needle 2 holds instep stitches. Work back and forth on 35 stitches for heel flap.

Complete as for Right Sock, working pattern from Chart B.

Twist

*intermediate*

Women's S
**A** 7"
**B** 8½"

10cm/4"

52
38

over stockinette stitch

 2 3 4 5 6

Super Fine weight
400 yds

Five 2.25mm/US 1,
or size to obtain gauge

**&**

cable needle (cn)

Shown in
*ZITRON* Trekking XXL
in color 66

# Interlochen Cables

## Angela Sivers     Lincoln City, Oregon

### Leg
Cast on 80 stitches and arrange 16 stitches each on Needles 1 & 2 and 24 stitches each on Needles 3 & 4. Join to work in the round.

*Begin Chart.* Work Rounds 1–16 of chart 5 times, end last round 3 stitches before end of round. Slip these 3 stitches to Needle 1. Slip first 3 stitches from Needle 3 to Needle 2. Needles 1 & 2 now hold 19 stitches each; Needles 3 & 4 hold 21 stitches each.

### Heel flap
Combine stitches from Needles 1 & 2 on one needle. Work back and forth on these 38 stitches for heel flap. *Row 1* [Sl 1, k1] around. *Row 2* Sl 1, purl to end of row. Repeat last 2 rows 19 more times.

### Turn heel
*Row 1* (RS) K21, SSK, k1, turn. *Row 2* Sl 1, p5, p2tog, p1, turn. *Row 3* Sl 1, k6, SSK, k1, turn. *Row 4* Sl 1, p**7**, p2tog, p1, turn. *Row 5* Sl 1, k**8**, SSK, k1, turn. Continue working 1 more stitch before decreases every row until *Row 16* Sl 1, p19, p2tog, p1, turn—22 stitches.

### Gussets
With a spare needle, k11. Place marker for beginning of round. With Needle 1, k11, then pick up and k20 along side of heel flap; with Needles 2 & 3, continue Chart pattern as established (instep); with Needle 4, pick up and k20 along side of heel flap, then knit to end of round—104 stitches; beginning of round is at center of heel. *Round 1* **Needle 1** Knit to last 3 sts, k2tog, k1; **Needles 2 & 3** p2, k2, work 2 repeats of Chart, k2 p2; **Needle 4** k1, SSK, knit to end of round. *Round 2* **Needle 1** Knit; **Needle 2 & 3** same as Round 1; **Needle 4** knit. Repeat last 2 rounds 10 more times—82 stitches.

### Foot
Work even in stockinette stitch and chart pattern as established until foot measures approximately 7" from back of heel, or 1½" less than desired length, end with Round 8 or 16 of chart.

### Toe
*Round 1* [Knit to last 3 stitches on needle, k2tog, k1; k1, SSK, knit to end of needle] twice. *Round 2* Knit. Repeat last 2 rounds 9 more times, then work Round 1 eight more times—10 stitches. Cut yarn, draw through remaining stitches, pull tight, and fasten off.

NOTES
*1 See page 168 for any unfamiliar techniques. 2 Sock is worked top down on double-pointed needles.*

**Chart**

16
15
14
13
12
11
10
9
8
7
6
5
4
3
2
1

— 16-st repeat —

**Stitch key**

☐ Knit

■ Purl

⧄⧄ **2/4 LPC** Sl 2  to cn and hold to front, k2, p2
(knitting the purls and purling the knits); k2 from cn

Adult M
**A** 7½"
**B** 9"

10cm/4"

52

36

over stockinette stitch

 2 3 4 5 6

Super Fine weight
350 yds

Two 2mm/US 1, 50cm (20")
or longer
or size to obtain gauge

**&**

2 cable needles (cn)

Shown in
*ELLEN'S ½ PINT FARM*
Merino/Bamboo
in Spring Green

# Luck O' the Irish

*Cindy Craig*   Kansas City, Missouri

## Cuff

Cast on 60 stitches. Arrange 30 stitches on each needle. Join to work in the round. *Round 1* K1, p1, [k2, p1] to last stitch, k1. Work k2, p1 rib as established for 1". *Next round* [Yo, k6] around—70 stitches.

**Chart A**

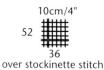

14-st repeat

## Leg

*Begin Chart A* Work 14-stitch repeat 5 times around. Work Rounds 1–12 three times.

## Ankle

Slip first stitch from Needle 1 to Needle 2; Needle 1 holds 34 stitches for heel and sole of foot; Needle 2 holds 36 stitches for instep and top of foot. *Next round* **Needle 1** Work Round 1 of Chart B; **Needle 2** continue pattern as established. Continue as established through Round 28 of Chart B.

## Heel

*Note* See page 65 for making yo at beginning of row and reorienting yo (RYO). Begin working back and forth on Needle 1 only. *Next row* (RS) Work Row 29 of Chart B; turn. *Next row* (WS) Maintaining twisted rib pattern as established, work to 1 stitch before end of row, turn. *Next row* Yo, work to 1 before end of row, turn. *Next row* Yo, work to 1 before previous yo, turn. Repeat last row 12 more times—5 stitches remain unworked in center of heel. *Next row* Yo, work 5 stitches in pattern as established, turn. *Next row* (WS) Yo, work to first yo, RYO, p2tog, turn. *Next row* Yo, work to next yo, reorient mount of both yo's, one at a time, k3tog, turn. *Next row* Yo, work to next yo, SSSP, turn. Repeat last 2 rows until all yo's have been worked—33 stitches on Needle 1. With yarn in back, slip last stitch from Needle 2 to Needle 1, bring yarn to front, slip stitch back to Needle 2. Turn.

## Foot

Resume working in the round. *Next round* Work Round 61 of Chart C. Slip yo at end of Needle 1 to Needle 2 and p2tog with first stitch on Needle 2. Continue Chart A on Needle 2, beginning with second stitch of chart. Continue as established through Round 90 of Chart C. *Next round* **Needle 1** K14, slip 1 stitch to a cn and hold in front, slip next stitch to another cn and hold in back, k1, kf&b stitch on back cn, knit stitch from front cn, knit to end; **Needle 2** work in pattern. Work in stockinette stitch on Needle 1 and Chart A on Needle 2 until foot measures 7½" from back of heel, or 1½" less than desired length, end with Round 12 of Chart A.

## NOTES

*1 See page 168 for any unfamiliar techniques. 2 Sock is worked cuff down on 2 circular needles.*

## Toe

*Round 1* **Needles 1 & 2** K1, SSK, knit to last 3 stitches, k2tog, k1. *Round 2* Knit. Repeat last 2 rounds 5 times more, then repeat Round 1 eight times— 14 stitches. Graft toe.

## Stitch key

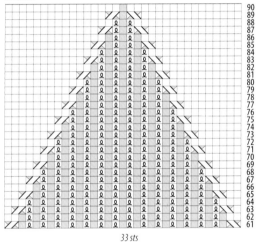

☐ Knit
▨ Purl
☒ K1 tbl on RS, pl tbl on WS
▧▧ **1/1 RC** *Slip 1 to cn and hold to back, k1; k1 from cn*
▨▨ **1/1 LC** *Slip 1 to cn and hold to front, k1; k1 from cn*
▧▧ **2/1 RC** *Slip 1 to cn and hold to back, k2; k1 from cn*
▨▨ **2/1 LC** *Slip 2 to cn and hold to front, k1; k2 from cn*

**Chart C**

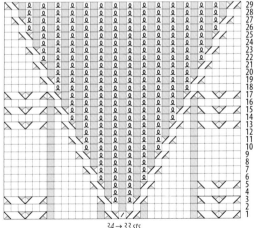

*33 sts*

**Chart B**

*34 → 33 sts*

Adult M
**A** 7½"
**B** 9"

10cm/4"

48
36

over stockinette stitch

 2 3 4 5 6

Super Fine weight
375 yds

Two 2.5mm/US 1½,
or size to obtain gauge,
50cm (20") or longer

**&**

Stitch markers
Cable needle (cn)

Shown in
*REGIA* Silk in color 032

# Ruby Slippers

*Inna Zakharevich*     *Cambridge, Massachusetts*

## Toe

Using Judy's Magic Cast-on, cast 15 stitches onto each of 2 circular needles—30 stitches. *Round 1* Knit. *Round 2* [K1, right lifted increase (R inc), knit to last stitch on needle, left lifted increase (L inc), k1] 2 times. Repeat last 2 rounds 7 more times—62 stitches. *Next round* K12, p1, R inc, k2, L inc, p1, R inc, k2, L inc, p1, knit to end—66 stitches; 35 stitches on Needle 1 for top of foot and 31 stitches on Needle 2 for sole of foot.

## Foot

*Next round* **Needle 1** K12, p1, work Round 1 of Chart B, p1, work Round 1 of Chart A, p1, k12; **Needle 2** knit. Continue in patterns as established for approximately 2½", end with a Round 4 of Chart.

## Instep

*Round 1* **Needle 1** K12, p1, work Chart B, place marker (pm), yo, knit into front and back of stitch (kf&b), yo, pm, work Chart A, p1, k12; **Needle 2** knit—69 stitches. *Round 2* **Needle 1** Work to first marker, k4, work to end; **Needle 2** knit. Continue to work in established patterns and work on **Needle 1** between markers as follows: *Round 3* Work Round 1 of Chart C. *Round 4* Yo, k4, yo. *Round 5* K1, work Round 1 of Chart C, k1. *Round 6* K6. *Round 7* Yo, k1, work Chart C,

k1, yo. *Round 8* K2, work Chart C, k2. *Round 9* Yo, k2, work Chart C, k2, yo. Repeat Rounds 2–9 until there are 36 stitches between the markers, increasing on Rounds 4, 7, and 9, and incorporating new stitches into Chart C pattern as soon as possible—70 stitches on Needle 1, 31 on Needle 2.

## Turn heel

*Set-up round* **Needle 2** Work following stitches from Needle 1: [K3, R inc] 4 times, p1, SSK, k2tog, remove marker; **Needle 1** work 36 stitches in Chart C, remove marker; **Needle 2** work following stitches from Needle 1: p1, SSK, k2tog, [L inc, k3] 4 times—Needle 1 holds 36 instep stitches, Needle 2 holds 69 heel stitches. Work back and forth on Needle 2 as follows: *Row 1* K48, wrap next stitch and turn work (W&T). *Row 2* P27, W&T. *Row 3* Knit to 1 stitch before wrapped stitch, W&T. *Row 4* Purl to 1 stitch before wrapped stitch, W&T. Repeat last 2 rows 6 more times—8 wrapped stitches on each side of 13 center stitches. *Row 17* Knit to first wrapped stitch, k7, hiding wraps, SSK (including last wrap), turn. *Row 18* Purl to first wrapped stitch, p7, hiding wraps, p2tog (including last wrap), turn.

**Chart A**

4
3
2
1
4-sts

**Chart B**

4
3
2
1
4-sts

**Chart C**

2
1
4-st
repeat

**Chart D**

2
1
4-st
repeat

### Stitch key
 Knit
 Purl
Sl 1, k1, yo, pass slipped stitch over both knit and yo
*2/2 LC* Sl 2 to cn and hold to front, k2; k2 from cn
*2/2 RC* Sl 2 to cn and hold to back, k2; k2 from cn

## NOTES

*1 See page 168 for any unfamiliar techniques. 2 Sock is worked toe up on 2 circular needles.*

## Heel flap

*Row 1* Sl 1, k27, SSK. *Row 2* Sl 1, p27, p2tog.
Repeat last 2 rows until 33 stitches remain on
Needle 2; turn. Sl 1, k27, SSK, k1. Do not turn.
Resume working in the round. *Round 1* **Needle 1**
Work in Chart C; **Needle 2** k1, k2tog, knit to end.

## Leg

*Round 1* **Needle 1** Work in Chart C; **Needle 2** k1,
[R inc, k7] 4 times, R inc, k2—36 stitches on Needle
2. *Round 2* Work Chart C on both needles. Continue
in Chart C until leg measures 5" above heel.

## Cuff

*Next round* Change to Chart D. Work until cuff
measures 1½". *Picot bind-off* [Bind off 1, cable
cast-on 2, bind off 5] to end of round.

Adult L
**A** 9"
**B** 10½"
**C** 11½"

circumference at top of leg 14"

10cm/4"

44

34

over stockinette st

**1** 2 3 4 5 6

Super Fine weight
875 yds

2.75mm/US 2

Five 2.75mm/US 2
or size to obtain gauge

**&**

Cable needle (cn)

four ¾" (19mm)

Shown in
*ZITRON* Trekking XXL in
color 90

# Celtic Pride Kilt Hose

*Vanessa Malone*   *Syracuse, New York*

## RIGHT SOCK

### Cuff

Using straight needles, cast on 144 stitches. *Row 1* (WS) P3, work Row 1 of Chart A 9 times, k3, p3. *Row 2* K3, p3, work Row 2 of Chart A 9 times, k3. Continue in rib and chart pattern as established. AT SAME TIME, on Rows 6 and 18, make buttonholes as follows: K3, bind off 3, continue as established to end of row. On following row, cast on 3 stitches over bound-off stitches. Continue until 27 rows are complete. *Row 28* Bind off 8, p1, [k3, p6, k3, p3] to end—136 stitches.

### Leg

Turn work so WS is facing. Change to double-pointed needles and arrange stitches as follows: **Needle 1** 27 stitches; **Needle 2** 45 stitches; **Needle 3** 51 stitches; **Needle 4** 13 stitches. Join to work in the round. *Set-up round* **Needle 1** K1, p3, k6, p3, k3, p2, k6, p3; **Needle 2** [k6, p3, k3, p3] 3 times; **Needle 3** [k6, p3, k3, p3] 3 times, k6. Slip stitches from Needle 4 onto Needle 1 (new beginning of round). *Round 1* **Needle 1** Chart C; **Needle 2** Chart A 3 times; **Needle 3** Chart A 3 times, then Stitches 1–6. Continue as established, through Round 82 of Chart C—118 stitches. Changing to Chart D on Needle 1 and continuing to work Chart A on Needles 2 and 3, work through Round 37 of Chart D—100 stitches. *Next round* **Needle 1** Work Round 38 of Chart D; **Needle 2** work in pattern to last 3 stitches, p3tog; **Needle 3** [k6, p3tog, k3, p3tog] 3 times, k6, turn—85 stitches.

**Chart A**

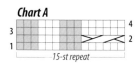

15-st repeat

**Chart B**

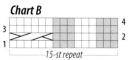

15-st repeat

**Chart C**

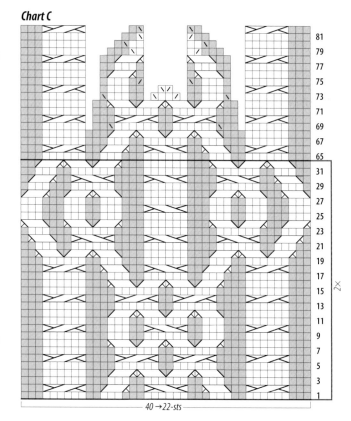

40 →22-sts

## NOTES

*1 See page 168 for any unfamiliar techniques. 2 Sock is worked cuff down: back and forth on straight needles for cuff, then around on double-pointed needles.*

## Chart D

37
35
33
31
29
27
25
23
21
19
17
15
13
11
9
7
5
3
1

22 → 3-sts

### Stitch key

☐ Knit on RS, purl on WS

▨ Purl on RS, knit on WS

◿ **K2tog**

◺ **P2tog**

◹ **SSK**

**3/3 LC** Sl 3 to cn and hold to front, p1; k3 from cn

**3/3 RC** Sl 3 to cn and hold to back, k3; k3 from cn

**3/1 LPC** Sl 3 to cn and hold to front, p1; k3 from cn

**3/1 RPC** Sl 1 to cn and hold to back, k3; p1 from cn

**3/2 LPC** Sl 3 to cn and hold to front, p2; k3 from cn

**3/2 RPC** Sl 2 to cn and hold to back, k3; p2 from cn

**6/2 LPC decrease** Sl 6 to cn, hold to front, p2; [SSK from cn] 3×

**6/2 RPC decrease** Sl 2 to cn, hold to back, [k2tog] 3×; p2 from cn

### Heel flap

*Next row* P44. Work back and forth on these stitches for heel flap. Place remaining 41 stitches on hold for instep. *Next row* (RS) [Sl 1, k1] to end. *Next row* Sl 1, purl to end. Repeat last 2 rows 21 more times.

### Turn heel

*Row 1* (RS) K24, SSK, k1, turn. *Row 2* Sl 1, p**5**, p2tog, p1, turn. *Row 3* Sl 1, k**6**, SSK, k1, turn. *Row 4* Sl 1, p**7**, p2tog, p1, turn. *Row 5* Sl 1, k**8**, SSK, k1, turn. Continue working 1 more stitch before p2tog or SSK each row until *Row 20* Sl 1, p**22**, p2tog, turn—24 stitches.

### Gussets

Knit 12 heel stitches (new beginning of round). *Next round* **Needle 1** Knit 12 remaining heel stitches; pick up and k22 along left side of heel; **Needle 2** p2tog, p1, work Chart A pattern twice, then work Stitches 1–8; **Needle 3** pick up and k22 along right side of heel, knit to end of round—108 stitches. *Next round* **Needle 1** Knit to last 3 stitches, k2tog, k1; **Needle 2** continue in pattern as established; **Needle 3** k1, SSK, knit to end. *Next round* Knit. Repeat last 2 rounds 9 more times—88 stitches.

### Foot

Work even in stockinette stitch on Needles 1 & 3 and Chart A on Needle 2 until foot measures 8" from back of heel, or 2½" less than desired length.

### Toe

Slip last 2 stitches from Needle 1 to Needle 2; slip first 2 stitches from Needle 3 to Needle 2—Needles 1 & 3 each hold 22 stitches; Needle 2 holds 44 stitches. *Round 1* **Needle 1** Knit; **Needle 2** k2, p40, k2; **Needle 3** knit. *Round 2* **Needle 1** Knit to last 3 stitches, k2tog, k1; **Needle 2** k1, SSK, knit to last 3 stitches, k2tog, k1; **Needle 3** k1, SSK, knit to end—84 stitches. *Round 3* Knit. Repeat last 2 rounds 10 more times, then Round 2 eight times—12 stitches. Knit across Needle 1; slip stitches from Needle 3 to Needle 2. Graft toe.

## LEFT SOCK

### Cuff

Using straight needles, cast on 144 stitches. *Row 1* (WS) P3, k3, work Row 1 of Chart B 9 times, p3. *Row 2* K3, work Row 2 of Chart B 9 times, p3, k3. Continue in rib and Chart pattern as established. AT SAME TIME, on Rows 6 and 18, make buttonholes as follows: Work in pattern to last 6 stitches, bind off 3, k3. On following row, cast on 3 stitches over bound-off stitches. Continue until 27 rows are complete. *Row 28* Bind off 8, turn—136 stitches.

### Leg

Turn work so WS is facing. Change to double-pointed needles and arrange stitches as follows, beginning on the end of piece away from the working yarn: **Needle 1** 21 stitches; **Needle 2** 45 stitches; **Needle 3** 51 stitches; **Needle 4** 19 stitches. Join to work in the round. *Set-up round* **Needle 1** K4, p3, k3, p2, k6, p3; **Needle 2** [k6, p3, k3, p3] 3 times; **Needle 3** [k6, p3, k3, p3] 3 times, k6. Slip stitches from Needle 4 onto Needle 1 (new beginning of round). Work same as for Right Sock through Round 37 of Chart C. *Next round* **Needle 1** Work Round 38 of Chart C; **Needle 2** [k6, p3tog, k3, p3tog] 3 times; **Needle 3** k6, p3tog, k3, turn. Slip remaining stitches from Needle 3 to Needle 1. Work in pattern as established to end—85 stitches. Turn work.

Work heel flap, heel turn, foot, and toe same as for Right Sock.

## Natalia Vasilieva   Moscow, Russia

Adult M
**A** 7½"
**B** 9"

10cm/4"

48 ⊞ 34

over stockinette stitch

 2 3 4 5 6

Super Fine weight
375 yds

2.5mm/US 1½,
80 cm (32") or longer

Five 2.5mm/US 1½
or size to obtain gauge

**&**

Stitch holder
Stitch markers
2 Cable needles (cn)

Shown in
*REGIA* Silk in color 0052

### NOTES
*1 See page 168 for any unfamiliar techniques. 2 Sock is worked toe up on double-pointed needles for toe and changing to 1 circular needle using Magic Loop method for foot, heel, and leg.*

## Toe

Using double-pointed needles, circle cast on 8 stitches. Arrange on 4 needles and join to work in the round. *Round 1* [K1 tbl, p1] around. *Round 2* [K1 tbl, M1P, p1] around. *Round 3* [K1 tbl, M1P, p2] around. *Round 4* [K1 tbl, M1P, p3] around. *Round 5* [K1 tbl, M1P, p4] around. *Round 6* [K1 tbl, M1P, p5] around—28 stitches. *Round 7* [K1 tbl, M1, p6] around. *Round 8* [K2 tbl, p6] around. *Round 9* [K1 tbl, M1P, T2L, p5] around—36 stitches. *Round 10* [K1 tbl, p2, k1 tbl, p5] around. *Round 11* [K1 tbl, M1P, p2, T2L, p4] around. *Round 12* [K1 tbl, p4] around. *Round 13* [K1 tbl, M1P, p4, T2L, p3] around. *Round 14* [K1 tbl, p6, k1 tbl, p3] around. *Round 15* [K1 tbl, M1P, p6, T2L, p2] around. *Round 16* [K1 tbl, p8, k1 tbl, p2] around. *Round 17* [K1 tbl, M1P, p8, T2L, p1] around. *Round 18* [K1 tbl, p10, k1 tbl, p1] around. *Round 19* [K1 tbl, M1P, p10, T2L] around—56 stitches. *Round 20* [K1 tbl, p12, k1 tbl] around. *Round 21* K1 tbl, [M1P, p12, T2L] around, twisting last stitch with first stitch from next round—60 stitches.
*Next round* With circular needle, purl.

## Foot

Arrange for Magic Loop technique, with 30 stitches on first needle for instep and 30 stitches on second needle for sole. *Begin Charts, Round 1* **Needle 1** Work Flame Cable A, p2, work Zigzag A, p2, work Flame Cable B; **Needle 2** purl. Work in Reverse Stockinette St and chart patterns as established for 60 rounds, or until foot measures 3" less than desired length.

### Gussets

*Next round* **Needle 1** Work in patterns as established; **Needle 2** work Gusset A, p26, work Gusset B. Continue as established through Round 16 of Gusset charts— 76 stitches; 30 on Needle 1 and 46 on Needle 2.

### Heel

Work back and forth on Needle 2 for heel.
*Next row* (WS) K36, turn. *Next row* P26, turn. *Next row* K26, turn. Repeat last 2 rows 6 more times. *Next row* P26, turn. *Next row, set-up row for Diamond chart* (WS) K11, p2, M1P, p2, k4, SSK, turn. *Row 1* Sl 1, work Row 1 of Diamond chart, p2tog, turn. *Row 2* Sl 1, work next row of Diamond, SSK, turn. *Row 3* Sl 1, work next row of Diamond, p2tog, turn. *Rows 4–9* Repeat last 2 rows 3 more times. *Row 10* Sl 1, work Row 10 of Diamond, pick up and p8 along side of heel flap. Turn. *Row 11* (RS) Sl 1, p2, work Row 11 of Diamond to second cable; sl 2 to cable needle (cn) hold in front, pick up and k2 from side of gusset, k2 from cn, and k6 along side of heel flap, turn—31 stitches between gussets. Turn. *Row 12* (WS) Sl 1, k2, work next row of Diamond, k2, SSK, turn. *Row 13* (RS) Sl 1, p2, work next row of Diamond, p2, p2tog, turn. *Rows 14–31* Repeat last 2 rows 9 more times—31 stitches on Needle 2. Resume working in the round.

**Flame Cable B**

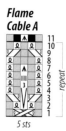

5 sts

**Flame Cable A**

5 sts

**Diamond** Work Rows 1–37, then Rounds 38–69.

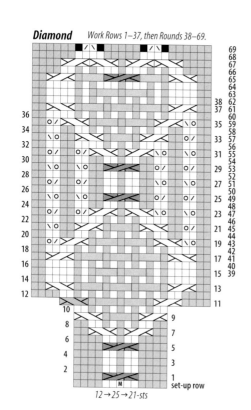

12 → 25 → 21-sts

**Gusset B**

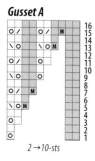

2 → 10-sts

**Gusset A**

2 → 10-sts

## Leg

*Next round* **Needle 1** Work in patterns as established; **Needle 2** p3, work Diamond chart, p3. *Next round* **Needle 1** Work in patterns as established; **Needle 2** p2, work Rib A chart, work Diamond, work Rib B chart, p2. Continue in patterns as established. After 6 rounds of Rib charts there are 73 stitches. Continue through 69 rounds of Diamond chart and Round 11 of Flame chart— 65 stitches.

## Cuff

*Set-up round for right sock* **Needle 1** [P1, k1 tbl] 10 times, p1, k2tog tbl, p1; **Needle 2** k1 tbl, p1, work Rib A, [p1, k1 tbl] 10 times, p1, work Rib B, p1, k1 tbl—64 stitches.

*Set-up round for left sock* **Needle 1** P1, k2tog tbl, [p1, k1 tbl] 10 times, p1; **Needle 2** k1 tbl, p1, work Rib A, [p1, k1 tbl] 10 times, p1, work Rib B, p1, k1 tbl—64 stitches.

Continue in k1 tbl, p1 rib and Ribs A and B for 1½", or to desired length. Bind off loosely.

**Rib B**

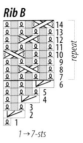

1→7-sts

**Rib A**

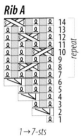

1→7-sts

**Zigzag Charts**

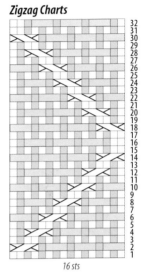

16 sts

*For ZigZag A, repeat Rounds 1—32.*
*For ZigZag B, work Rounds 17—32, then repeat Rounds 1—32.*

### Chart Note

For left sock, use Zigzag B and on Diamond chart, work 2/1/2 LPC instead of 2/1/2 RPC. **2/1/2 LPC** Slip 2 to first cn and hold to front, slip 3rd stitch to second cn and hold to back, k2; purl stitch from second cn; k2 from cn.

### Stitch key

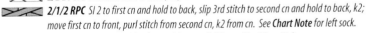

| | | | |
|---|---|---|---|
| ☐ Knit on RS, purl on WS | | ☑ K2tog | |
| ▨ Purl on RS, knit on WS | | ☒ SSK | |
| O Yarn over (yo) | | ▲ S2KP2 | |
| ℧ K1 tbl | | ■ No stitch | |
| Ⓜ M1 purl on RS | | Ⓜ M1 knit on WS | |

**T2R** Sl 1 to cn and hold to back, k1 tbl; p1 from cn.

**T2L** Sl 1 to cn and hold to front, p1; k1 tbl from cn.

**Cable 1/1/1 R** Sl 1 to cn and hold to back, sl 1 to second cn and hold to back, k1 tbl; move first cn to front, p1 from second cn, k1 tbl from remaining cn .

**Cable 1/1/1 L** Sl 1 to cn and hold to front, sl 1 to second cn, hold to back, k1 tbl; p1 from second cn, k1 tbl from remaining cn .

**k-yo-k** through back of the same stitch

**2/2 RC** Sl 2 to cn and hold to back, k2; k2 from cn.

**2/2 LC** Sl 2 to cn and hold to front, k2; k2 from cn.

**2/1/2 RPC** Sl 2 to first cn and hold to back, slip 3rd stitch to second cn and hold to back, k2; move first cn to front, purl stitch from second cn, k2 from cn. *See* **Chart Note** *for left sock.*

**Green** Sl 2 to cn and hold to front, pick up and k1 from side of flap; k2 from cn.

**Yo cable** With right needle pick up third stitch and pass over the first 2 stitches; k-yo-k.

**Japanese flame stitch** *Rows 1–3* Knit. *Row 4* K-yo-k the stitch 3 rows below first stitch on left needle, drop stitch off left needle. *Row 5* K3. *Row 6* S2KP2.

**experienced**

Adult M
**A** 7½"
**B** 9"

10cm/4"

48  34

over stockinette stitch with smaller needles

**1** 2 3 4 5 6

Super Fine weight

**MC** 350 yds
**CC** 20 yds

Two 2.5mm/US 1½, or size to obtain gauge

Two 3mm/US 2½

 3.5mm/US E-4

**&**

Stitch markers
Stitch holder
Small amount waste yarn
4 pewter bee beads 5/16" (8mm) long
Sewing thread to match MC
Two 1" coilless safety pins
Two 6mm gold pearl beads
Swarovski crystal beads: 24 citrine 3mm bicone and
12 jonquil 4mm bicone
96 pearl size 11 seed beads
Size 12 beading needle
Size D beading thread

Shown in
*CLAUDIA HAND PAINTED YARNS*
Fingering 55 Jungle (MC)
and Begonia (CC)

# Bees & Blossoms

*Amy C Rutter*   *Marietta, Georgia*

## Toe

With smaller needles and MC and using Judy's Magic Cast-on, cast 12 stitches onto each of 2 circular needles—24 stitches. *Round 1* Knit. *Round 2* [K1, left lifted increase, knit to last stitch, right lifted increase, k1] 2 times. Repeat last 2 rounds 9 more times—64 stitches.

## Foot

Work in stockinette stitch until sock measures 7½", or 1½" less than desired length.

## Heel

*Round 1* K32 from Needle 1; place 32 stitches from Needle 2 on holder. With crochet cast-on and waste yarn, cast 33 stitches onto Needle 2. Knit to last new stitch; knit that stitch together with first stitch to join—64 stitches. Mark beginning of round. *Round 2* Knit. *Round 3* [SSK, knit to last 2 stitches on needle, k2tog] 2 times. Repeat last 2 rounds 9 more times—24 stitches. Graft heel.

## Leg

Remove waste yarn and place 32 recovered stitches on Needle 1. Replace 32 instep stitches from holder to Needle 2. Join yarn to heel stitches with RS facing. Change to larger needles and rearrange stitches as follows: With larger Needle 1, knit 16 heel stitches. With larger Needle 2, knit 16 heel stitches, then knit 16 instep stitches; slip remaining 16 instep stitches to Needle 1. Beginning of round is at center of instep. *Begin Chart* **Note** that on Round 3 and every following 6th round, the first and last stitches of each needle are crossed, forming a mini cable. Work through end of chart.

## NOTES
*1 See page 168 for any unfamiliar techniques. **2** Sock is worked toe up on 2 circular needles.*

**Chart**

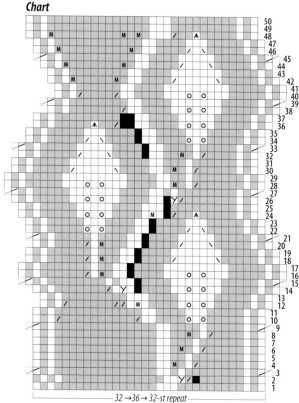

*32 →36 → 32-st repeat*

**Stitch key**

| | | | |
|---|---|---|---|
| ☐ | Knit | ⊙ | Yarn over (yo) |
| ▨ | Purl | Ⓜ | M1 knitwise |
| ⟋ | K2tog | Ⓜ | M1 purlwise |
| ⟋ | P2tog | ⋏ | S2KP2 |
| ⟍ | SSK | Ⴗ | Knit front & back |
| ■ | Stitches do not exist in these areas of chart | | |
| ⟋⟍ | Cross stitches between needles as follows: sl last stitch from needle k-wise, sl first stitch from next needle k-wise, sl both stitches back to left needle; knit second stitch tbl but leave on needle; knit both stitches together tbl; sl second stitch back to new right-hand needle. | | |

## Cuff

*Next round* With smaller needles,*[p1, k1] 5 times, M1P, [k1,
p1] 10 times, cross stitches between needles; repeat from *
once—66 stitches. *Next round* (First stitch already knit into cross
from preceding round) P1, [k1, p1] 15 times, k2, [p1, k1] 16 times.
*Next 4 rounds* *K1, [p1, k1] 16 times; repeat from* once. *Next round*
Continue rib as established, but cross stitches between needles.
*Next round* Continue in rib as established. Bind off loosely.

**Narcissus** With smaller needle, crochet hook, waste yarn and using a temporary cast-on, cast on 6 stitches. *Row 1* With CC, knit. *Row 2* K3, yo, k3—7 stitches. *Row 3 and all odd-numbered rows 5–11* Knit. *Row 4* K3, yo, k4—8 stitches. *Row 6* K3, yo, k5—9 stitches. *Row 8* K3, yo, k6—10 stitches. *Row 10* K3, yo, k7—11 stitches. *Row 12* K3, yo, k8—12 stitches. *Row 13* Bind off 6, knit to end—6 stitches. Repeat Rows 2–13 four more times. Remove waste yarn and place 6 stitches from cast-on edge on spare needle. Graft final row to cast-on row. Weave strand of yarn through eyelets and pull tight, leaving an opening about ¼" in diameter for center of flower.

*Beaded Flower Pins—see diagrams*
Thread beading needle with 48" length of beading thread. String a 6mm pearl and 6 small crystals, leaving a 12" tail. Pass needle through pearl, forming a half circle of crystals around pearl—*diagram A*. Pick up 6 more small crystals and pass needle through pearl, forming a second half circle—*diagram B*. Pass needle through a crystal adjacent to hole in pearl. Pick up 4 seed beads, 1 large crystal, and 4 seed beads and pass needle through small crystal to right of first crystal, then through first small crystal again, forming a petal of seed beads with a large crystal in the middle—*diagram C*. *Pass needle through next 2 small crystals. Pick up 4 seed beads, 1 large crystal, and 4 seed beads and pass needle through last 2 small crystals, forming another petal—*diagram D*. Repeat from* 4 more times, so pearl is surrounded by 6 petals of crystals and seed beads. Weave needle through one of petals and into another petal. Tie a few half hitch knots between beads. Cut thread. Carefully straighten one of the safety pins. Slide pearl onto straightened pin until it lies near clasp. Carefully bend pin back into shape; round nose pliers make this task easier.

**Finishing**
Use sewing thread to sew bee beads near leaves on leg of sock. Insert beaded flowers into center of knitted flowers and pin into place near cuffs of your socks. Remove or change the flowers to suit your mood or your ensemble.

Kirsten Hall    Rockville, Maryland

*experienced*

Women's M (L)
**A** 8 (9)"
**B** 9 (10)"

10cm/4"

48

36
over stockinette stitch

**1** 2 3 4 5 6
Super Fine weight
380 (425) yds

Four 2.25mm/US 1
or size to obtain gauge

**&**

Stitch markers
Cable needle (cn)

Shown in
*REGIA* Cotton in color 0152

## NOTES

*1 See page 168 for any unfamiliar techniques. 2 Sock is worked toe up on double-pointed needles.*

## Toe

Cast on 3 stitches. Do not turn work. Slide stitches back to other end of needle, bring yarn across the back of the stitches. *Round 1* Knit in front and back of stitch (kf&b) 3 times—6 stitches; arrange 3 stitches on each of 2 needles. *Round 2* Kf&b 6 times—12 stitches; arrange 4 stitches on each of 3 needles. Mark beginning of round. *Round 3* [K1, kf&b, place marker (pm), k1, kf&b] 3 times—18 stitches. *Round 4* Knit. *Round 5* [Knit to marker, L inc, slip marker, knit to end of needle, L inc] 3 times—24 stitches. *Rounds 6–11* Repeat Rounds 4 & 5—42 stitches. *Rounds 12 & 13* Knit. *Round 14* Repeat Round 5. *Rounds 15–23* Repeat Rounds 12–14—66 stitches. *Size L only* Repeat Rounds 12–14 once—72 stitches. *All sizes, next round* Knit.

## Foot

*Next round* K1, pm, work Round 1 of Chart A, pm, knit to end of row—70 (76) stitches. Continue as established, working Chart A between markers and stockinette stitch on sole of sock through Round 62 of Chart—94 (100) stitches. *Next round* K1, work Round 63 of Chart, rearrange stitches so 61 stitches of chart are held on 2 needles for instep. Work heel back and forth on remaining 33 (39) stitches.

## Heel

*Row 1* (RS) K6 (7), [k1, sl 1] 10 (12) times, k1, turn; 6 (7) stitches remain unworked. *Row 2* Sl 1 wyif, yo, p20 (24), turn. Note that Sl 1 and yo form a pair. *Row 3* Sl 1 wyib, yo, k2, [sl 1, k1] to 2 stitches before last sl 1/yo pair, k2, turn. *Row 4* Sl 1 wyif, yo, purl to last stitch before next pair, turn. *Row 5* Sl 1 wyib, yo, [k1, sl 1] to 1 stitch before next pair, k1, turn. *Row 6* Repeat Row 4. Repeat Rows 3–6 once, then work Rows 3–5 once. Do not turn. There are 6 sl 1/yo pairs on each side of center 9 (13) stitches.

## Heel flap

*Continue with RS row* [K1tbl, k1] 5 times, k1tbl, SSK, turn. *Next row* Sl 1 wyif, purl to first yo, [p1tbl, p1] 5 times, p1tbl, p2tog, turn. Move first 11 and last 11 stitches from instep needles to heel needles—39 stitches remain on hold for instep. *Next row* Sl 2 wyib, [k1, sl 1] 16 (18) times, SSK, turn. *Next row* Sl 1 wyif, p31 (35), p2tog, turn. Repeat last 2 rows until 1 stitch remains to be joined on either side of heel flap. *Next row* (RS) Work to last 4 stitches of heel flap; place marker for new beginning of round.

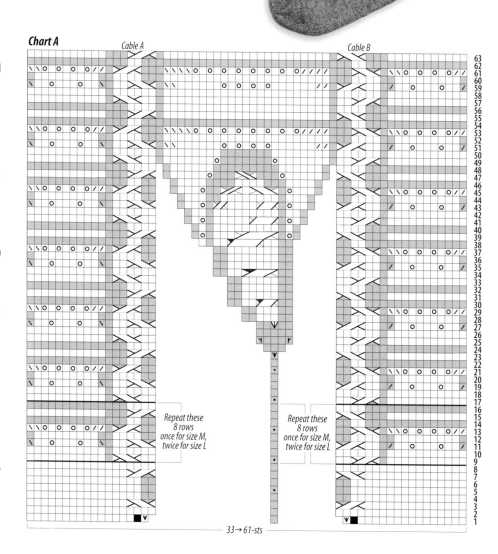

**Chart A**

Cable A

Cable B

Repeat these 8 rows once for size M, twice for size L

Repeat these 8 rows once for size M, twice for size L

33→61-sts

## Chart B

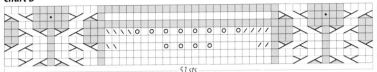

*51 sts*

## Chart C

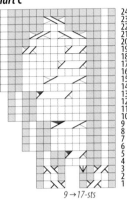

*9 → 17-sts*

## Cuff chart, size L

*11-st repeat*

## Cuff chart, size M

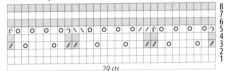

*29 sts*

### Leg

*Round 1* K1, k1-yo-k1 into next stitch (kok inc), k1, SSK, p3, k4, p25, k4, p3, k2tog, k1, kok inc, knit to end of round—76 (80) stitches. *Round 2* Work Round 1 of Chart B over next 51 stitches, *p1, k1; repeat from* to last stitch, p1. Continue in Chart B and p1, k1 rib as established, working Rounds 1–8 of Chart 4 times.

*Next round* Work Round 1 of Chart B, [p1, k1] 4 (5) times, work Round 1 of Chart C over next 9 stitches, [k1, p1] 4 (5) times. Continue in patterns as established through Round 24 of Chart C—84 (88) stitches.

### Cuff

*Next round* Continue Chart B on instep stitches, then work Round 1 of Cuff Chart for your size on back of leg. Continue in patterns as established, working Rounds 1–8 once, then working Rounds 1–5. *Next round* Purl. *Next round* Knit. Bind off loosely.

### Stitch key

- ☐ Knit
- ☐ Purl
- ◯ Yarn over (yo)
- ⟋ K2tog
- ⟋ P2tog
- ⟍ SSK
- **R inc** Purl into right loop of stitch in row below then p1 (right lifted inc)
- **L inc** P1 then purl into left loop of stitch in row below (left lifted inc)
- **⅓** K3tog
- **⅓** SK2P
- **•** **Pebble** K-yo-k into stitch. Slip 3 to left needle; k3, slip 3 to left needle; sl 2tog k-wise, sl 1 k-wise, p2sso
- ⱴ **kok inc** k1-yo-k1 into stitch
- ⱴ **pop inc** p1-yo-p1 into stitch
- ▓ Stitches do not exist in these areas of chart
- ⟋ **2/1 RC** Slip 1 to cn and hold to back, k2; k1 from cn
- ⟍ **2/1 LC** Slip 2 to cn and hold to front, k1; k2 from cn
- ⟍ **2/2 LC** Sl 2 to cn and hold to front, k2; k2 from cn
- ⟍ **2/2 RC** Sl 2 to cn and hold to back, k2; k2 from cn
- ⟋ **1/1 RPC** Slip 1 to cn and hold to back, k1; p1 from cn
- ⟍ **1/1 LPC** Slip 1 to cn and hold to front, k1; p1 from cn
- ⟋ **1/2 RPC** Slip 2 to cn and hold to back, k1; p2 from cn
- ⟍ **1/2 LPC** Slip 1 to cn and hold to front, p2; k1 from cn
- ⟋ **2/1 RC inc** Slip 1 to cn and hold to back, k2; kok inc from cn
- ⟍ **2/2 RPC** Slip 2 to cn and hold to back, k2; p2 from cn
- ⟍ **2/2 LPC** Slip 2 to cn and hold to front, p2; k2 from cn
- ◣ **2/3 RC inc** Sl 2 to cn and hold to back, k3; k1, kok inc from cn
- ⟋ **3/1 RC** Sl 1 to cn and hold to back, k3; k1 from cn
- ⟋ **4/1 RC inc** Sl 1 to cn and hold to back, k4; kok inc from cn
- ⟋ **4/2 RC** Sl 2 to cn and hold to back, k4; k2 from cn

*intermediate*

Adult M
**A** 8"
**B** 10"

10cm/4"

46
32

over stockinette stitch

**1** 2 3 4 5 6

Super Fine weight
400 yds

Two 2.25mm/US 1,
or size to obtain gauge,
40cm (16") or longer

2.25mm/US B-1

**&**

Mini compass ¾"
diameter mounted on a
rectangular base 1" × 2"
Small stitch holder

Shown in
*UNIVERSAL YARNS* Ditto in
Bryce Canyon Black

# Find Your Way Home

*Wendy Gaal*   Encinitas, California

## Toe

Use Judy's Magic Cast-on to cast 17 stitches onto each needle—34 stitches.
*Round 1* **Needle 1** Knit; **Needle 2** knit through back loop. *Round 2* [K1, M1, knit to last stitch on needle, M1, k1] 2 times. *Round 3* Knit. Repeat last 2 rounds 8 more times—70 stitches. Move first 3 and last 2 stitches from Needle 1 to Needle 2—30 stitches on Needle 1 for sole, 40 stitches on Needle 2 for top of foot.

## Foot

*Round 1* **Needle 1** Knit;
**Needle 2** work Round 1
of Chart for left or right
sock. Work as established
until foot measures
8", or 2" shorter than
desired length. Move
first 6 and last 6 stitches
from Needle 2 to Needle
1—42 stitches on Needle
1 for heel, 28 stitches on
Needle 2 for instep.

**Chart, left sock**

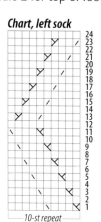

10-st repeat

**Chart, right sock**

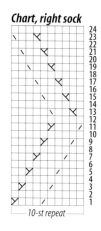

10-st repeat

☐ Knit on RS, purl on RS
☑ K2tog
◫ SSK
☒ Right lifted increase
☒ Left lifted increase

## Heel

*Note* See technique box on next page for making yo at beginning of row and reorienting yo (RYO).
Work back and forth on Needle 1. *Row 1* (RS) K41, turn. *Row 2* (WS) Yo, purl to last stitch, turn. *Row 3* Yo, knit to 1 stitch before previous yo, turn. *Row 4* Yo, purl to 1 stitch before previous yo, turn. Repeat last 2 rows 10 more times. *Row 25* Yo, knit to first yo, RYO, k2tog, turn. *Row 26* Yo, purl to first yo, SSP, turn. *Row 27* Yo, knit to next yo, RYO twice, k3tog, turn. *Row 28* Yo, purl to next yo, SSSP, turn. Repeat last 2 rows until all yo's have been worked—42 stitches on Needle 1. Move first 6 and last 6 stitches from Needle 1 to Needle 2—30 stitches on Needle 1 for back of leg, 40 stitches on Needle 2 for front of leg.

## Leg

Work all stitches in Chart pattern, continuing from where you left off on instep. For left sock, work until leg measures 6½", then work cuff. For right sock, work until leg measures 2½", then work compass pocket.

## NOTES

*1 See page 168 for any unfamiliar techniques. 2 Sock is worked toe up on 2 circular needles.*

## Compass pocket

With RS facing, using a separate ball of yarn, pick up and k1 in purl bump behind last 12 stitches on Needle 2. Work these 12 stitches back and forth in stockinette stitch for 2¾". Then put on hold and cut yarn, leaving a long tail.

*Next round, attach pocket lining* **Needle 1** Work in pattern; **Needle 2** work 27 stitches, pick up a stitch from edge of lining and work it together with next stitch, work 10, pick up a stitch from opposite edge and work together with next stitch. Continue to attach pocket every other round or every RS row. After approximately ½", end with an odd-numbered row of Chart. *Next row* K63, bind off 2, knit to end. *Next row* Work to 2 stitches before bound-off stitches, k2tog, turn. *Next row* P2tog, purl to 2 stitches before bound-off stitches, SSP, turn. *Next row* SSK, work to last 2 stitches, k2tog. *Next row* Purl to last 2 stitches, SSP. *Next row* Work to end. *Next row* P1, M1P, purl to end. *Next row* K1, M1, work in pattern to last stitch, M1, k1. *Next row* P1, M1P, purl to last stitch, M1P, p1. *Next row* K1, M1, work to end, cast on 2, rejoin to work in the round and work to end of Needle 2. Work around leg, attaching pocket lining, then continue until leg measures 6½".

### Cuff
Work in k1, p1 rib for 1½". Bind off loosely.

### Finishing
With crochet hook, work 1 round single crochet around compass opening. Place compass in pocket and graft top of pocket lining closed.

Reorientation of yarn over (RYO)

**Yo beginning of a knit row**
With yarn in front of needle, knit first stitch: right leg of yo is in front of needle.

**Yo beginning of a purl row**
With yarn in back of needle, bring it over the needle to the front of work and around needle to purl the stitch: right leg of yo is in back of needle.

1      2      3

*1* When the right leg of a stitch (or yo) is at back of the needle, slip to right needle as if to purl.
*2* Return to left needle as if to knit.
*3* Now the right leg of the stitch is ready to be worked.

**experienced**

Adult S
**A** 7"
**B** 9"

10cm/4"

36

36

over Chart pattern

**1** 2 3 4 5 6

Super Fine weight
**A** 275 yds
**B** 200 yds

2.25mm/US 1, 80cm (32") long
or size to obtain gauge

**&**

Cable needle (cn)

Shown in
*REGIA* 4-fädig Mosaik
in color 5568 (A) and
Design Line by Kaffe Fassett
in color 4255 (B)

# Twisted Mosaic

*Janice Talkington*    Saginaw, Michigan

## Toe

Use Straight-wrap Cast-on and A to cast on 34 stitches. Arrange for Magic Loop with 17 stitches on each needle. *Round 1* Knit. *Round 2* [K1, M1, *p1, k1; repeat from* to last 2 stitches on needle, p1, M1, k1] twice. *Round 3* [K2, *p1, k1; repeat from* to last stitch on needle, k1] twice. *Round 4* [K1, M1, *k1, p1; repeat from* to last stitch on needle, M1, k1] twice. *Round 5* [*K1, p1; repeat from* to last stitch on needle, k1] twice. Repeat Rounds 2–5 four more times— 74 stitches; 37 sole stitches on Needle 1, 37 instep stitches on Needle 2.

## Foot

*Begin Chart* Work Rounds 1–40, then work Rounds 1–23.

## Arch expansion

*Next round* Maintaining pattern as established, work 13, place marker (pm), work 11, pm, work to end of round. *Next round, increase round* (Round 25 of Chart) Work to first marker, M1, slip marker (sm),k1, M1, work to 1 stitch before 2nd marker, M1, k1, sm, M1, work to end of round. Continue as established, working increase round every 8th round 4 more times—57 stitches on Needle 1; 94 stitches total. End with Round 22 of Chart.

## Heel turn

K14 with A. Move these stitches to Needle 2; move last 14 stitches from Needle 1 to Needle 2—Needle 1 now holds 29 heel stitches; Needle 2 holds 65 instep stitches. With A, work back and forth on Needle 1.

*Row 1* (RS) K3, [sl 1, k1] to last 2 stitches, wrap next stitch and turn work (W&T). *Row 2* Purl to last 2 stitches, W&T. *Row 3* [K1, sl 1] to 1 stitch before last wrapped stitch, W&T. *Row 4* Purl to 1 stitch before last wrapped stitch, W&T. *Row 5* [Sl 1, k1] to 1 stitch before last wrapped stitch, W&T. *Row 6* Repeat Row 4. Repeat Rows 3–6 twice more—7 wrapped stitches on each side. *Next row* (RS) [K1, sl1] to first wrapped stitch, k6 hiding wraps, SSK next stitch and its wrap together with following stitch, turn. *Next row* Slip 1, purl to first wrapped stitch, p6 hiding wraps, p2tog next stitch and its wrap with following stitch—27 stitches on heel needle.

## Back of heel

*Set-up row* Place a marker at each end of Needle 2. Slide first 10 and last 10 stitches from Needle 1 to ends of Needle 2—Needle 1 now holds 45 instep stitches; Needle 2 holds 47 heel stitches. With RS facing, slip first 10 stitches and marker of Needle 2 so working yarn is accessible and you are ready to work across heel turn stitches. *Row 1* (RS) [Slip 1, k1] to 1 stitch before marker, SSK, remove marker (rm), turn. *Row 2* Sl 1, purl to 1 stitch before marker, p2tog, rm, turn. *Row 3* [Slip 1, k1] to 1 stitch before previous turn, SSK, turn. *Row 4* Sl 1, purl to 1 stitch before previous turn, p2tog, turn. Repeat Rows 3 and 4 seven more times—1 stitch remains unworked on each end, 29 stitches on Needle 2.

## NOTES

*1 See page 168 for any unfamiliar techniques. 2 Sock is worked toe up on 1 circular needle using Magic Loop method.*

**Chart**

Working yarn

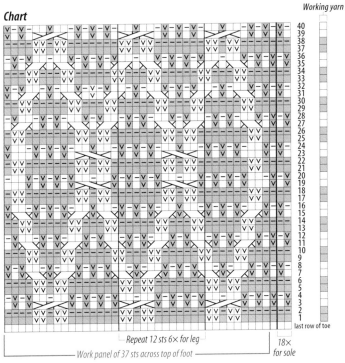

*Repeat 12 sts 6× for leg*
18× for sole
*Work panel of 37 sts across top of foot*

last row of toe

## Leg

*Next row* (RS) [Sl 1, k1] until 1 stitch before previous turn, SSK. Resume working in the round. *Next Round* **Needle 1** Work Round 23 of Chart pattern as established; **Needle 2** SSK, [slip 1, k1]. Work 12-stitch repeat of Chart pattern around 72 stitches of leg for approximately 5½", or to desired length, end with Round 20 or Round 40 of Chart. Cut B.

## Cuff

*Next 6 rounds* With A, work k1, p1 rib. Bind off loosely.

# Color

*easy +*

Adult M
**A** 7½"
**B** 9½"

10cm/4"

42 | 30

over stockinette stitch

 2 3 4 5 6

Super Fine weight
**A** 190 yds
**B** 170 yds
**C, D, E** 34 yds each

Two 2mm/US 0
or size to obtain gauge
40cm/16" or longer

2.25mm/B-1

Yarn needle

Shown in
*SHIBUI* Sock Deep Mossy
Green (A), Wasabi (B),
Honey (C)

*CLAUDIA HANDPAINTED
YARNS* Fingering Honey (D),
Last Night's Wine (E)

# A Tad Bit O' Plaid

*Karen Wohlen*    *Spokane, Washington*

## Toe

Use A and Judy's Magic Cast-on to cast on 12 stitches. Arrange 6 stitches on each needle: Needle 1 holds instep stitches; Needle 2 holds sole/heel stitches.

*Round 1* [K1, M1L, knit to last stitch on needle, M1R, k1] twice. *Rounds 2–4* Repeat Round 1—28 stitches. *Round 5* Knit. *Round 6* Repeat Round 1. Repeat last 2 rounds 6 times—56 stitches.

## Foot

*Begin Chart A* **Needle 1** Work Chart A; **Needle 2** work same color sequence in stockinette stitch; continue until sock measures 6½" from beginning, or 3" less than foot length, end with Round 12.

## Gussets

*Round 1* **Needle 1** Work Chart A; **Needle 2** k1, M1L, knit to last stitch, M1R, k1. *Round 2* **Needle 1** Work Chart A; **Needle 2** knit. Repeat last 2 rounds 8 times—28 instep and 46 heel stitches. Work across Needle 1 in pattern.

## Heel turn

With A, work back and forth on Needle 2 only: *Row 1* (RS) K32, knit in front and back of next stitch (kf&b), k1, wrap next stitch and turn work (W&T). *Row 2* (WS) P21, purl into front and back of next stitch (pf&b), p1, W&T.

*Row 3* K19, kf&b, k1, W&T. *Row 4* P17, pf&b, p1, W&T. Continue working 2 fewer stitches before each increase until *Row 10* P5, pf&b, p1, W&T—56 stitches on Needle 2. *Row 11* Knit, hiding wraps. Work across Needle 1 in pattern.

## Heel flap

With A, work back and forth on Needle 2 only: *Row 1* (RS) K41, hiding remaining wraps, SSK, turn. *Row 2* (WS) Sl 1, p26, p2tog, turn. *Row 3* Sl 1, [k1, sl 1] 13 times, SSK, turn. Repeat last 2 rows 12 times, then work Row 2 once—28 stitches on Needle 2. *Next row* Knit.

## Leg

Resume working in rounds, maintaining color sequence, and working Chart A on all stitches until leg measures approximately 5½" above heel flap, end with Round 6.

## Cuff

With A, work k3, p1 rib for 1". Bind off using elastic bind-off (see technique box on next page).

## Vertical stripes

Using crochet hook and placing colors as shown in Chart B, chain in every purl stitch from toe to cuff on instep/front of leg and from top of heel to cuff on back of leg.

## NOTES

*1 See page 168 for any unfamiliar techniques. **2** Sock is worked toe up on 2 circular needles.*

**1** Knit 2 stitches.
**2** Insert left needle into 2 stitches on right needle (from left to right) …

… and knit them together (through back loops):

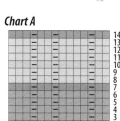

1 stitch bound off (see above).
**3** Knit 1 more stitch.
**4** Repeat Steps 2–3.

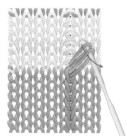

**Chart A**

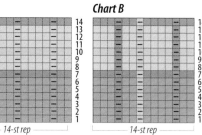

└─ 14-st rep ─┘

**Chart B**

14
13
12
11
10
9
8
7
6
5
4
3
2
1

└─ 14-st rep ─┘

**Stitch key**
☐ Knit
⊟ Purl

**Color key**
▨ A
▨ B
▨ C
▨ D
▨ E

**Chart Note**
When knitting the sock, follow Chart A. Chart B shows the vertical stripes crocheted over the purls.

Adult S
**A** 7"
**B** 8"

10cm/4"

48

32

over stockinette stitch

**1** 2 3 4 5 6

Super fine weight
375 yds

2.5mm/US 1½, 80 cm (32") or
longer or size to obtain gauge

Shown in
*REGIA* 4-fädig in color 5048

*Natalia Vasilieva*   *Moscow, Russia*

## ESTONIAN SPIRAL SOCK

### Leg
Cast on 60 stitches. Arrange stitches for Magic Loop technique and join to work in the round. *Spiral Stitch, all rounds* [K2, yo, k1, k2tog] around. Work in Spiral Stitch until piece measures 6" from cast-on.

### Heel
*Next row* Knit 30. Work back and forth on these stitches only for heel. Work 11 more rows in stockinette stitch, end with WS row.

### Heel turn
*Row 1* K**18**, SSK, k**10**. *Row 2* P**17**, p2tog, p**10**. *Row 3* K**17**, SSK, k**9**, *Row 4* P**16**, p2tog, p**9**. *Row 5* K**16**, SSK, k**8**. *Row 6* P**15**, p2tog, p**8**. *Row 7* K**15**, SSK, k**7**. *Row 8* P**14**, p2tog, p**7**. *Row 9* K**14**, SSK, k**6**. *Row 10* P**13**, p2tog, p**6**—20 stitches. *Row 11* K**14**, SSK, turn. *Row 12* P**7**, p2tog, turn. *Row 13* K**7**, SSK, turn. Repeat last 2 rows 4 more times, then work Row 12 once—8 stitches.

### Foot
*Next round* Knit 8 heel stitches. Pick up and k11 along left side of heel. Continue Spiral Stitch pattern on 30 instep stitches. Pick up and k11 along right side of heel—60 stitches. Work Spiral Stitch on all stitches until foot measures 7" from back of heel, or 1" less than desired length.

### Toe
*Round 1* [K3, k2tog] around. *Round 2, 4, 6* Knit. *Round 3* [K2, k2tog] around. *Round 5* [K1, k2tog] around. *Round 7* [K2tog] around. Cut yarn and draw through 12 remaining stitches. Pull tight and fasten off.

## NOTES
*1 See page 168 for any unfamiliar techniques. 2 Socks are worked cuff down on 1 circular needle using Magic Loop method.*

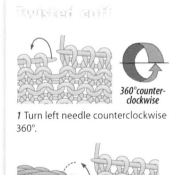

Twisted cuff

360°counter-clockwise

**1** Turn left needle counterclockwise 360°.

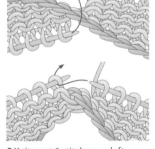

**2** Knit next 6 stitches on left needle. *Note* Sock cuff is worked in seed, not garter stitch.

## FAIR ISLE SOCK

### Cuff

Cast on 60 stitches. Do not join to work in the round. *Row 1* [K1, p1] around. *Row 2* [P1, k1] around. Repeat last 2 rows twice more. *Row 7* *[K1, p1] 3 times, rotate left needle 360 degrees counterclockwise, making a twist in the work between the needles; repeat from*. Join to work in the round. *Round 1* [P1, k1] around. *Round 2* [K1, p1] around. Repeat last 2 rounds once more.

### Leg

Join second strand of yarn. Begin Chart. Work 4-row repeat of pattern 12 times.

**Chart**

6-st repeat

**Stitch key**

☐ A
☐ B

### Chart Note

The stranded colorwork pattern is worked using 2 strands of the same multi-colored yarn, one labeled A and the other B. In order to maintain contrast, be sure to start each strand in a different place in the color sequence. Carry the color not in use loosely across the WS of the work.

## Heel

*Next row* **Needle 1** Work pattern over next 29 stitches, slip last stitch to Needle 2; **Needle 2** work pattern over next 31 stitches. Working back and forth on Needle 2 stitches only, work 17 more rows in Chart pattern, end with WS row.

## Heel turn

Drop B; continue heel with A only. *Row 1* K16, SSK, k1, turn. *Row 2* Sl 1, p**2**, p2tog, p1, turn. *Row 3* Sl 1, k**3**, SSK, k1, turn. *Row 4* Sl 1, p**4**, p2tog, p1, turn. *Row 5* Sl 1, k**5**, SSK, k1, turn. *Row 6* Sl 1, p**6**, p2tog, p1, turn. *Row 7* Sl 1, k**7**, SSK, k1, turn. *Row 8* Sl 1, p**8**, p2tog, p1, turn. *Row 9* Sl 1, k**7**, SSK, turn. *Row 10* Sl 1, p**7**, p2tog, turn. Repeat last 2 rows 6 more times—9 stitches.

## Foot

Beginning with Row 1, Stitch 5 of Chart, work 9 heel stitches in pattern. Continuing in pattern, pick up and k11 along left side of heel, knit across 29 instep stitches, and pick up and k11 along right side of heel—60 stitches. Continue in pattern as established until foot measures 6½", or 1½" less than desired length.

## Toe

Cut B; continue toe with A only. *Round 1* [K4, SSK, k4] around. *Round 2, 4, 6, 8, 10* Knit. *Round 3* [K4, k2tog, k3] around. *Round 5* [K3, SSK, k3] around. *Round 7* [K3, k2tog, k2] around. *Round 9* [K2, SSK, k2] around. *Round 11* [K2, k2tog, k1] around. *Round 12* [K1, SSK, k1] around. *Round 13* [K1, k2tog] around. *Round 14* [SSK] around. Cut yarn, draw through remaining stitches, pull tight, and fasten off.

## Entrelac cuff & leg

*Tier 3* Work rectangles with RS facing.

*Tier 2* Work rectangles with WS facing.

*Tier 1* Work garter stitch rectangles.

〰️ live stitches
—— picked-up stitches
〰️〰️ joined edge

◇ RS rectangle

◆ WS rectangle

74

## ENTRELAC SOCKS

**WS Rectangles, set-up row** With WS facing, pick up and p5 along left edge of rectangle in Tier round. *Row 1* (RS) K5, turn. *Rows 2, 4, 6 & 8* (WS) Sl 1, p3, p2tog, turn. *Rows 3, 5, 7, & 9* Sl 1, k4, turn. *Row 10* Sl 1, p3, p2tog.

**RS Rectangles, set-up row** With RS facing, pick up and k5 along left edge of rectangle in previous Tier. *Row 1* (WS) P5, turn. *Rows 2, 4, 6 & 8* Sl 1, k3, k2tog, turn. *Rows 3, 5, 7 & 9* Sl 1, p4, turn. *Row 10* Sl 1, k3, k2tog.

### Cuff
**Tier 1** *Use knit cast-on to cast on 5 stitches; knit 8 rows—1 garter stitch rectangle complete. Do not turn. Repeat from *7 more times—8 rectangles complete. Work 1 additional row on last rectangle to begin next Tier, turn work.

### Leg
**Tier 2** Work 7 WS Rectangles, then work 1 more, joining to first rectangle of Tier 1 AND working extra RS row, turn work.
**Tier 3** Work 8 RS Rectangles, working extra WS row on last rectangle, turn work. Continue as established, alternating Tiers of RS and WS Rectangles until 16 Tiers are complete.

### Heel
**Heel tier 1** Work 5 RS Rectangles; work extra WS row. **Heel tier 2** Work 4 WS Rectangles; work extra RS row. **Heel tier 3** Work 3 RS Rectangles; work extra WS row. **Heel tier 4** Work 2 WS Rectangles. Pick up and p5, turn work. **Heel tier 5** Work 3 RS rectangles: begin first on Row 2 and join third to side of Tier 3 rectangle (see illustration). Pick up and p5, turn work. **Heel tier 6** Work 4 WS rectangles: begin first on Row 2 and join fourth to side of Tier 2 rectangle. Do not turn work.

### Foot
Resume working Tiers of rectangles as for leg. Continue until foot measures 7¼", or about ¾" less than desired length, end with a Tier of WS Rectangles.

### Toe
Work 1 RS Rectangle. **Next rectangle, set-up row** *Pick up and k5 along left edge of next rectangle in previous round. *Row 1* (WS) P4, p2tog, turn. *Rows 2, 4, 6 & 8* Sl 1, k3, k2tog, turn. *Rows 3, 5, 7 & 9* Sl 1, p3, p2 tog. *Row 10* Sl 1, k3, k2tog. Repeat from *6 more times. Bind off. Cut yarn, leaving a long tail. With a tapestry needle, sew bound-off edge to side of first rectangle in final Tier. Run tail through corners of rectangles at toe, pull tight, fasten off.

**Entrelac heel**

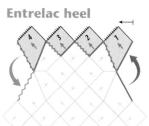

*Heel tier 6* Make 4 WS rectangles, picking up first addjoining last to sides of Tier 2.

*Heel tier 5* Make 3 RS rectangles, picking up first adjoining last to sides of Tier 3.

*Heel tier 4* Make 2 WS rectangles.

*Heel tier 3* Make 3 RS rectangles.

*Heel tier 2* Make 4 WS rectangles.

*Heel tier 1* Make 5 RS rectangles.

*intermediate*

Adult M
**A** 8"
**B** 10"

10cm/4"
44
35
over Foot Pattern

  2 3 4 5 6

Super Fine weight
3 or more colors
400 yds total

Five 2.25mm/US 1
or size to obtain gauge

Shown in
*CHERRY TREE HILL/LOUET*
Gems Fingering in Old
Rose, Monet, Sugar Maple,
Green Mountain Madness,
Blueberry Hill, Country
Garden, Champlain Sunset,
and Fall Foliage.

# Drip Candles

*Kirsten Hall*   Rockville, Maryland

**Foot Pattern** (Over a multiple of 2 stitches)
*Rounds 1 and 3* With A, knit. *Round 2* [K1 with A, k1 with B] to end of round. *Rounds 4–6* [K1 with B, k1 with A] to end of round. *Round 7* With B, knit. *Round 8* [K1 with A, k1 with B] to end of round. *Rounds 9–16* Repeat Rounds 1–8 EXCEPT with B (instead of A) and C (instead of B) as shown in Foot Color Sequence. *Rounds 17–24* Repeat Rounds 1–8 EXCEPT with C (instead of A) and A (instead of B) as shown in Foot Color Sequence. Repeat these 24 rounds for 3-color sock, or changing colors in an expanded sequence or as desired for more colors.

**Ankle Pattern** (Over a multiple of 4 stitches)
*Round 1* With A, knit. *Round 2* With B, [k1, slip 1 purlwise with yarn on WS (sl 1), k1, p1] to end of round. *Rounds 3–30* Repeat last 2 rounds, changing colors as shown in Ankle Stripe Sequence for 3-color sock, or changing colors in an expanded sequence or as desired for more colors.

**Ankle Stripe Sequence**
Work 1 row each: A, *(B, A, B, A, B) twice, (C, B, C, B, C) twice, (A, C, A, C, A) twice; repeat from*.

**Toe**
Use A and Judy's Magic Cast-on to cast on 16 stitches. Arrange 4 stitches on each of 4 needles; Needles 1 & 2 will be instep stitches, Needles 3 & 4 will be heel stitches. Join to work in the round.

**Foot Color Sequence**

| | | |
|---|---|---|
| A | C | 24 |
| A | | 23 |
| C | A | 22 |
| C | A | 21 |
| C | A | 20 |
| C | | 19 |
| A | C | 18 |
| C | | 17 |
| C | B | 16 |
| C | | 15 |
| B | C | 14 |
| B | C | 13 |
| B | C | 12 |
| B | | 11 |
| C | B | 10 |
| B | | 9 |
| B | A | 8 |
| B | | 7 |
| A | B | 6 |
| A | B | 5 |
| A | B | 4 |
| A | | 3 |
| B | A | 2 |
| A | | 1 |

*Round 1* [K1, make 1 left (M1L), knit to last stitch on needle, make 1 right (M1R), k2] twice. *Rounds 2 & 3* Repeat Round 1—28 stitches. *Round 4* Knit. Repeat last 2 rounds 11 more times—72 stitches.

**Foot**
Work even in Foot Pattern until foot measures approximately 6" from beginning of toe, or 4" less than foot length, end with a single-color round.

**Gussets**
*Note* Work increases on 2-color rounds. The pattern will be disrupted at the increases; it may be necessary to knit 2 stitches of the same color next to one another. Take care to maintain pattern between increases.

*Round 1* **Needles 1 & 2** Work in pattern; **Needles 3 & 4** k1, M1L, work in pattern to last stitch, M1R, k1. *Round 2* Work in pattern. Repeat last 2 rounds 11 more times—36 instep stitches, 60 heel stitches.

## NOTES
*1 See page 168 for any unfamiliar techniques. 2 Sock is worked toe up on double-pointed needles. 3 The stitch pattern is written as a sequence of 3 colors designated A, B, and C. Feel free to use more colors and change them at random or in order you wish; the sample socks were made with the 8 colors listed.*

## Heel turn

Work 36 instep stitches in pattern. Continue with heel in one color only: *Row 1* K18, [k1, sl 1] 11 times, k2, turn. *Row 2* P2tog, p22, turn. *Row 3* K2tog tbl, [sl 1, k1] 10 times, k1, turn. *Row 4* P2tog, p20, turn. *Row 5* K2tog tbl, [sl1, k1] 9 times, k1, turn. *Row 6* P2tog, p18, turn. *Row 7* K2tog tbl, [sl1, k1] 8 times, k1, turn. *Row 8* P2tog, p16, turn. *Row 9* K2tog tbl, [sl1, k1] 7 times, k1, turn. *Row 10* P2tog, p14, turn. *Row 11* K2tog tbl, [sl1, k1] 6 times, k1, turn. *Row 12* P2tog, p12, turn. *Row 13* K2tog tbl, [sl1, k1] 5 times, k1, do not turn—12 stitches in short-row section of heel with 18 gusset stitches unworked on each side.

## Heel flap

*Row 1* Pick up and k12 along side of heel turn, knitting 12th stitch together with adjoining gusset stitch, turn. *Row 2* P24, pick up and p12 along side of heel, purling 12th stitch together with gusset stitch, turn. Continue decreasing last stitch of heel flap with gusset stitch as follows: *Row 3* [Sl 1, k1] 17 times, sl 1, SSK, turn. *Row 4* P35, p2tog, turn. *Row 5* Sl 1, [sl 1, k1] 17 times, SSK, turn. *Row 6* P35, p2tog, turn. Repeat Rows 3–6 seven more times— 38 stitches on heel needle. *Joining round* [Sl 1, k1] 17 times, sl 1, SSK, k36 instep stitches, k2tog, knit to end of heel needle— 72 stitches.

Work in Foot Pattern for 1".

## Leg

Work in Ankle Pattern for 5".

## Cuff

Using the color of your choice, work k1, p1 rib for 1". Bind off using tubular bind-off.

Adult M
**A** 8"
**B** 9½"

10cm/4"

50  

36

over stockinette stitch

 1 2 3 4 5 6

Super Fine weight
**MC** 250 yds
**CC** 180 yds

2.25mm/US 1,
or size to obtain gauge
23cm/9" long

Four 2.25mm/US 1

**&**

Stitch marker

Shown in
*CHERRY TREE HILL* Supersock
in Natural (MC) and
Cabin Fever (CC)

# Fair Isle Made Easy

Laurie Kynaston     Spokane, Washington

## Corrugated Rib
*Every round* K2 with CC, p2 with MC.

## Stripe Pattern
Knit 3 rounds with MC, knit 3 rounds with CC.

## Cuff
With MC and circular needle, cast on 72 stitches. Place marker (pm) for beginning of round and join. Work in Corrugated Rib for 1".

## Leg
With MC, knit 2 rounds. **Begin Chart** Work Rounds 1–20 of chart 4 times. Place last 36 stitches worked on hold for instep.

## Heel flap
With CC, work back and forth in rows on remaining 36 stitches. *Row 1* (RS) [Sl 1, k1] to end. *Row 2* (WS) Sl 1, purl to end. Repeat last 2 rows 17 more times—36 rows.

## Turn heel
*Row 1*(RS) Sl 1, k19, SSK, k1, turn. *Row 2* Sl 1, p**5**, p2tog, p1, turn. *Row 3* Sl 1, k**6**, SSK, k1, turn. *Row 4* Sl 1, p**7**, p2tog, p1, turn. *Row 5* Sl 1, k**8**, SSK, k1, turn. Continue working 1 more stitch before decrease every row, end sl 1, p**17**, p2tog, p1, turn—20 stitches.

## Gussets
K10. Change to MC and k10, then pick up and k19 along side of heel flap, pm, knit instep stitches from hold, pm, pick up and k19 along side of heel flap, then k10—94 stitches; beginning of round is at center of heel.

*Round 1* Knit to 3 stitches before marker, k2tog, k1, knit to next marker, k1, SSK, knit to end of round. *Round 2* Knit. Change to CC and Stripe Pattern. AT SAME TIME, repeat last 2 rounds until 72 stitches remain.

## Foot
Work even in Stripe Pattern until foot measures approximately 7½" from back of heel, or 2" less than desired length.

## Toe
Change to CC and double-pointed needles. *Round 1* **Needle 1** K15, k2tog, k1; **Needle 2** k1, SSK, k30, k2tog, k1; **Needle 3** k1, SSK, knit to end of round. *Round 2* Knit. *Round 3* **Needle 1** Knit to last 3 stitches, k2tog, k1; **Needle 2** k1, SSK, knit to last 3 stitches, k2tog, k1; **Needle 3** k1, SSK, knit to end of round. *Round 4* Knit. Repeat last 2 rounds 8 more times, then work Round 3 four more times—16 stitches.

## Finishing
With Needle 3, knit stitches from Needle 1. Graft toe.

**Chart**

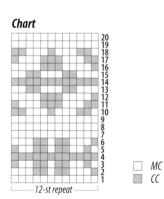

□ MC
▨ CC

———12-st repeat———

## NOTES
*1 See page 168 for any unfamiliar techniques. 2 Socks were worked top down on 9" circular needles, with double-pointed needles used for the toes only. If you prefer, use double-pointed needles for the entire sock.*

**intermediate**

Adult M
**A** 8"
**B** 8½"

10cm/4"

36

32

over Chart A pattern
with larger needle

**1** 2 3 4 5 6

Super Fine weight

**A** 180 yds
**B** 150 yds

2.75mm/US 2, 80cm (32") long
or size to obtain gauge
2.0mm/US 0, 80cm (32") long

Shown in
*COLINETTE YARNS* JitterBug
Velvet Olive (A) and
Velvet Plum (B)

# Mirrored Fair Isle

*Cathy Leffingwell*   *Eau Claire, Wisconsin*

## Cuff
With Tubular Cast-on, smaller needle, and A, cast on
62 stitches. Arrange for Magic Loop method with 31
stitches on each needle, join to work in the round. Change
to larger needle and work k1, p1 rib for 1½". Knit 1 round.

## Leg
*Begin Chart A.* Work 8-row repeat of chart until piece
measures approximately 4" from beginning, end
with Row 3.

## Gusset
*Next round* Work Round 1 of Chart B, then Chart A as
established. Continue through Round 29 of Chart B,
completing round with Chart A—91 stitches; 59 stitches
on Needle 1, 32 stitches on Needle 2.

## Turn heel
Work back and forth in short rows for heel, maintaining color
pattern established in Gusset. *Row 1* (RS) K17, k2tog tbl, k1,
turn. *Row 2* Sl 1, p**6**, p2tog, p1, turn. *Row 3* Sl 1, k**7**, k2tog tbl,
k1, turn. *Row 4* Sl 1, p**8**, p2tog, p1, turn. *Row 5* Sl 1, k**9**, k2tog
tbl, k1, turn. Continue as established, working 1 more stitch before
decrease each row until *Row 27* Sl 1, k**31**, k2tog tbl—64 stitches.

## Foot
Resume working in the round. *Begin Chart C* Repeat 8
rows of chart for 3" or until sock is about 2½" less than
desired length.

## Toe
Work stitches on top of foot in A, weaving B on every
other stitch. Maintain color pattern as established on
sole of foot. Round begins with stitches on top of foot.
*Round 1* Knit. *Round 2* [K1, k2tog tbl, knit to 3 stitches
before end of needle, k2tog, k1] twice. *Round 3* Knit.
Repeat last 2 rounds 7 more times, then work Round 2
three times—20 stitches. Graft toe closed.

### NOTES
*1* See page 168 for any unfamiliar techniques. *2* Sock is worked cuff down on 1 circular needle using Magic Loop method.

**Chart A**

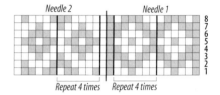

**Chart B**

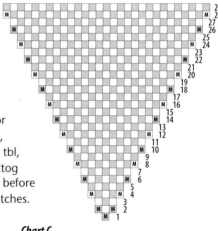

**Chart C**

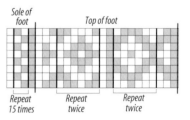

### Stitch key
☐ Knit with A on first sock, B on second sock
▨ Knit with B on first sock, A on second sock
Ⓜ Make 1
Ⓜ Make 1, purl

80

Adult M
**A** 8"
**B** 9"

10cm/4"

42 [grid] 38

over stranded colorwork
pattern

 2 3 4 5 6

Super Fine weight
**A–B** 220 yds each

2mm/US 0, or size to obtain
gauge, 80cm (32") or longer

**&**

Stitch markers

64 size 8/0 seed beads
Transparent Crystal

Shown in
*ZITRON* Trekking XXL
in color 66 (A)
and 94 (B)

**Stitch key**
[ ] Knit
[M] Make one (M1)
[•] Knit and draw on a bead

**Color key**
[ ] A
[ ] B

# Snow Under Cedars

## Leslie Comstock    El Cerrito, California

## RIGHT SOCK

### Cuff
Using Braided Cast-on, and leaving 6" tails of
each yarn, loosely cast on 81 stitches. Join to
work in the round by passing last stitch over
first stitch. Using Magic Loop method, move
40 stitches to Needle 1
and 40 to Needle 2. Work
6 rounds of k1B, p1A rib.
*Next round* Work 2-color
Braid. With A, knit 1 round.
Work Chart A. With A, knit
2 rounds, decreasing 4
stitches on final round—
76 stitches. *Next round*
Work 2-color braid.

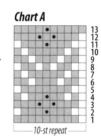

**Chart A**

10-st repeat

### Leg
Arrange stitches so there are 35 on Needle 1 for
front of leg/instep and 41 on Needle 2 for back
of leg/sole. Work Rounds 1–36 of Chart B (page
85). *Round 37* **Needle 1** Work Chart B; **Needle
2** work Heel Flap.

### Heel flap
Work Row 1 of Chart
D—43 stitches. Working
back and forth in rows,
work Rows 2 and 3 of
chart 10 times—21 rows.

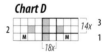

**Chart D**

2   14x 3
M   M
18x   1

### Turn heel
Keep 4 edge stitches at beginning and end of
row in pattern and maintain alternating color
stripes as established in flap. *Row 1 (WS)* Sl 1,
p27, p2tog, p1, turn. *Row 2* Sl 1, k14, SSK, k1,
turn. *Row 3* Sl 1, p15, p2tog, p1, turn. *Row 4*

Sl 1, k**16**, SSK, k1, turn. *Row 5* Sl 1, p**17**, p2tog,
p1, turn. Continue as established, working 1
more stitch before decrease every row until
*Row 14* Sl 1, k**26**, SSK, k1—29 stitches.

### Foot
*Begin Chart E, Round 1* Beginning as marked,
pick up and k21 in pattern from left side of heel
flap; mark beginning of round. *Round 2* Work
instep stitches, pick up and k21 in pattern from
right side of heel flap, work across heel—
106 stitches. Continue through Round
58 of chart, decreasing on sole as
shown—76 stitches.

### Toe
Work Chart G—26 stitches.

### Finishing
To close toes, arrange 13 stitches on each
needle, with a B stitch at each end. Turn
sock inside out and work 3-needle bind-off,
maintaining stripe pattern by working each
pair of stitches with the corresponding color.
To make hanging loop at cuff, make a twisted
cord with ends from cast-on. Sew loose ends
of cord to inside of cuff.

## LEFT SOCK
Work as right sock EXCEPT:

### Leg
Arrange stitches so there are 41 on Needle 1 for
back of leg/sole and 35 on Needle 2 for front of
leg/instep. Work Rounds 1–36 of Chart C (page
84). Work Heel Flap on Needle 1.

## NOTES
*1 See page 168 for any unfamiliar techniques. **2** Sock is worked top down with 1 circular needle. **3** Place
beads using the crochet hook method.*

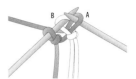

**1** Place a slipknot of A and a slipknot of B on left needle (first 2 stitches cast on).

**2** Knit B stitch with A yarn, then bring A yarn to front of work between needles.

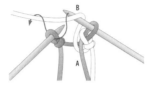

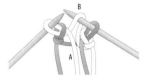

**3a** Bring B yarn under A strand, in front of work, behind right needle and over it (from back to front) then knit next (A) stitch.

**3b** Slip stitch back to left needle and bring yarn to front of work.

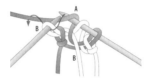

**4a** Bring A yarn under B strand, in front of work, behind right needle and over it (from back to front) then knit next (B) stitch.

**4b** Slip stitch back to left needle and bring yarn to front of work.

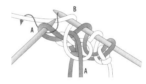

**5a** Bring B yarn under A strand, in front of work, behind right needle and over it (from back to front) then knit next (A) stitch.

**5b** Slip stitch back to left needle and bring yarn to front of work.

Repeat Steps 4 and 5.

**1** With one of the colors, work a Make 1 increase and slip increased stitch to left needle. **2** Bring right needle behind first stitch on left needle…

…and with same color, knit second stitch through back loop, but do not remove it from left needle.

**3** With the other color, knit the first stitch and pull both stitches off left needle. **4** Slip stitch just knit to left needle. Repeat Steps 2–4.

At end of round, pass last stitch over first stitch to restore stitch count.

## Foot

*Begin Chart F, Round 1* Beginning as marked, pick up and k21 from left side of heel flap, work across instep stitches; mark beginning of round. *Round 2* Pick up and k21 from right side of heel flap, work across heel—106 stitches.

**Chart C, left leg**

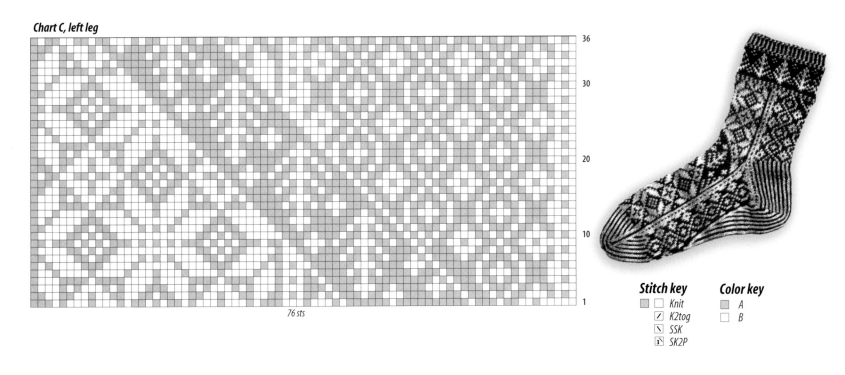

76 sts

**Stitch key**
- Knit
- ✓ K2tog
- ＼ SSK
- ₃＼ SK2P

**Color key**
- A
- B

**Chart F, left foot**

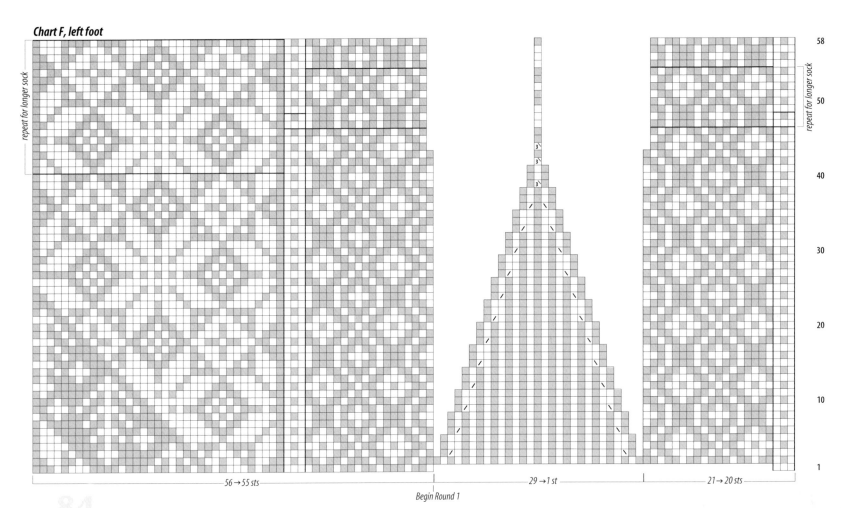

repeat for longer sock

56 → 55 sts

Begin Round 1

29 → 1 st

21 → 20 sts

repeat for longer sock

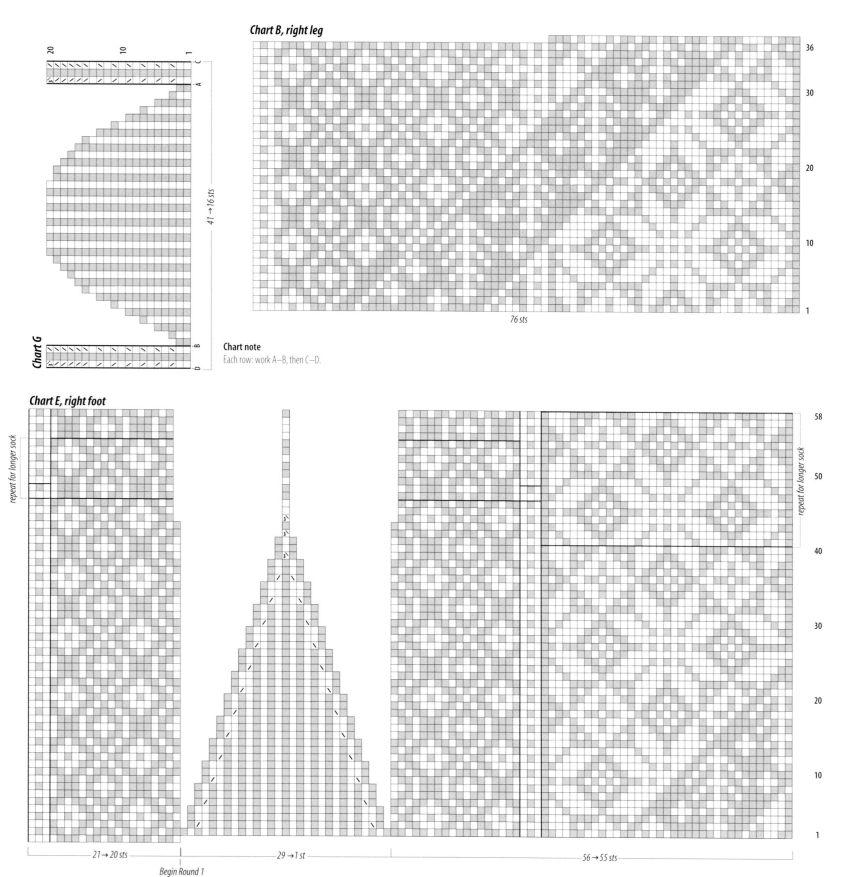

**Chart B, right leg**

20  10  1  C

41 → 16 sts

*Chart G*

A

76 sts

B

D

**Chart note**
Each row: work A–B, then C–D.

**Chart E, right foot**

repeat for longer sock

58

50

40

3
3
3

30

20

repeat for longer sock

10

1

21 → 20 sts

29 → 1 st

56 → 55 sts

*Begin Round 1*

*intermediate*

Adult M
**A** 7½"
**B** 9"

10cm/4"

40
36

over Chart pattern

 2 3 4 5 6

Super Fine weight

**MC** 230 yds

**CC** 150 yds

Two 2.75mm/US 2, or size
to obtain gauge, 40cm (16")
or longer

Shown in
*REGIA* 4 fädig in color
2177 (MC) and Design Line
by Kaffe Fassett in color
4253 (CC)

# Union Jack Argyle

*Janice Talkington    Saginaw, Michigan*

## STRIPE PATTERN
*Every row* [K1 with MC, k1 with CC] to last stitch, end k1 with MC.

## Toe
With MC and Judy's Magic Cast-on, cast 17 stitches onto each of 2 circular needles—
34 stitches. *Round 1* Knit. *Round 2* K2, [sl 1, k1] 6 times, sl 1, k2 on each needle. *Round 3*
[K1, right lifted increase (R inc), knit to last stitch on needle, left lifted increase (L inc), k1]
twice. *Round 4* [K1, sl 1; repeat from* to last stitch on needle, k1] twice. *Round 5* Repeat
Round 3. *Round 6* [K2, *sl 1, k1; repeat from* to last stitch on needle, k1] twice. Repeat
Rounds 3–6 three more times—66 stitches.

## Foot
Needle 1 holds 33 stitches for top of foot and Needle 2 holds 33 stitches for sole of
foot. *Join CC and begin Chart: Next round* **Needle 1** Work Round 1 of Chart; **Needle 2**
work Stripe Pattern. Continue in patterns as established until sock measures 7½", or 1½"
shorter than desired length. Work across Needle 1 in Chart pattern.

## Heel
With MC, work back and forth on **Needle 2** as follows: *Row 1* (RS) [K1, sl 1] 15 times,
k1, wrap next stitch and turn work (W&T). *Row 2* P29, W&T. *Row 3* [K1, sl 1] to 1 stitch
before last wrapped stitch, W&T. *Row 4* Purl to 1 stitch before last wrapped stitch, W&T.
Repeat last 2 rows 6 more times—15 stitches remain between wrapped stitches. **Note**
As you reverse the short row shaping, you will be wrapping stitches a second time. When
these stitches are worked on subsequent rows, work both wraps together with their stitch
(hide wrap). *Row 17* [K1, sl 1] to first wrapped stitch, hide wrap, W&T. *Row 18* Purl to
first wrapped stitch, hide wrap, W&T. *Row 19* [K1, sl 1] to next wrapped stitch, hide
wraps, W&T. *Row 20* Purl to next wrapped stitch, hide wraps, W&T. Repeat last 2 rows
until all wrapped stitches have been worked.

## Leg
Resume working in the round, working Chart pattern on **Needle 1** and Stripe Pattern on
**Needle 2** for 1". *Next round* Repeat Chart pattern around leg, for 5".

## Cuff
With MC, work k1, p1 rib for 2". Bind off loosely in rib.

## NOTES
*1 See page 168 for any unfamiliar techniques.* **2** *Sock is worked toe up on 2 circular needles.*

**Chart**

22-st repeat

22
21
20
19
18
17
16
15
14
13
12
11
10
9
8
7
6
5
4
3
2
1

back of leg

top of foot/
front of leg

**Color key**

☐ MC
▨ CC

**experienced**

Adult M
**A** 8"
**B** 9"

10cm/4"
40
36
over Chart pattern
using smaller needles

1 **2** 3 4 5 6

Fine weight

**A** 275 yds
**B** 225 yds

2.5mm/US 1½ ,or size to obtain
gauge; 3mm/US 2½, for heel;
both 80 cm (32") or longer

Shown in
*CHERRY TREE HILL* Supersock
Wild Cherry (A) and Green
Mountain Madness (B)

## NOTES
*1 See page 168 for any unfamiliar
techniques. 2 Sock is worked from
cuff down on 1 circular needle
using Magic Loop method. 3 Heel
is worked with larger needle.*

## Pattern Play

*Linda McGibbon*    *Beaverton, Michigan*

### Cuff
With smaller needle and using 2–Color Long-tail Cast-On,
cast on 78 stitches, alternating 3 stitches B with 3 stitches A.
Arrange 39 stitches on each needle. Join to work in the round.
*Next 14 rounds* [K3 with B, p3 with A] around.

### Leg
Work Rows 1–91 of Chart A.

## Chart A

**Color key**
☐ A
▨ B

**Stitch key**
▨ ☐ Knit
⊟ Purl

Work these rows twice

91
89
87
85
83
81
79
77
75
73
71
45 69
43 67
41 65
39 63
37 61
35 59
33 57
31 55
29 53
27 51
25 49
23 47
21
19
17
15
13
11
9
7
5
3
1
Last round of ribbing

Needle 2, Front of leg — Needle 1, Back of leg

### Heel flap

Change to larger needle and work back and forth on heel stitches. Leave Needle 2 stitches on hold for instep. *Row 1* (RS) With A, [sl 1, k1] to end. Do not turn; slide stitches back to other end of needle (slide). *Row 2* (RS) With B, [k1, sl 1] to end. Turn. *Row 3* (WS) With A, [p1, sl 1] to end. Do not turn; slide. *Row 4* (WS) With B, [sl 1, p1] to end. Turn. Repeat last 4 rows 11 more times.

### Turn heel

Alternate 1 stitch A with 1 stitch B throughout heel turn to maintain checkerboard pattern. *Row 1* (RS) K22, SSK, k1, turn. *Row 2* Sl 1, p**6**, p2tog, p1, turn. *Row 3* Sl 1, k**7**, SSK, k1, turn. *Row 4* Sl 1, p**8**, p2tog, p1, turn. *Row 5* Sl 1, k**9**, SSK, k1, turn. Continue working 1 more stitch before decrease every row, end sl 1, p**20**, p2tog, p1 — 23 stitches.

### Gussets and foot

*Begin Chart B* With smaller needle, work Round 1 of chart (next page) across heel stitches. Pick up and k12 down side of heel flap, continuing alternation of colors. Work chart across Needle 2. *Round 2* Pick up and k12 up side of heel flap, work chart — 86 stitches. *Arrange stitches* Needle 1 holds 47 stitches for gussets and sole and Needle 2 holds 39 stitches for instep. Work through Round 50 of Chart, decreasing for gussets as shown — 78 stitches.

### Toe

*Round 1* **Needle 1** With A, k1, SSK; [k1B, k1A] to last 3 stitches; with A, k2tog, k1; **Needle 2** with B, k1, SSK; [k1A, k1B] to last 3 stitches; with B, k2tog, k1. *Round 2* **Needle 1** K2A, [k1A, k1B] to last 2 stitches, k2A; **Needle 2** k2B, [k1B, k1A] to last 2 stitches, k2B. Repeat last 2 rounds 8 more times, then Round 1 four times — 26 stitches. Graft toe.

## Color key
□ A
▧ B

## Stitch key
▧ □ Knit
− Purl
▨ ▧ K2tog
◣ ◺ SSK

**Chart B**

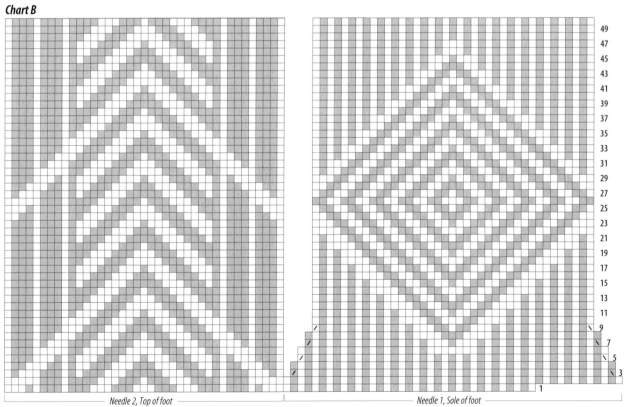

49
47
45
43
41
39
37
35
33
31
29
27
25
23
21
19
17
15
13
11
9
7
5
3
1

Needle 2, Top of foot | Needle 1, Sole of foot

## Kate Hedstrom    *Fairbanks, Alaska*

*experienced +*

Adult M
**A** 7½"
**B** 9"

10cm/4"

40

36

over Chart pattern in
stockinette stitch

**1** 2 3 4 5 6

Super Fine weight

**A** 200 yds
**B** 250 yds
**C1–C5** 15 yds each

Two 2.25mm/US 1 or size to
obtain gauge, 60 cm (24")
or longer

Shown in
*ZITRON* Trekking Pro Natura
dyed (see Note 3)

## NOTES
*1 See page 168 for any unfamiliar techniques. 2 Sock is worked toe up on 2 circular needles. 3 This sock was made with yarn dyed with natural dyes. Color A, a deep purple, was dyed with logwood. Color B, a variegated green, was first dyed yellow with marigold, tansy and coreopsis, then overdyed with Japanese indigo. Color C is small amounts of 5 different pink and orange tones dyed with madder root and cochineal. You can get a similar look with commercially hand-dyed semi-solid and variegated yarns.*

## Intarsia in the round

*Stranded round* Knit first (and every alternate) round of flower motif in 2-color stranded technique, working flower stitches with 3rd color, then dropping flower yarn and completing round with the 2 other yarns.

*Inlay round* Next round, flower yarn is at left side of motif. First work across motif with 2 stranding yarns, knitting MC stitches and slipping flower stitches. Drop 2 stranding yarns. Turn work to WS, and work across motif with flower yarn, purling flower stitches and slipping MC stitches. Drop flower yarn. Turn work to RS, slip all stitches across motif, and complete round with 2 stranding yarns.

**Note** Always pick up intarsia yarn from under other stranded yarn.

**Chart A**

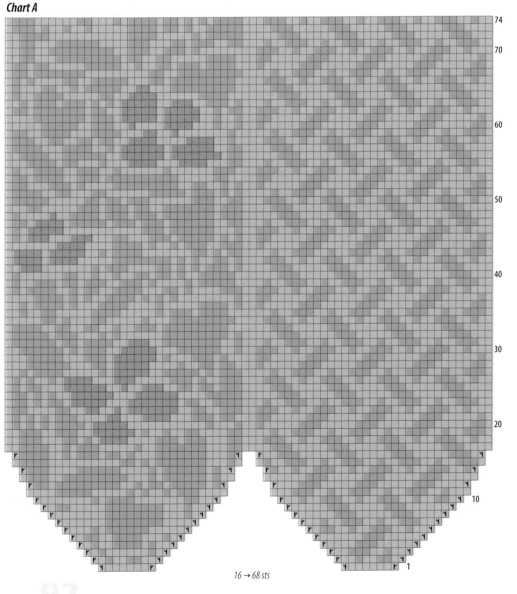

16 → 68 sts

### Color key
- A
- B
- C1 - C5

### Stitch key
- M  M1
- r  R lifted inc
- L  L lifted inc

**Chart B**

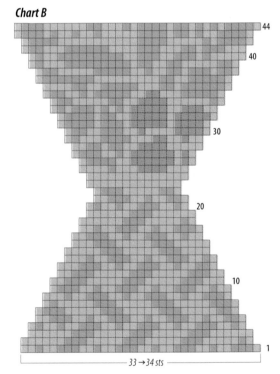

33 → 34 sts

**Chart Note:**
This sock is worked in 2-color stranded colorwork combined with intarsia in the round. Colors A and B are used throughout, with the color not in use carried loosely across back of work. A separate bobbin or butterfly of a color C is used to work each flower motif using intarsia in the round. Color C is not carried across back of work.

92

## Toe and Foot

Using Judy's Magic Cast-On and A, cast 8 stitches onto each of 2 needles—16 stitches. Knit 1 round. Work Chart A, Rows 1–74—68 stitches.

## Heel

Following Chart B, work short-row heel as follows: *Row 1* **Needle 2** K**33**, wrap next stitch and turn work (W&T). *Row 2* P**32**, W&T. *Row 3* Sl 1, knit to 1 stitch before wrapped stitch, W&T. *Row 4* Sl 1, purl to 1 stitch before wrapped stitch, W&T. Continue as established, working 1 fewer stitch before turn on each row, until 12 stitches remain unworked in center of heel between wrapped stitches. *Row 23* Knit across to first wrapped stitch and knit it together with its wrap, W&T. *Row 24* Purl across to first wrapped stitch and purl it together with its wrap, W&T. *Row 25* Knit across to double-wrapped stitch and knit it together with both its wraps, W&T. *Row 26* Purl across to double-wrapped stitch and purl it together with both its wraps, W&T. Repeat last 2 rows until all heel stitches have been worked.

## Leg

Resume working in the round and follow Chart C, Rows 1–75—80 stitches.

## Cuff

*Round 1* With A, knit. *Round 2* Purl. *Round 3* Knit, increasing 1 stitch—81 stitches. *Round 4* Using 3 different color C variations, [k1 C1, k1 C2, k1 C3] around. *Round 5* [K1 C2, k1 C3, k1 C1] around. *Round 6* [K1 C3, k1 C1, k1 C2] around. *Rounds 7 and 8* With A, knit. *Round 9* Purl. Bind off using EZ's sewn bind-off. Make a braid at cuff with tails of A and C. Finish braid with an overhand knot.

**Chart C**

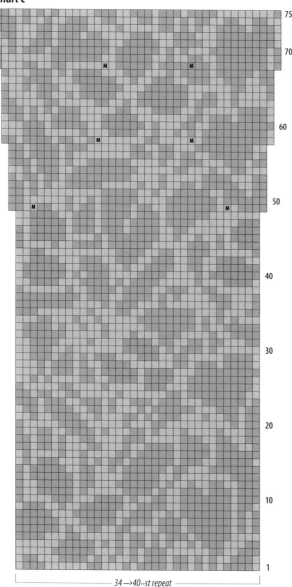

34 →40–st repeat

*intermediate*

Adult M
**A** 8"
**B** 9"

10cm/4"

48

34

over stockinette stitch

**1** 2 3 4 5 6

Super Fine weight

**MC** 225 yds
**CC** 175 yds

Two size 2.25mm/US 1,
60cm (24") long
or size to obtain gauge

**&**

Stitch marker

Shown in
*NEIGHBORHOOD FIBER
CO. STUDIO* Sock Logan
Circle (MC) and
Variegated Berry (CC)

# Raspberries & Green

*Virginia R. Jones*   *Greenbelt, Maryland*

## Toe

Using Judy's Magic Cast-on with MC and leaving a long tail, cast 3 stitches onto each of 2 needles—6 stitches. *Round 1* With working yarn and tail held together, knit. There are 2 stitches in each original stitch—12 stitches total. Drop tail. *Round 2* Knit. *Round 3* [K1, knit into front and back of next stitch (kf&b)] to end—18 stitches. *Round 4* Knit. *Round 5* [K2, kf&b] to end—24 stitches. *Rounds 6 & 7* Knit. *Round 8* [K3, kf&b] to end—30 stitches. *Rounds 9–11* Knit. Continue as established, working 1 more stitch before increase every 4th round until *Round 32* [K9, kf&b] to end—66 stitches.

## Foot

Arrange 34 stitches on Needle 1 for instep and 32 stitches on Needle 2 for sole. *Round 1* With MC, [p1, k1 tbl] twice, p1, join CC and work Row 1 of Chart 3 times, [p1, k1 tbl] twice, p1, knit to end. *Round 2* With CC, [p1, k1 tbl] twice, p1, change to MC and work Row 2 of Chart 3 times, [p1, k1 tbl] twice, p1, knit to end. Continue as established, changing color on every round as directed by Chart, until piece measures 4½".

## Arch expansion

Place a marker on each side of 4 center stitches on Needle 2. *Next round* **Needle 1** Work rib and Chart pattern as established; **Needle 2** knit to first marker, slip marker (sm), left lifted increase (L inc), knit to marker, right lifted increase, sm, knit to end. *Next 2 rounds* **Needle 1** Work as established; **Needle 2** Knit. Continue as established, working increases between markers every third round, until 34 stitches are between markers, end with CC—96 stitches.

## Heel turn

*Set-up row* **Needle 1** Work as established; **Needle 2** k15, slip these 15 stitches to Needle 1. Slip last 15 stitches from Needle 2 to Needle 1; Needle 1 now holds 64 instep stitches and Needle 2 holds 32 heel stitches. With MC, work back and forth on Needle 2. *Row 1* (RS) K1, L inc, k1, [sl 1, k1] to last 2 stitches, wrap next stitch and turn work (W&T). *Row 2* Purl to last 2 stitches, W&T. *Row 3* [K1, sl 1] to 1 stitch before last wrapped stitch, W&T. *Rows 4 & 6* Purl to 1 stitch before last wrapped stitch, W&T. *Row 5* [Sl 1, k1] to 1 stitch before last wrapped stitch, W&T. Repeat Rows 3–6 three more times—9 wrapped stitches on each side. *Next row* (RS) [K 1, sl1] to first wrapped stitch, k8, hiding wraps, SSK next stitch and its wrap together

**Chart**

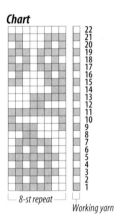

22
21
20
19
18
17
16
15
14
13
12
11
10
9
8
7
6
5
4
3
2
1

⌐ 8-st repeat ¬        Working yarn

☐ MC
▨ CC

## Chart note

Work each row with the color indicated. For example, work Row 1 with CC, knitting the CC stitches (the shaded squares) and slipping the MC stitches (the unshaded squares) with the yarn in back.

## NOTES

*1 See page 168 for any unfamiliar techniques. 2 Sock is worked toe up on 2 circular needles. 3 The chart design is a Barbara Walker mosaic pattern.*

with the following stitch, turn. *Next row* Sl 1, purl to first wrapped stitch, p8 hiding wraps, p2tog (next stitch with its wrap and following stitch)—31 stitches on heel needle.

## Back of heel

*Set-up row* Place a marker at each end of Needle 2. Slide first 15 and last 15 stitches from Needle 1 to ends of Needle 2; Needle 1 now holds 34 instep stitches; Needle 2 holds 61 heel stitches. With RS facing, slip first 15 stitches on Needle 2 to other end of Needle 2 so working yarn is accessible and ready to work across heel; turn stitches. *Row 1* (RS) [Sl 1, k1] to 1 stitch before marker, SSK, removing marker, turn. *Row 2* Sl 1, purl to 1 stitch before marker, p2tog, removing marker, turn. *Row 3* [Sl 1, k1] until 1 stitch before previous turn, SSK, turn. *Row 4* Sl 1, purl to 1 stitch before previous turn, p2tog, turn. Repeat Rows 3 and 4 twelve more times—1 stitch remains unworked on each end.

## Leg

*Next row* (RS) [Sl 1, k1] until 1 stitch before previous turn, SSK. Resume knitting in the round. *Next round* **Needle 1** Work rib and Chart pattern as established, changing to CC at beginning of Chart; **Needle 2** k2tog, p1, k1 tbl, M1P, work Chart pattern 3 times, [p1, k1 tbl] twice—Needle 1 now holds 34 front-of-leg stitches; Needle 2 holds 32 back-of-leg stitches. Work even in rib and Chart pattern as established until leg measures approximately 4" above top of heel, end with Row 22 of Chart.

## Cuff

*Round 1* [K1 with MC, k1 with CC] to end of round. *Round 2* With both yarns in front, p1 with MC, [bring CC in front of MC and p1 with CC, bring MC in front of CC and p1 with MC] around. *Round 3* With both yarns in front, p1 with MC, [bring CC behind MC and p1 with CC, bring MC behind CC and p1 with MC] to end of round.

## Finishing

Cut both yarns, leaving a tail of MC 1 yard long. Work EZ's sewn bind-off.

*intermediate +*

Adult S, long
**A** 7"
**B** 10"

10cm/4"
68 ▦
36

over Chart pattern

 2 3 4 5 6

Super Fine weight

**MC** 300 yds

**CC** 200 yds

Five 2.75mm/US 2,
or size to obtain gauge

Shown in
*REGIA* 4-fädig in Black (MC) and
Design Line by Kaffe Fassett in
Mirage Carribean (CC)

# Mosaic Miters

*Lina Forner*   *Waterloo, Ontario, Canada*

## Toe
Use MC and a temporary cast–on to cast on 32 stitches. *Row 1* (WS) Purl. *Row 2* (RS) Sl 1, k**30**, turn. *Row 3* Sl 1, p**29**, turn. *Row 4* Sl 1, k**28**, turn. *Row 5* Sl 1, p**27**, turn. Continue working back and forth in stockinette stitch, slipping the first stitch and working 1 fewer stitch every row until *Row 17* Sl 1, p**15**, turn. *Row 18* Sl 1, k**13**, twisted SSK (TSSK), turn. *Row 19* Sl 1, p**13**, twisted p2tog (Tp2tog), turn. *Row 20* Sl 1, k**14**, TSSK, turn. *Row 21* Sl 1, p**15**, Tp2tog, turn. Continue working 1 more stitch before decrease every row until *Row 34* Sl 1, k**28**, TSSK, turn. *Row 35* Sl 1, purl to end. *Row 36* Sl 1, knit to end. With another needle, k32 from cast-on—64 stitches. Place marker for beginning of round. Arrange 16 stitches on each of 4 double-pointed needles: Needles 1 & 2 for top of foot; Needles 3 & 4 for sole.

## Foot
*Rounds 1 & 2, 5 & 6, 9 & 10, 13 & 14* With MC, **Needles 1 & 2** work Chart; **Needles 3 & 4** knit. *Rows 3 & 4* **Needles 1 & 2** With RS facing and CC, work Chart Row 3; turn; yo, with WS facing, work Chart Row 4; **Needles 3 & 4** with WS facing and MC, purl, turn; slip 1 from Needle 3 to Needle 2, pass yo over slipped stitch, then return stitch to Needle 3; with RS facing, k1 hiding yo wrap, knit across. *Short rows 7 & 8* **Needles 1 & 2** With RS facing and CC, work Chart Row 7, turn; with WS facing, work Chart Row 8, turn. Do not work Needles 3 & 4. *Rows 11 & 12* **Needles 1 & 2** Work as Rows 3 & 4 EXCEPT chart Rows 11 & 12.

*Short rows 15 & 16* **Needles 1 & 2** With RS facing and CC, work Chart Row 15, turn; with WS facing, work Chart Row 16, turn. Do not work Needles 3 & 4. Repeat Rounds 1–16 until foot measures 5" from tip of toe, or about 4" less than desired length.

## Gussets
Continue in pattern, increasing 1 stitch after first stitch of Needle 3 (MIR) and before last stitch of Needle 4 (MIL) every Round 1, Row 4, Rounds 5 & 9, Row 12, and Round 13 until Needles 3 & 4 hold 35 stitches each—102 stitches total, end with a CC row. Cut CC yarn. *Next round* With MC, work as established.

## Heel
*Heel set-up, Row 1* With **Needles 1 & 2** work chart; continue with **Needle 2** and k19 from Needle 3; with another needle, k16 from Needle 3 and k15 from Needle 4, slip 1 from Needle 4 to Needle 3. slip remaining stitches from Needle 4 to Needle 1—35 sts each on Needles 1 & 2, 32 stitches on Needle 3. *Row 2* (WS) Slip 1 with yarn in back, bring yarn forward, P30, W&T. *Row 3* K28, W&T. *Row 4* P**26**, W&T. *Row 5* K24, W&T. Continue working back and forth on heel, working 2 fewer stitches each row until *Row 11* K12, W&T. *Row 12* Purl to last stitch, hiding wraps; purl last stitch together with edge stitch from Needle 2, turn. *Row 13* Knit to last stitch, hiding wraps, knit last stitch together with edge stitch from Needle 1. *Row 14* Sl 1, purl to last stitch, purl last stitch together with edge stitch from Needle 2.

## NOTES
*1 See page 168 for any unfamiliar techniques. 2 Sock is worked toe up on double-pointed needles.*
*3 The top of the foot is worked in the Chart pattern, while the sole of the foot is worked in stockinette stitch. A pair of short rows are worked only across the top of the foot every 8 rows to compensate for the difference in row gauge between the stitch patterns.*

## Chart, left sock

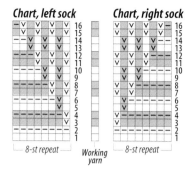

## Chart, right sock

8-st repeat | Working yarn | 8-st repeat

**Chart Note:**
Work each row of chart with color indicated. For example, work Row 3 with CC, slipping MC stitches and knitting CC stitches.

### Color key
- ☐ MC
- ▨ CC

### Stitch key
- ▨ ☐ Knit
- ▬ – Purl
- ☑ ☑ Slip 1 with yarn at WS of work

## Heel flap

Join CC. Work back and forth in rows. *Row 1* (RS) Sl 1, [k1 CC, k1 MC] to last stitch on needle; with MC, knit last stitch together with edge stitch from Needle 1. *Row 2* Sl 1, [p1 MC, p1 CC] to last stitch; with MC, purl last stitch together with edge stitch from Needle 2. Repeat last 2 rows until all gusset stitches have been worked—64 stitches; place 16 on each needle.

## Leg

Resume working all stitches in the round in chart pattern until leg measures approximately 7" from top of heel flap, end with Round 16 of chart. Cut CC yarn.

## Cuff

With MC, knit 1 round. Work k2, p2 rib for 2". Bind off using EZ's Sewn Bind-off.

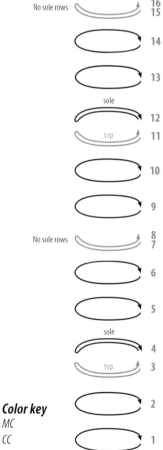

No sole rows — 16 / 15
14
13
sole — 12
top — 11
10
9
No sole rows — 8 / 7
6
5
sole — 4
top — 3
2
1

### Color key
← MC
← CC

**Chart Note:**
Yarn path for rows & rounds on foot of sock.

## Twisted Knit (TKnit)

**1** Slip 1 stitch as if to knit, insert right needle into right leg of stitch in row below as if to purl.

**2** Slip left needle into these 2 stitches from left to right and knit them together.

**3** You are ready to turn your work for the next short row.

## Twisted Purling (TPurling)

**1** Slip 1 stitch as if to purl, insert right needle into right leg of stitch in row below as if to knit.

**2** Slip left needle into these 2 stitches from left to right and purl them together.

**3** You are ready to turn your work for the next short row.

*intermediate +*

Adult M
**A** 7"
**B** 8"

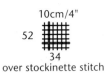

10cm/4"

52
34

over stockinette stitch

**1** 2 3 4 5 6

Super Fine weight

**A** 160 yds
**B** 110 yds
**C, E** 60 yds each
**D** 40 yds

Five 2.25mm/US 1
or size to obtain gauge

**&**

Small amount smooth waste yarn
Stitch markers

Shown in
*CHERRY TREE HILL* Supersock in
Sapphire (A), Azalea (B), Quarry
Hill (C), Cornflower (D), and
Country Garden (E)

# Fancy Garter

*Mary Tanti*    *Salt Spring Island, British Columbia, Canada*

## Entrelac Cuff

*Hem rectangles for Tier 1* With A *knit cast-on 6 stitches (counts as Row 1). *Row 2* (WS) P6. *Row 3* Sl 1, k5. *Row 4* Sl 1, p5. Repeat Rows 3 & 4 three more times, then work Row 3 again. Leave these 6 stitches on the needle. Repeat from* 6 more times—7 rectangles are complete.

*Tier 1 Arrange work into a circle* Slip 2 rectangles each onto Needles 1 & 2, 3 rectangles onto Needle 3. With RS facing and a another needle, *pick up and k6 along edge (from cast-on to tip) of first rectangle (6th stitch is picked up along side of last stitch on left needle. *Row 1* (WS) P6. *Row 2* Sl 1, k4, SSK. *Row 3* Sl 1, p5. Repeat last 2 rows 4 more times, then work Row 2 again. Repeat from* until all 7 rectangles have been worked.

*Tier 2* Attach B at tip of last rectangle. *With WS facing, pick up and p6 down side of rectangle *Next row* K6. *WS rows* Sl 1, p4, p2tog. *RS rows* Sl 1, k5. Repeat last 2 rows 5 more times. Repeat from* until 7 rectangles are complete. Put 6 stitches from final rectangle on hold.

*Tier 3 (5, 7)* Attach A at tip of last rectangle worked. *With RS facing, pick up and k6 along side of rectangle; turn, p6. *RS rows* Sl 1, k4, SSK. *WS rows* Sl 1, p5. Repeat last 2 rows 5 more times. Repeat from* until 6 (4, 2) color A rectangles are complete. Put 6 stitches from final rectangle on hold.

*Tier 4 (6, 8)* Attach C (D, E) at tip of last rectangle worked. *With WS facing, pick up and p6 along side of rectangle. *Next row* K6. *WS rows* Sl 1, p4, p2tog. *RS rows* Sl 1, k5. Repeat last 2 rows 5 more times. Repeat from* until 5 (3, 1) C (D, E) rectangles are complete. Put 6 stitches from final rectangle on hold.

## Leg

Attach A to held stitches from Tier 2 (center back of sock). [K6 from holder, pick up and k6 along side of block in next tier] 3 times, k5 from Tier 8 holder, yo, knit last Tier 8 stitch, pick up and k1 at side of Tier 8, yo, pick up and k5 more along side of Tier 8, [k6 from holder, pick up and k6 along side of block in next tier] 3 times,

**Entrelac Cuff**

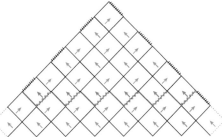

**Tier 3** *Continue alternating RS and WS rectangles working 6 rectangles for Tier 3, then 5, 4, 3, 2, and 1 rectangles for Tiers 4–8.*

**Tier 2** *Work rectangles with WS facing*

**Tier 1** *Work rectangles with RS facing*

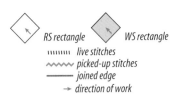
RS rectangle     WS rectangle
ıııııı *live stitches*
⋀⋀⋀ *picked-up stitches*
—— *joined edge*
→ *direction of work*

## NOTES

*1 See page 168 for any unfamiliar techniques. 2 Sock is worked cuff down on double-pointed needles.*

pick up and k1 from Tier 1 block—87 stitches.

*Next round, Ridge round* P42, k2, p42, k1. *Chevron round 1* K42, yo, k2, yo, k41, S2KP2 (last 2 stitches of round with first stitch of next round). *Chevron round 2* Knit. Repeat last 2 rounds 3 more times. Work Ridge round. Change to C. Work 8 Chevron rounds. Change to B. Work Chevron round 1. Work Ridge round. Work 8 Chevron rounds. Work Ridge round. Change to E. Work 8 Chevron rounds. Change to D. Work Chevron round 1. Work Ridge round. Work 2 Chevron rounds. *Round 44* K37, yo, k2, yo, k8, yo, k2, yo, k36, S2KP2. *Round 45* Knit. *Round 46* K37, yo, k12, yo, knit to end of round. Change to A. *Round 47* Knit. *Round 48* P39, yo, p10, yo, purl to end of round—91 stitches.

## Back of heel

Slip last 2 stitches onto left needle. Join B. *Row 1* (RS) K4, turn. *Row 2* Sl 1, k**3**, sl 1, turn. *Row 3* With A, [k1, sl 1] **3** times, turn. *Row 4* P1, k**5**, sl 1, turn. *Row 5* With B, [k1, sl 1] **4** times, turn. *Row 6* P1, k**7**, sl 1, turn. *Row 7* With A, [k1, sl 1] **5** times, turn. *Row 8* P1, k**9**, sl 1, turn. Continue as established, changing color every other row and working one more stitch each row, until *Row 64* P1, k**65**, sl 1, turn—24 instep stitches remain unworked.

### Turn heel

For extra reinforcement, weave color not in use along wrong side of work, catching yarn every other stitch. *Row 1* (RS) With B, k37, SSK, k1, turn. *Row 2* Sl 1, p9, p2tog, change to A, p1, turn. *Row 3* Sl 1, k**10**, SSK, k1, turn. *Row 4* Sl 1, p**11**, p2tog, change to B, p1, turn. *Row 5* Sl 1, k**12**, SSK, k1, turn. *Row 6* Sl 1, p**13**, p2tog, change to A, p1, turn. Continue, working 1 more stitch before decrease on each row and changing color just before the last stitch on each WS row, until *Row 28* With A, sl 1, p**35**, p2tog, p1, turn—38 heel stitches, 24 instep stitches. Cut B.

### Foot

*Next round* With A, k38, M1, k24, M1—64 stitches. Knit 4 more stitches and place marker (pm) for new beginning of round. *Next round, set up spiral stripe* **Needle 1** With A, k16; **Needle 2** with second strand of A, k16; **Needle 3** with C, k16; **Needle 4** with E, k16. Return to beginning of Needle 4 and, with C, k14, sl 2. Return to beginning of Needle 3 and, with A, k28, sl 4. Return to beginning of Needle 2 and, with A, k42, sl 6. Work spiral stripe as follows, taking care not to twist the colors. *Next round* Beginning with Needle 1 and E, k56, sl 6. Continue with C, which is waiting for you after the 6 slipped stitches. Continue as established, working each color in turn, until foot measures approximately 6½" from back of heel, or 1½" less than desired length. Pm for side of toe.

### Toe

Continue in spiral stripe pattern. *Round 1, decrease round* K1, SSK, knit to 3 sts before side marker, k2tog, k2, SSK, knit to 3 stitches before end, k2tog, k1. *Round 2* Knit. Repeat these 2 rounds 7 more times—32 stitches. Graft toe.

### Finishing

Turn sock inside out, graft hem rectangles along join between Tiers 1 & 2, making sure to shape each point as you work along.

# Aztec Pottery

*Sandra R. Merrill*   Richfield, Minnesota

**intermediate**

Adult L
**A** 9"
**B** 9"

10cm/4"

40  32
over Chart pattern

 2 3 4 5 6

Super Fine weight
**MC** 370 yds
**CC** 185 yds

Two size 2.25mm/US 1,
or size to obtain gauge,
40cm (16") or longer

Shown in
LOUET Gems Fingering in
Black (MC) and CHERRY
TREE HILL Gems in Indian
Summer (CC)

## NOTES
*1 See page 168 for any unfamiliar techniques. 2 Sock is worked cuff down on 2 circular needles.*

## Cuff

With MC, cast 36 stitches onto each of 2 needles—72 stitches. Join to work in the round. Work k2, p2 rib for 1½".

## Leg

*Begin Chart A* Work Rounds 1–70. Note that pattern is the same for both needles for Rounds 1–56, then changes for Needle 2 on Rounds 57–70.

## Heel flap

With CC, work back and forth on Needle 2 for the heel; Needle 1 holds 36 instep stitches. *Row 1* (RS) [Sl 1, k1] to end. *Row 2* Sl 1, purl to end. Repeat last 2 rows 17 more times.

## Turn heel

*Row 1* (RS) Sl 1, k20, SSK, k1, turn. *Row 2* Sl 1, p**7**, p2tog, p1, turn. *Row 3* Sl 1, k**8**, SSK, k1, turn. *Row 4* Sl 1, p**9**, p2tog, p1, turn. *Row 5* Sl 1, k**10**, SSK, k1, turn. Continue working 1 more stitch before decrease every row until *Row 14* Sl 1, p**19**, p2tog, p1, turn. *Row 15* Knit—22 stitches.

## Gussets

Continuing with heel needle and CC, pick up and k16 along left side of heel flap. With instep needle, knit instep stitches. With heel needle, pick up and k16 along right side of heel flap, then knit to end of heel needle—90 stitches; Needle 1 holds 36 instep stitches, Needle 2 holds 54 heel and gusset stitches. *Round 1* With CC, knit. *Round 2* With MC, **Needle 1** knit; **Needle 2** k1, SSK, knit to last 3 stitches, k2tog, k1. Repeat last 2 rounds 8 more times—72 stitches.

## Foot

*Begin Chart B* Work Rounds 1–41 on Needle 1 and alternate rounds of CC and MC on Needle 2, weaving the carried yarn on the WS. Then work 1-round stripes on both needles until foot measures 7½" from back of heel, or 1½" less than desired length.

## Toe

*Decrease round* [K1, SSK, knit to last 3 stitches, k2tog, k1] twice. Work 8 Decrease rounds, maintaining 1-round stripes. Cut CC and work 6 Decrease rounds with MC only—12 stitches, 6 on each needle. Graft toe.

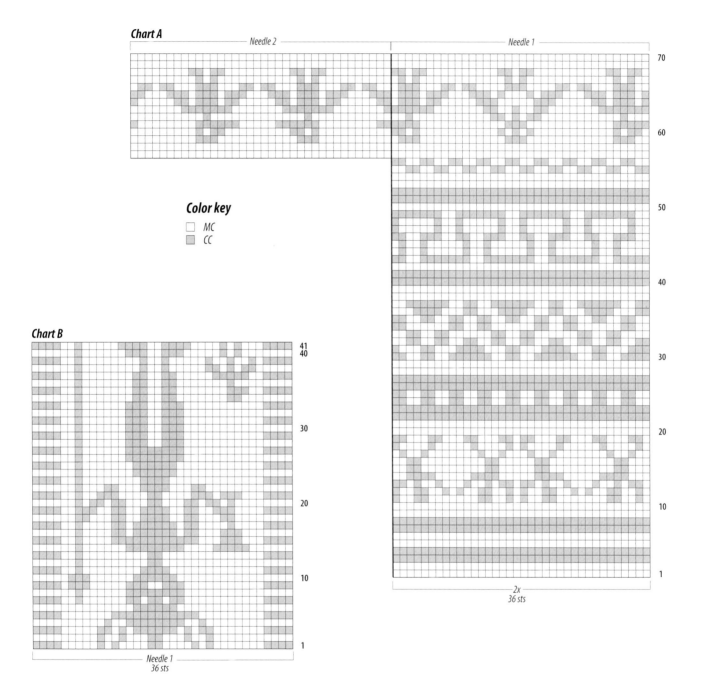

**Chart A**

Needle 2 — Needle 1

**Color key**
- ☐ MC
- ▨ CC

**Chart B**

Needle 1
36 sts

2x
36 sts

*intermediate*+

S (M, L, XL)
**A** 6½ (7½, 8½, 9½)"
**B** 7½ (9, 10, 11)"

10cm/4"

46 ⊞ 34

*over stockinette stitch*

*A hexagon beginning
with 60 stitches measures
2-1/8" across*

 **1** 2 3 4 5 6

Super Fine weight
450 yds

Five 2.25mm/US 1, or
size to obtain gauge

2.2mm/US 2

**&**

Stitch markers
Yarn needle

Shown in
*REGIA* Design Line
by Kaffe Fassett in
Landscape Storm

Stretchy Sock Shown in
REGIA Design Line by
Kaffe Fassett in Exotic
Turquoise

# Hexagons

*Kirsten Hall*    Rockville, Maryland

## CHOOSING YOUR HEXAGON SIZE

### Measuring your foot

Measure around ball of foot and ankle, then match larger of those measurements with nearest sock circumference; do not add any ease. The sock circumference is 4 times the distance between centers of 2 adjoining hexagons. The hexagons are a multiple of 6 stitches, but it is still easy to finesse the sizing. For a 9" sock, cast on 66 (the next larger size), decrease 6 stitches in the first round, then proceed with Round 1 of the pattern. Or, reduce any hexagon by 2 rows by skipping Round 1—just be sure to place the center-of-needle markers as you work Round 2.

| FOR THIS SOCK CIRCUMFERENCE | CAST ON THIS NUMBER OF STITCHES FOR HEXAGON |
|---|---|
| 6½" | **48** (16 per needle) |
| 7½" | **54** (18 per needle) |
| 8½" | **60** (20 per needle) |
| 9½" | **66** (22 per needle) |

### Knitting first hexagon

Use long-tail cast-on to cast on the number of stitches needed for your size. Arrange stitches evenly on 3 needles and join to work in the round.

*SMOOTH HEXAGON, Round 1* Knit, placing marker (pm) in center of each needle. *Round 2* \*K2tog, knit to 2 stitches before marker, SSK, k2tog, knit to last 2 stitches on needle, SSK; repeat from\*—12 stitches decreased. *Rounds 3 & 4* Knit. *Round 5* Repeat Round 2. Repeat Rounds 3–5 until either 12 or 18 stitches remain. If 18 stitches remain, knit 1 round. *Next Round* [K2tog, k1] around—12 stitches. Cut yarn, draw through remaining stitches twice, pull tight, and fasten off.

*STRETCHY HEXAGON, Round 1* Purl, pm at center of each needle. *Round 2* [K2tog, knit to 2 stitches before marker, SSK, k2tog, knit to last 2 stitches on needle, SSK] 4 times—12 stitches decreased. *Rounds 3 & 4* Knit. *Round 5* Purl. *Round 6* Repeat Round 2. *Round 7* Knit (purl, purl, purl). *Round 8* Knit. *Round 9* **Small only** [K2tog, SSK]—12 stitches, end of Small. **For M (L, XL)** Knit. *Round 10* Repeat Round 2—18 (24, 30) stitches. *Round 11* Knit. *Round 12* **For Medium only** [K2tog, k1] 6 times—12 stitches, end of M. **For Large and XL** Knit. *Round 13* **For Large only** [K2tog, SSK] around—12 stitches, end of large. **XL only** [K2 tog, k1, SSK] around—18 stitches *Round 14* [K2tog, K1] around—12 stitches, end of XL. **For all sizes** Cut yarn, draw through remaining stitches twice, pull tight, and fasten off.

## NOTES

*1 See page 168 for any unfamiliar techniques. 2 To avoid a gap at corners where 3 or more hexagons meet, pick up corner stitch through corner stitches of both adjoining units. 3 Mark heel unit with a safety pin and mark which end of the sock will be the toe. You may want to carry along a reinforcing thread when knitting the heel unit—or whichever unit that falls where you wear out socks. 4 When trimming ends on the WS, don't trim them too short. Tails that are left long are less likely to migrate to RS of the sock.*

## First hex

Cast on 48 (54, 60, 66) sts on 3 dpn—16 (18, 20, 22) sts, 2 sides of hex, on each.

## Second hex

Cast on 5 sides— 40 (45, 50, 55) sts; pick up and k8 (9, 10, 11) sts from 1 side of first hex .

## Third hex

Work as previous hex.

## Fourth hex

*Cast on 2 sides—16 (18, 20, 22) sts; pick up 1 side; repeat from*. This hex completes the first tier and forms the tube.

## Knitting the subsequent hexagons

Each hexagon has 8 (9, 10, 11) stitches on each of its 6 sides. When starting a new hex, first cast on, then pick up stitches from adjoining sides. Pick up the first and third stitches after the cast-on with the tail, then weave the tail in as you pick up 1 stitch in every cast-on stitch.

To join a hex between 2 others (see fourth hex in first tier), cast on 2 sides, then pick up and knit along side of third hex, alternating tail and working yarn; cast on 2 sides, then pick up the final side along first hex. Continue to build your sock, 1 hexagon at a time, until you have 3 tiers of 4 hexagons for leg, 3 tiers of 4 hexagons for foot, and 3 hexagons for back and bottom of heel.

*This sock can be knit from nearly any direction. Begin with any hexagon on the diagram and add to it. As you build your sock, compare it to the diagram so you can see where the next hexagon should go. Heavy lines and colored dots indicate pick-up edges where hexagons meet.*

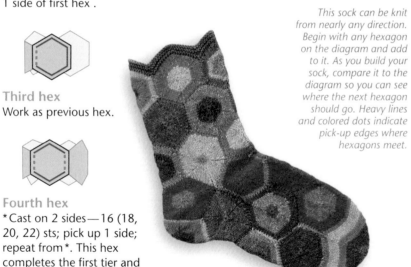

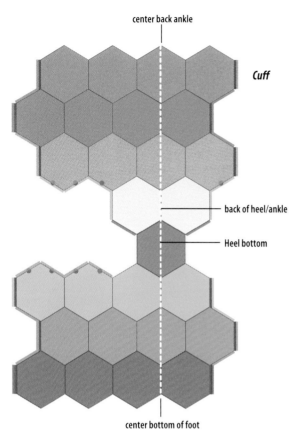

center back ankle

*Cuff*

back of heel/ankle

Heel bottom

center bottom of foot

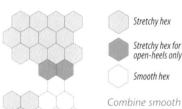

Stretchy hex

Stretchy hex for open-heels only

Smooth hex

*Combine smooth hexagons (for foot) and stretchy hexagons (for leg) for custom comfort.*

## Next tier: First hex

Cast on 4 sides—32 (36, 40, 44) sts; pick up 2 sides.

## Second hex

Cast on 3 sides—24 (27, 30, 33) sts; pick up 3 sides.

## Third hex

Work as previous hex.

## Fourth hex

Cast on 2 sides—16 (18, 20, 22) sts; pick up 4 sides.

—— Cast-on stitches
- - - - Pick-up stitches

## Cuff

Starting with dpn at peak of 1 hexagon, pick up 1 stitch in every cast-on stitch down to valley between hexagons and up to peak of next hexagon—a total of 16 (18, 20, 22) stitches on needle. Repeat from* with 3 more needles—48 (54, 60, 66) stitches. *Round 1* Purl, pm at center of each needle. *Round 2* Knit. *Round 3* [M1, knit to 2 stitches before marker, SSK, slip marker (sm), k2tog, knit to end of needle, M1] 4 times. *Round 4* Purl. *Round 5* Knit. *Round 6* Repeat Round 3. Bind off loosely in purl.
Stretchy hexagon sock cuffs are finished with 10 rows.

## Toe

The length of toe shaping is equal to distance between centers of 2 adjacent hexagons. Try on sock before beginning toe. If more length is needed, work several rows of cuff edging pattern before beginning toe shaping, replacing the purl rounds with knit rounds for a smoother finish. To shorten toe, omit Rounds 2 & 4. Pick up stitches at toe end of sock same as for cuff. *Next round* Knit, placing a marker at center of each needle. Knit one round. *Decrease round* [Knit to 2 stitches before marker, SSK, k2tog, knit to end of needle] 4 times. Work Decrease round every 3rd round until number of stitches has been reduced by half, then every other round until 8 stitches remain. Cut yarn, draw through remaining stitches twice, pull tight and fasten off.

*Completed sock showing back of leg and sole with heel turned up (on left) and heel turned down (on right).*

*Nancy Hazen*    *Kirkland, Washington*

*intermediate*

Adult M
**A** 8"
**B** 9"
**C** 12"

10cm/4"

48 ▦
24

over Garter stitch using
3.25mm/US 3 needles

Mitered square measures 2"
from point to point

1 2 **3** 4 5 6

Light weight
525 yds

Four 3.25mm/US 3
or size to obtain gauge

Four 3.5mm/US 4
Two 3.75mm/US 5

**&**

Stitch markers

Shown in
*MOUNTAIN COLORS*
Bearfoot in Ruby River

### Foot and Leg

Work squares and triangles in the order shown on the diagram, using needle size indicated.

*Square 1* With size 3.25mm/US 3 needles, cable cast on 19 stitches. Mark center stitch. *Row 1* (WS) Sl 1, knit to last stitch, p1. *Row 2* (RS) Sl 1, knit to 1 stitch before center stitch, SK2P, knit to last stitch, p1—2 stitches decreased. Repeat Rows 1–2 until 3 stitches remain. *Next RS row* SK2P. Do not cut yarn; remaining stitch becomes first stitch of next square.

*Squares 2, 6, 21, 30, 38, 46* With RS facing, pick up and k8 along upper left side of previous square or triangle; cast on 10—19 stitches. Work same as Square 1 EXCEPT cut yarn and fasten off.

*Squares 3, 7, 12* Work same as Square 1.

*Squares 4, 5, 8–10, 13–17, 20, 23, 25–29, 33–37, 40–45, 49–53, 56–58, 61* With RS facing, pick up and k8 along upper left side of previous square; cast on 10—19 stitches. Work same as Square 1. NOTE *Squares 37, 43, 45, 50, 52, 57* Needle size changes after third decrease row.

*Triangles 11, 47, 54, 59, 62* Pick up and k8 along upper left side of previous square—9 stitches. *Row 1* (WS) Sl 1, k7, p1. *Row 2* Sl 1, k2tog, k5, p1—8 stitches. *Row 3 and all WS rows* Sl 1, knit to last stitch, p1. *Row 4* Sl 1, k2tog, k4, p1—7 stitches. *Row 6* Sl 1, k2tog, k3, p1—6 stitches. *Row 8* Sl 1, k2tog, k2, p1—5 stitches. *Row 10* Sl 1, k2tog, k1, p1—4 stitches. *Row 12* Sl 1, k2tog, p1—3 stitches. *Row 14* Sl 1, k2tog—2 stitches. *Row 16* K2tog. Cut yarn leaving an 8" tail.

*Triangle 18* With RS facing, pick up and k9 along lower left side of Square 17. *Row 1* (WS) Sl 1, knit to last stitch, p1. *Row 2* Sl 1, knit to last 3 stitches, k2tog, p1—1 stitch decreased. Repeat Rows 1–2 until 2 stitches remain. *Next row* K2tog. Cut yarn and fasten off.

*Square 19* With RS facing, pick up and k9 along upper left side of Triangle 18; cast on 10—19 stitches. Work same as Square 2.

*Square 22 (31, 39, 48, 55, 60)* Cast on 10; pick up and knit along upper right side of

### NOTES

*1 See page 168 for any unfamiliar techniques. 2 Sock is worked in garter stitch miters with stockinette heel and toe on double-pointed needles. 3 Use cable cast-on throughout. 4 The two top tiers of squares for these socks are made with needles 1 and 2 sizes larger than rest of sock to provide extra room for calf. 5 To make smaller socks, use needles 1 size smaller and make toes a couple of rows shorter. To make larger socks, use needles 1 size larger and make toes a couple of rows longer.*

## Sock body chart

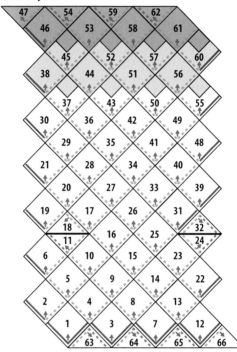

Square 13 (25, 31, 40, 49, 56)—19 stitches. Work same as Square 1.

*Triangle 24* With WS facing, pick up and k8 along upper right side of Square 23—9 stitches. *Row 2* (RS) Sl 1, knit to last 3 stitches, k2tog, p1—1 stitch decreased. *Row 2* Sl 1, knit to last stitch, p1. Repeat Rows 1–2 until 2 stitches remain. *Next row* K2tog. Cut yarn and fasten off.

*Triangle 32* With RS facing, pick up and k9 along lower right side of Square 31. Work same as Triangle 11.

*Triangle 63 (64, 65, 66)* With RS facing, pick up and k9 along lower right side of Square 1 (3, 7, 12). Work same as Triangle 11.
Sew free edges of all triangles along upper and lower edges to adjacent squares. Bring sides of piece together to form a tube and sew back of leg seam and bottom of foot seam. Leave heel opening free.

### Heel

With 3.25mm/US 3 needles and 2 strands of yarn held together, beginning at junction of Triangles 24 and 11, pick up and k12 along edge of each triangle at heel opening—48 stitches. Arrange stitches so 12 stitches from Triangle 24 are on Needle 1, 24 stitches from Triangles 32 and 18 are on Needle 2, and 12 stitches from Triangle 11 are on Needle 3. Join to work in the round. Knit 2 rounds. *Next round* **Needle 1** Knit to last 3 stitches, k2tog, k1; **Needle 2** k1, SSK, knit to last 3 stitches, k2tog, k1; **Needle 3** k1, SSK, knit to end of round. Work last round 7 more times—16 stitches. Knit stitches from Needle 1 onto Needle 3. Graft stitches on Needle 2 to stitches on Needle 3.

### Toe

With 3.25mm/US 3 needles and a single strand of yarn, work same as for heel.

### Cuff

With 3.5mm/US 4 needles and RS facing, pick up and k17 along edge of each triangle at upper edge of sock—68 stitches. Arrange stitches on 3 needles and join to work in the round. Work 9 rounds of k1, p1 rib. Bind off loosely in rib.

Adult M
**A** 8½"
**B** 9½"

10cm/4"

56
26

over garter stitch

1 2 **3** 4 5 6

Light weight

**A–C** 100 yds each

2.5mm/US 1½, or size to
obtain gauge, 80cm (32")
or longer

2.5mm/US 1½,
or size to obtain gauge

2.75mm/C-2

**&**

Small amount smooth waste yarn
Stitch markers
Safety pin

Shown in
*REGIA* 6-fädig in Jacquard
Color 5275 (A), 1936 (B),
and 2143 (C)

# 'Round the Bend

*Arden Okazaki*    *Deep River, Ontario, Canada*

**DOUBLE DECREASE (DD)** K2tog, k1, slip marker, k1, SSK.

## Center strip

With A and a straight needle, cast-on 9 stitches. Cut 2 strands of waste yarn, each 30" long, to mark turning loops at end of each row (see illustrations 1 and 2, page 124). *Row 1* (RS) Knit. Mark RS with safety pin. *Row 2* Knit; one ridge complete. Repeat these 2 rows until there are 166 ridges, and 166 turns are caught on waste yarn on each edge of strip. Bind off loosely on RS.

## Left side

With B, circular needle, and RS facing, pick up and k1 at a corner of center strip, k166 loops from waste yarn, pick up and p1 at corner—168 stitches. *Row 1* (WS) Sl 1, k24, place instep marker (IM), k44, place toe marker (TM), k59, place heel marker (HM), k39, p1. *Rows 2, 4* Sl 1, knit to **3** before **HM**, DD, knit to **3** before **TM**, DD, knit to end. *Row 3 and all WS rows* Sl 1, knit to end. *Row 6* With C, sl 1, k25, k2tog, k7, DD, k7, SSK, knit to **3** before **TM**, DD, knit to end. *Row 8, 10* With B, sl 1, knit to **3** before **HM**, DD, knit to **7** before **TM**, k2tog, k2, DD, k2, SSK, knit to end. *Row 12* Sl 1, k25, k2tog, k3, DD, k3, SSK, knit to **7** before **TM**, k2tog, k2, DD, k2, SSK, knit to **3** before **IM**, knit into front and back of stitch (kf&b), k3, kf&b, knit to end.

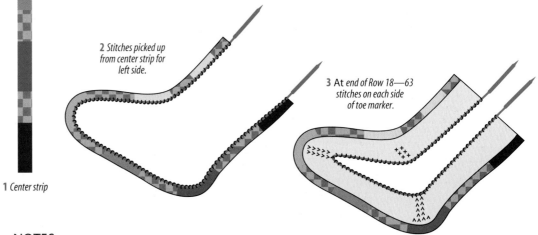

**2** *Stitches picked up from center strip for left side.*

**3** *At end of Row 18—63 stitches on each side of toe marker.*

**1** *Center strip*

## NOTES

*1 See page 168 for any unfamiliar techniques. 2 Sock begins with a long strip which forms front of leg, top of foot, center of sole, and back of leg. Sides of the sock are worked from stitches picked up from sides of strip and shaped with increases and decreases at heel and toe. 3 Markers indicate position of heel, toe, and instep. It is helpful to label these markers, or use different colored markers for each position. 4 Work all slipped stitches as if to knit.*

*Row 14* With C, sl 1, k28, DD, knit to **7** before **TM**, k2tog, k2, DD, k2, SSK, knit to **3** before **IM**, kf&b, k3, kf&b, knit to end. *Row 16* With B, sl 1, k17, DD, knit to **6** before **TM**, k2tog, k1, DD, k1, SSK, knit to **3** before **IM**, kf&b, k3, kf&b, knit to end. *Row 18* Sl 1, k26, DD, knit to **2** before **TM**, k2tog, SSK, knit to **3** before **IM**, kf&b, k3, kf&b, knit to end—126 stitches, 63 on each side of TM. *Row 20* With C, sl 1, knit to **TM**, fold sock at toe, with needle points parallel to one another. Cut yarn with long tail and graft from toe to cuff. Secure end.

## Right side

With C and RS facing, pick up and k168 along other side of strip. *Row 1* (WS) Sl 1, k39, place HM, k59, place TM, k44, place IM, k24, p1. *Row 2* Sl 1, knit to **3** before **TM**, DD, knit to **3** before **HM**, DD, knit to end. *Row 3 and all WS rows* Sl 1, knit to end. *Row 4* With B, repeat Row 2. *Row 6* With C, sl 1, knit to **3** before **TM**, DD, knit to **12** before **HM**, k2tog, k7, DD, k7, SSK, knit to end. *Row 8* Sl 1, knit to **7** before **TM**, k2tog, k2, DD, k2, SSK, knit to **3** before **HM**, DD, knit to end. *Row 10* With B, repeat Row 8. *Row 12* With C, sl 1, knit to **3** before **IM**, kf&b, k3, kf&b, knit to **7** before **TM**, k2tog, k2, DD, k2, SSK, knit to **8** before **HM**, k2tog, k3, DD, k3, SSK, knit to end. *Row 14* Sl 1, knit to **3** before **IM**, kf&b, k3, kf&b, knit to **7** before **TM**, k2tog, k2, DD, k2, SSK, knit to **3** before **HM**, DD, knit to end. *Row 16* With B, sl 1, knit to **3** before **IM**, kf&b, k3, kf&b, knit to **6** before **TM**, k2tog, k1, DD, k1, SSK, knit to **3** before **HM**, DD, knit to end. *Row 18* With C, sl 1, knit to **3** before **IM**, kf&b, k3, kf&b, knit to **2** before **TM**, k2tog, SSK, knit to **3** before **HM**, DD, knit to end. *Row 19* Sl 1, knit to **TM**— 63 stitches on either side of TM. Graft as for Left Side.

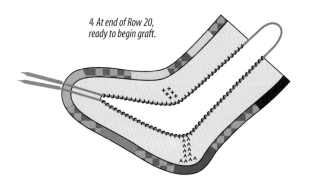

**4** At end of Row 20, ready to begin graft.

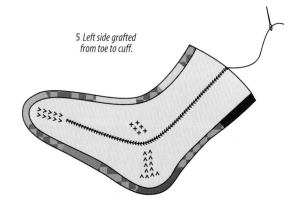

**5** Left side grafted from toe to cuff.

# A-Step Socks

Arden Okazaki    Deep River, Ontario, Canada

easy

Women's M
**A** 8½"
**B** 9½"

10cm/4"
64
32
over garter stitch

**1** 2 3 4 5 6
Super fine weight

**A** 400 yds
**B** 50 yds

2mm/US 0, or size to obtain gauge, 80cm (32") or longer

**&**

Stitch markers
Safety pin
Small amount smooth waste yarn

Shown in
AUSTERMANN Step 1 in Peat
(A) and Vulcan (B)

## NOTES

*1 See page 168 for any unfamiliar techniques. 2 Cast-on runs down center back leg, around end of toes and up center front leg. Long rows are worked out to sides from this cast-on. Sides are grafted closed. 3 Sample sock was worked primarily in color A, with sections of color B inserted at random to provide more color variation. You can change colors in a regular pattern or at random—knitter's choice.*

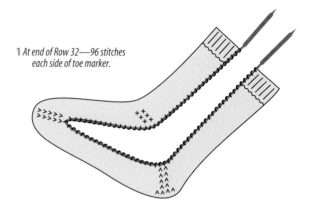

**1** At end of Row 32—96 stitches each side of toe marker.

**DOUBLE DECREASE (DD)** K2tog, k1, slip marker, k1, SSK.

### Side one

With A and long-tail cast-on, loosely cast on 256 sts. *Row 1* (RS) Sl 1, k71, place heel marker (HM), k80, place toe marker (TM), k56, place instep marker (IM), k47, p1. Mark RS with safety pin. *Row 2* (WS) Sl 1, knit to last stitch, p1. *Row 3* Sl 1, k18, knit into front and back of stitch (kf&b), knit to last 20 stitches, kf&b, k18, p1—258 sts. *Row 4, 7, 10, 16, 22, 28* Sl 1, p18, sl 1, p1, knit to last 21 stitches, sl 1, purl to end. *Row 5, 6, 8, 12, 14, 18, 20, 24, 26* Sl 1, k18, sl 1, p1, knit to last 21 stitches, sl 1, p1, k18, p1. *Row 9* Sl 1, k18, sl 1, p1, knit to **11** before **HM**, k2tog, k6, DD, k6, SSK, knit to **3** before **TM**, DD, knit to last 21 stitches, sl 1, p1, k18, p1. *Row 11* Sl 1, k18, sl 1, p1, knit to **3** before **HM**, DD, knit to **3** before **TM**, DD, knit to last 21 stitches, sl 1, p1, k18, p1. *Row 13* Sl 1, p18, sl 1, p1, knit to **10** before **HM**, k2tog, k5, DD, k5, SSK, knit to **3** before **TM**, DD, knit to last 21 stitches, sl 1, purl to end. *Row 15* Sl 1, k18, sl 1, p1, knit to **3** before **HM**, DD, knit to **3** before **TM**, DD, knit to last 21 stitches, sl 1, p1, k18, p1. *Row 17* Sl 1, k18, sl 1, p1, knit to **9** before **HM**, k2tog, k4, DD, k4, SSK, knit to **6** before **TM**, k2tog, k1, DD, k1, SSK, knit to last 21 stitches, sl 1, p1, k18, p1. *Row 19* Sl 1, p18, sl 1, p1, knit to **3** before **HM**, DD, knit to **6** before **TM**, k2tog, k1, DD, k1, SSK, knit to last 21 stitches, sl 1, p1, purl to end. *Row 21* Sl 1, k18, sl 1, p1, knit to **8** before **HM**, k2tog, k3, DD, k3, SSK, knit to **6** before **TM**, k2tog, k1, DD, k1, SSK, knit to **3** before **IM**, kf&b, k3, kf&b, knit to last 21 stitches, sl 1, p1, k18, p1. *Row 23 and 27* Sl 1, k18, sl 1, p1, knit to **3** before **HM**, DD, knit to **6** before **TM**, k2tog, k1, DD, k1, SSK, knit to **3** before **IM**, kf&b, k3, kf&b, knit to last 21 stitches, sl 1, p1, k18, p1. *Row 25* Sl 1, p18, sl 1, p1, knit to **7** before **HM**, k2tog, k2, DD, k2, SSK, knit to **6** before **TM**, k2tog, k1, DD, k1, SSK, knit to **3** before **IM**, kf&b, k3, kf&b, knit to last 21 stitches, sl 1, purl to end. *Row 29* Sl 1, k18, sl 1, p1, knit to **6** before **HM**, k2tog, k1, DD, k1, SSK, knit to **6** before **TM**, k2tog, k1, DD, k1, SSK, knit to **3** before **IM**, kf&b, k3, kf&b, knit to last 21 stitches, sl 1, p1, k18, p1. *Row 30* Sl 1, k18, k2tog, knit to last 21 stitches, k2tog, k18, p1. *Row 31* Sl 1, knit to **3** before **HM**, DD, knit to **6** before **TM**, k2tog, k1, DD, k1, SSK, knit to **3** before **IM**, kf&b, k3, kf&b, knit to last stitch, p1. *Row 32* Sl 1, knit to last stitch, p1. *Row 33* Sl 1, knit to **2** before TM, k2tog, knit to last stitch, p1. *Row 34* Sl 1, knit to **2** before TM, k2tog—95 stitches on each side of TM. Fold sock at the toe, with needle points parallel to one another. Cut yarn with long tail and graft from toe to cuff. Secure end.

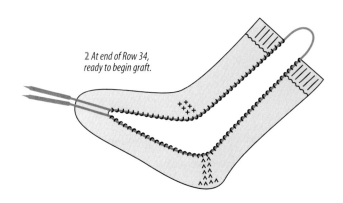

**2** At end of Row 34, ready to begin graft.

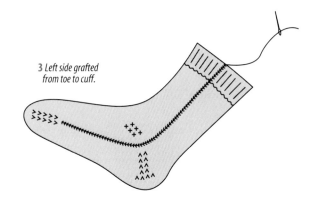

**3** Left side grafted from toe to cuff.

## Side two

With RS facing, pick up and knit 1 stitch in each stitch of cast-on—256 sts. *Next row* (WS) Sl 1, k71, HM, k80, TM, k56, IM, k47, p1.

*Width adjustment rows* The following 2 rows can be repeated as needed to add extra width to the sock. Each 2 row repeat will add about ¼" to the foot circumference. *Row 1* (RS) Sl 1, knit to last stitch, p1. *Row 2* (WS) Repeat Row 1. *Rows 3–8* Work as for Side 1 EXCEPT RS rows of Side 1 are WS rows of Side 2.

*Row 9* Sl 1, k18, sl 1, p1, knit to **3** before **TM**, DD, knit to **11** before **HM**, k2tog, k6, DD, k6, SSK, knit to last 21 stitches, sl 1, p1, k18, p1. *Row 11* Sl 1, k18, sl 1, p1, knit to **3** before **TM**, DD, knit to **3** before **HM**, DD, knit to last 21 stitches, sl 1, p1, k18, p1. *Row 13* Sl 1, p18, sl 1, p1, knit to **3** before **TM**, DD, knit to **10** before **HM**, k2tog, k5, DD, k5, SSK, knit to last 21 stitches, sl 1, purl to end. *Row 15* Sl 1, k18, sl 1, p1, knit to **3** before **TM**, DD, knit to **3** before **HM**, DD, knit to last 21 stitches, sl 1, p1, k18, p1. *Row 17* Sl 1, k18, sl 1, p1, knit to **6** before **TM**, k2tog, k1, DD, k1, SSK, knit to **9** before **HM**, k2tog, k4, DD, k4, SSK, knit to last 21 stitches, sl 1, p1, k18, p1. *Row 19* Sl 1, p18, sl 1, p1, knit to **6** before **TM**, k2tog, k1, DD, k1, SSK, knit to **3** before **HM**, DD, knit to last 21 stitches, sl 1, purl to end. *Row 21* Sl 1, k18, sl 1, p1, knit to **3** before **IM**, kf&b, k3, kf&b, knit to **6** before **TM**, k2tog, k1, DD, k1, SSK, knit to **8** before **HM**, k2tog, k3, DD, k3, SSK, knit to last 21 stitches, sl 1, p1, k18, p1. *Row 23* Sl 1, k18, sl 1, p1, knit to **3** before **IM**, kf&b, k3, kf&b, knit to **6** before **TM**, k2tog, k1, DD, k1,

SSK, knit to **3** before **HM**, DD, knit to last 21 stitches, sl 1, p1, k18, p1. *Row 25* Sl 1, p18, sl 1, p1, knit to **3** before **IM**, kf&b, k3, kf&b, knit to **6** before **TM**, k2tog, k1, DD, k1, SSK, knit to **7** before **HM**, k2tog, k2, DD, k2, SSK, knit to last 21 stitches, sl 1, purl to end. *Row 27* Sl 1, k18, sl 1, p1, knit to **3** before **IM**, kf&b, k3, kf&b, knit to **6** before **TM**, k2tog, k1, DD, k1, SSK, knit to **3** before **HM**, DD, knit to last 21 stitches, sl 1, p1, k18, p1. *Row 29* Sl 1, k18, sl 1, p1, knit to **3** before **IM**, kf&b, k3, kf&b, knit to **6** before **TM**, k2tog, k1, DD, k1, SSK, knit to **6** before **HM**, k2tog, k1, DD, k1, SSK, knit to last 21 stitches, sl 1, p1, k18, p1. *Row 31* Sl 1, knit to **3** before **IM**, kf&b, k3, kf&b, knit to **6** before **TM**, k2tog, k1, DD, k1, SSK, knit to **3** before **HM**, DD, knit to last stitches, p1—95 stitches on each side of TM.

*Rows 32–34* Work as for Side One. Graft as for Side One.

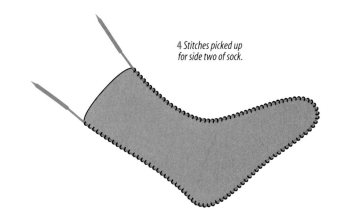

**4** Stitches picked up for side two of sock.

Adult M
**A** 8"
**B** 9"

10cm/4"
48
36
over stockinette st

**1** 2 3 4 5 6
Super Fine weight

**A** 330 yds
**B** 220 yds

2.25mm/US 1

Four 2.25mm/US 1
or size to obtain gauge

Shown in
*REGIA* 4-fädig in colors
1956 (A) and 1937 (B)

# Funny & Fancy

*Jeannette Kelley*   Cottonwood, Idaho

1

2

3

4

5

6

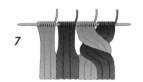

7

## 2/2 RIB
*Row 1* (RS) K1, [k1, p2, k2, p2, k1] to end.
*Row 2* (WS) [P1, k2, p2, k2, p1] to last stitch, p1.

## Leg
*1* Cast on 81 stitches as follows: [8A, 8B] 4 times, 8A, 9B. Work in 2/2 Rib for 12 rows, matching colors and twisting yarns at color change to connect strips.

*2* Work next 24 rows in pattern without twisting yarns at back of work so that strips are not connected.

*3* Slip first 2 strips to separate dpns.

*4* Work a left twist over first 2 strips as follows: Bring right strip over left strip…

*5*…then under left strip and back to its original position.

*6* Place stitches of left strip back on working needle…

*7*…then place stitches of right strip on working needle. Work in pattern across both strips, connecting strips. Repeat Steps 3–7 for each pair of strips. Work 11 rows connecting strips. Repeat from Step 3 once more. Work 2 more rows, connecting strips.

## NOTES
*1 See page 168 for any unfamiliar techniques. 2 Leg of sock is worked back and forth on straight needles, then foot is worked around on double-pointed needles. 3 Sock is worked using Intarsia technique. Before you begin, wind a separate bobbin or butterfly of yarn for each vertical stripe. You'll need five 20-yard bobbins of each color for each sock.*

## Heel flap
*Next row* (RS) With B only, [k2, p2] 10 times, M1, k1, turn. Work back and forth on these 42 stitches for heel. *Next row* (WS) [P2, k2] to last 2 stitches, p2. *Next row* [K2, p2] to last 2 stitches, k2. Repeat last 2 rows 11 more times.

## Heel turn
*Row 1* (WS) P24, p2tog, p1, turn.
*Row 2* Sl 1, k**7**, SSK, k1, turn. *Row 3* Sl 1, p**8**, p2tog, p1, turn. *Row 4* Sl 1, k**9**, SSK, k1, turn. *Row 5* Sl 1, p**10**, p2tog, p1, turn. Continue working 1 more stitch before decrease each row until *Row 17* Sl 1, p**22**, p2tog, turn. *Row 18* Sl 1, k22, SSK—24 stitches.

## Gussets
With double-pointed needle and A, pick up and k19 along left side of heel flap. With another needle, work across 40 instep stitches in rib, using A only. With another needle, pick up and k19 along right side of heel flap, then knit 12 heel stitches. Slip 12 remaining heel stitches to first needle. Slip first instep stitch from Needle 2 to Needle 1. Slip last instep stitch from Needle 2 to Needle 3; beginning of round is at center of heel. Needles 1 & 3 each hold 32 stitches; Needle 2 holds 38 stitches. *Next round* **Needle 1** Knit to last 2

stitches, k2tog; **Needle 2** [p2, k2] to last 2 stitches, p2; **Needle 3** SSK, knit to end. *Next round* Knit. Repeat last 2 rounds 13 more times—74 stitches.

## Foot
Continue as established, working stockinette stitch on Needles 1 & 3 and rib on Needle 2, until foot measures 7" from back of heel, or 2" less than desired length. Change to B and work 1 round. Move first stitch from Needle 2 to Needle 1.

## Toe
*Round 1* **Needle 1** Knit to last 3 stitches, k2tog, k1; **Needle 2** k1, SSK, knit to last 3 stitches, k2tog, k1; **Needle 3** k1, SSK, knit to end. *Round 2* Knit. Repeat last 2 rounds 7 more times, then work Round 1 six times—18 stitches. Knit stitches on Needle 1. Graft toe.

## Finishing
Sew side seam on leg of sock in 12-row segments, leaving openings to correspond to cable twists.

**intermediate +**

Adult M
**A** 8"
**B** 8"

10cm/4"
32 **▦** 
22
over stockinette stitch

 1 **2** 3 4 5 6
Fine weight
**A** 125 yds
**B** 125 yds
**C** 50 yds
Optional: small amounts of accent colors for Bobble Cuff.

3.5mm/US 4,
or size to obtain gauge

3.5mm/US E-4

Shown in
*COLINETTE* Cadenza in
Adonis Blue (A),
Velvet Damson (B), and
Elephants Daydream(C)

# Doublefun

*Leena Siikaniemi*    *Ilmajoki, Finland*

## NOTES
*1 See page 168, for any unfamiliar techniques. 2 Sock is worked cuff down. 3 See Notes on Double Knit in Color. 4 Always twist yarns at end of full rows. When working short rows, do not twist yarns in short row, but do twist yarns at end of return row.*

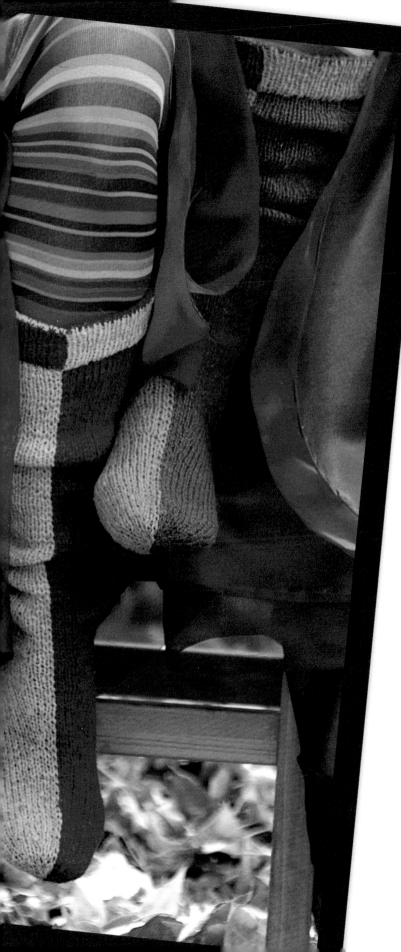

## Double Knit in Color

Double knitting is a way to work two layers of fabric at the same time on 1 pair of needles. It's simple if you think of the fabric as having two 'right' sides. All the knit stitches in a row make up one layer of fabric; the purl stitches in the same row form the other layer.

Knit stitches of the side that is facing you at any given time (Side A or B) and purl stitches for the opposite layer.

Think of the stitches as being in pairs: one knit and one purl. When the layers are joined at the beginning and end of the row, the work forms a tube and has great potential for socks.

### Side A facing

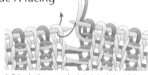

*1. Bring both yarns to back, knit A stitch with A.*

*2. Bring both yarns to front, purl B stitch. Repeat Steps 1 and 2.*

### Side B facing

*1. Bring both yarns to back, knit B with B.*

*2. Bring both yarns to front, purl A with A. Repeat Steps 1 and 2.*

*intermediate +*

Adult M
**A** 8"
**B** 8½"
**C** 13½"

10cm/4"
32
21
over stockinette stitch

1 **2** 3 4 5 6

Fine weight
**A–D** 110 yds each

3.25mm/US 3,
or size to obtain gauge

Five 3.25mm/US 3

**&**

Stitch marker

Shown in
*STUDIO MAISA TIKKANEN*
*KUITUVÄRJÄTTY VILLALANKA*
100% Finnish Lambswool in
colors 770, 730, 420, & 410

## NOTES

*1 See page 168 for any unfamiliar techniques. 2 Sock is worked cuff down. 3 See Notes on Double Knit in Color. 4 Always twist yarns at end of full rows. When working short rows, do not twist yarns in short row, but do twist yarns at end of return row.*

# BLUE-TONE SOCKS

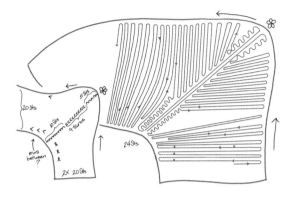

When A side is facing, the row is considered a RS row (A stitches are knit in this row).

*Double decrease (DD)*
Slip next (A) stitch, slip next 2 (1B, 1A) together as if to knit, then slip these 3 stitches back to left needle; first 4 stitches on needle are now arranged A, A, B, B: p2tog with A, SSK with B.

## Leg
Tie a slip knot with yarns A and B. Beginning with A, loop cast on, alternating 1 stitch A and 1 stitch B until you have 40 stitches, not counting slip knot. Do not twist yarns between stitches, but do twist yarns (front under back) at end of each row and tighten. *Row 1, B side* [Knit B stitch with B, purl A stitch with A] around. Remove slip knot from needle. *Row 2, A side* Knit A stitches with A, purl B stitches with B. Repeat last 2 rows 6 more times.

## Instep
*Increase row 1* With B facing, [k1B, p1A] twice, M1B, M1A, [k1B, p1A] to end. Work 5 rows even. *Increase row 2* [K1B, p1A] 3 times, M1B, M1A, [k1B, p1A] to end. Work 7 rows even. *Increase row 3* [K1B, p1A] 4 times, M1B, M1A, [k1B, p1A] to end. Work 5 rows even. *Increase row 4* [K1B, p1A] 17 times, M1B, M1A, [k1B, p1A] to end—48 stitches. *Next row* Work even.

## Heel
*Short-row heel, next row* With A facing, [k1A, p1B] 16 times; slip A and B, wrap B around B stitch and return to left needle, wrap A around A stitch and return to left needle, turn work without twisting yarns (W&TAB). *Next row* Work all stitches, twist yarns. [*Next row* Work to 2 stitches before wrapped stitches, W&TAB. *Next row* Work all stitches.] 9 times. *Next row* Work all stitches, hiding wraps and working firmly. *Next row* Work even. *Next row* [K1B, p1A] 5 times, W&TAB. *Next row* Work all stitches. [*Next row* Work to wrapped stitches, then work next 2 stitches, hiding wraps, W&TAB. *Next row* Work all stitches.] 9 times. *Next row* Work across all stitches hiding last wraps from previous row. Work 3 rows even.

*Instep decreases, next row* [K1A, p1B] 5 times, DD, [k1A, p1B] 12 times, DD, [k1A, p1B] to end. Work 6 rows even. *Next row* [P1B, k1A] 2 times, DD, [p1B, k1A] to end. Work 5 rows even. *Next row* P1B, k1A, DD, [p1B, k1A] to end—40 stitches. Work 5 rows even, twisting yarns at end of every row. *Exchange colors, next row* Work B stitches with A and A stitches with B. Work 10 rows even in colors as established.

## Toe
*Toe shaping, decrease row 1* [P1A, k1B ] twice, DD, *[p1A, k1B ] 3 times, DD, repeat from* 2 times more, p1A, p1B—32 stitches. Work 4 rows. *Decrease row 2* P1A, k1B , DD, *[p1A, k1B ] 2 times, DD, repeat from* 2 more times, p1A, k1B—24 stitches. Work 4 rows even. *Decrease row 3* [P1A, k1B, DD] 4 times—16 stitches. Work 2 rows even. *Final decrease row* [DD] 4 times—8 stitches. Cut yarn, leaving a 6" tail, thread through stitches, and pull tight.

## Bobble Cuff
*Bobble stitch* Work 5 double crochet (dc) into one stitch leaving last loop of each on hook, yarn over hook and pull through all 6 loops on hook.

*Cuff, first round* With crochet hook and one CC, chain (ch) 4. Work bobble into 2nd ch from hook. Ch 10. With RS facing, connect to back seam of sock with single crochet (sc). *Ch 2, skip a stitch from cast-on, work a bobble into next stitch, ch 2, skip a cast-on stitch, sc into next stitch, repeat from* around to back seam, join to first stitch with a slip stitch (sl st), sl st 6 along ch toward first bobble and work a bobble into next ch. Sl st into next ch and fasten off. Hide tails. *Next round* With a second CC, make bobble as for Round 1, [ch 5, make bobble in second ch from hook] twice, ch5, sc into sc at back seam, [ch 7, sc into next sc] around, end at back seam. Cut yarn, secure, and hide tails.

**2-color Tubular Cast-on**

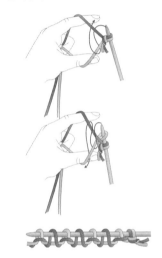

# MI-PARTI STOCKINGS

## Cuff

*Note* Cuff is worked in a double layer.

Make a slip knot with ends of both yarns, and work tubular cast-on, alternating A and B until you have 46 stitches (slip knot does not count as a stitch); twist yarns and alternately cast on with B and A until you have 46 more stitches—92 stitches. Cast-on counts as Row 1. *Begin Double Knitting, Row 2* With slip knot to your left, work first 46 stitches, knitting A stitches with A and purling B stitches with B. Twist B over A, knit B stitches with B and purl A stitches with A to end of row. Remove slip knot from needle. *Row 3* With slip knot to your right, [k1A, p1B] 23 times, then twist B over A, and [k1B, p1A] to end of row. With knot to the right, mark side of fabric facing you as outside of sock. Transfer stitches to 4 double-pointed needles, 23 stitches per needle. Join, begin working in the round. **Note** to work stitches firmly at beginning and end of needles. *Round 1* [K1A, p1B] 23 times, twist yarns, [k1B, p1A] 23 times. *Rounds 2–10* Twist yarns, [k1A, p1B] 23 times, twist yarns, [k1B, p1A] 23 times. *Join inner cuff to outer cuff* Both yarns are now at back seam. With side A facing, slip last A stitch from Needle 4 to Needle 1, and with yarn B only, *[k2tog] 3 times, M1 knitwise, repeat from* 6 more times, k2tog twice, slip remaining stitch to Needle 3. Drop B, and turn cuff inside out. With inside A fabric facing and yarn A only, *[p2tog] 3 times, M1 purlwise; repeat from* 6 more times, p2tog twice—60 sts. Turn cuff right side out, making sure yarns are on the outside. Transfer all A stitches to one needle and all B stitches to another; then with A color facing transfer all stitches onto 1 long double point or circular needle, first 1 A stitch then 1 B stitch.

## Leg

Work even in Double Knitting for 4½", making sure to twist yarns (front under back) at end of each row and tighten.

*Calf decreases row* With B facing, work to last 8 sts (4A and 4B), work DD (see Blue Socks), work to end. Work 5 rows even. Repeat last 6 rows 3 more times. [Work Decrease row, work 3 rows even] 4 times. Work Decrease row—42 stitches. Work 2" even. *Instep increase* With B facing, work to last 6 stitches (3A, 3B), M1A, M1B, work to end. Work 5 rows even. Repeat last 6 rows once more. *Next row* Work 14 stitches, M1A, M1B, work to last 8 stitches, M1A, M1B, work to end—50 stitches. *Next row* Work even.

## Heel

*Short-row heel, next row* With A facing, [K1A, p1B] 16 times; slip A and B, wrap B around B stitch and return to left needle, wrap A around A stitch and return to left needle, turn work without twisting yarns (W&TAB) *Next row* Work all stitches, twist yarns. [*Next row* Work to 2 stitches before wrapped stitches, W&TAB. *Next row* Work all stitches.] 10 times. *Next row* Work all stitches, hiding wraps and making sure to work firmly. *Next row* Work even. *Next row* [P1A, k1B]

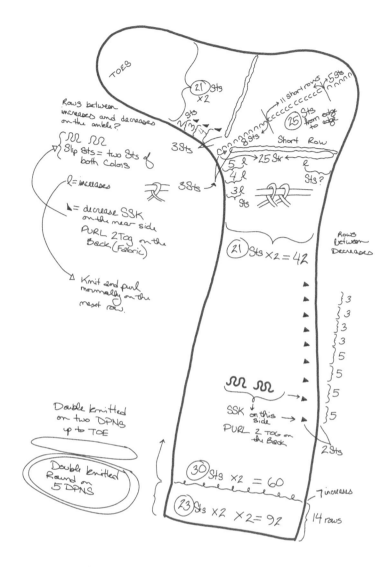

5 times, W&TAB. *Next row* Work all stitches. [*Next row* Work to wrapped stitches, then work next 2 stitches, hiding wraps, W&TAB. *Next row* Work all stitches.] 10 times. *Next row* Work across all stitches hiding last wraps from previous row. Work 3 rows even. *Instep decreases, next row* Work 12 stitches, DD, work to last 12 stitches, DD, work to end. Work 3 rows even. [*Next row* Work to last 10 stitches, DD, work to end. Work 3 rows even.] twice—42 stitches. Work even until 2" less than desired length.

## Toe

*Toe shaping, decrease row 1* [Work 6 stitches, DD] 4 times, work 2—34 stitches. Work 4 rows even. *Decrease row 2* [Work 4 stitches, DD] 4 times, work 2—26 stitches. Work 3 rows even. *Decrease row 3* [Work 2 stitches, DD] 4 times, work 2—18 stitches. Work 2 rows even. *Decrease row 4* [DD] 4 times, work 2—10 stitches. Work 1 row even. Cut yarn, leaving a 6" tail, thread through stitches, and pull tight.

Adult M
**A** 7½"
**B** 9"

10cm/4"

32
20

over stockinette stitch

1 2 3 **4** 5 6

Medium weight
175 yds

Two 3.75mm/US 5,
or size to obtain gauge,
80cm (32") or longer

3.75mm/US 5

**&**

Small amount smooth
waste yarn

Shown in
*PLYMOUTH* Boku in color 14

# Spiral Stripes

*Cathy Leffingwell*   Eau Claire, Wisconsin

## FIRST SOCK

### Toe

With circular needle and Judy's Magic Cast-on, cast 8 stitches onto each needle—16 stitches. *Round 1* Knit. *Round 2* [K1, M1L, knit to last stitch on needle, M1R, k1] 2 times. *Round 3* Knit. Repeat last 2 rounds 6 more times—44 stitches.

### Foot

*Begin Spiral Strip* Cut 1 strand of waste yarn to mark turning loops at beginning of each RS row (see technique box, page 124). Use straight or double-pointed needle in right hand. *Row 1* (RS) K1, M1L, turn. *Row 2* (WS) Sl 1, p1. *Row 3* K1, SSK. *Row 4 and all WS rows* Purl (or knit in reverse, see page 132). *Row 5* K1, SSSK. *Row 7* K1, M1L, SSK. *Row 9* K2, SSSK. *Row 11* K2, SSK. *Row 13* K2, M1L, SSSK. *Row 15* K3, SSK. *Row 17* K3, SSSK. *Row 19* K3, M1L, SSK. *Row 21* K4, SSSK. *Row 23* K4, SSK. *Row 25* K4, M1L, SSSK—
6 stitches on right needle. *Row 27* K5, SSK. *Row 29* K5, SSSK. *Row 31* Begin Chart pattern. AT SAME TIME, continue joining spiral strip to toe stitches, alternating SSK and SSSK at end, and catching turning loop at beginning of each RS row. After 30 rows of Chart, all toe stitches have been worked.

*Begin Sliding Loop* **Note** Join strips with Sliding Loop technique at end of every RS row throughout rest of sock unless otherwise indicated. Work 30 rows even in stockinette stitch for sole of foot, then work next 30 rows in chart pattern for top of foot. Repeat this 60-row sequence until 3 repeats of chart pattern are complete.

*Side gusset* Do not pick up new loop. *Next row* K6. *Next row* P6.

Work 30 rows of sole, 2 unattached rows for Side gusset, 30 rows of Chart, 2 unattached rows for Side gusset, 34 rows stockinette, 2 unattached rows for Side gusset, 30 rows of Chart.

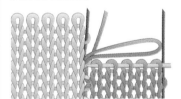

**Sliding loop join**

*Lay marking strand over working yarn.*

*1* and *2* Mark the joining loop as you knit. At the beginning of each right-side row, bring working yarn around a length of waste yarn.

*3* Knit up a sliding loop Insert free needle in first joining loop and pull up a long loop of working yarn. Remove loop from needle and turn work. Using yarn supplied by sliding loop, work 2 rows. Continue pulling up a loop in each joining loop and working 2 rows with yarn from each new loop.

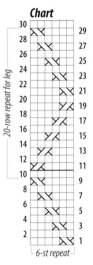

**Chart**

20-row repeat for leg

6-st repeat

**Stitch key**

☐ Knit on RS, purl on RS
⤬ 1/1 LT
⤬ 1/1 RT

## NOTES

*1 See page 168 for any unfamiliar techniques. 2 Sock is worked toe up. Magic Loop is used for toe, heel, and cuff. The foot and leg are worked in a long spiral strip which is joined using Sliding Loop technique. 3 It is helpful to work the wrong-side rows of the strip by "knitting in reverse". 4 A self-striping yarn works best for this sock.*

## Building a spiral sock

**3** Continue building spiral strip until all sole stitches of toe have been worked.

**2** With smaller dpn, begin spiral strip.

**1** Work toe.

**5** Continue, joining with Sliding Loop.

**4** Work spiral strip in chart pattern across remaining toe stitches (top of foot).

ıllıllı *live stitches*
—— *joined edge*

## Heel

*Next row* (RS) K1, M1L, knit to end. *Next row* Purl. Repeat last 2 rows 6 more times— 13 stitches. Work 10 rows even, continuing to join. *Next row* SSK, knit to last stitch. *Next row* Purl. Repeat last 2 rows 6 more times— 6 stitches. Work 30 rows of Chart across top of foot. *Next row* Knit to last stitch, M1R, k1. *Next row* Purl. Repeat last 2 rows 6 more times—13 stitches. Work 10 rows even. *Next row* Knit to last 2 stitches, k2tog. *Next row* Purl. Repeat last 2 rows 6 more times—6 stitches.
Work 30 rows of Chart pattern across top of foot, joining every row.

## Leg

Continue in Chart pattern around leg, decreasing at back of leg as follows: At end of Chart Rows 13, 21, 29, and 17, pick up next loop and place on right needle, pick up following loop for Sliding Loop, turn work and begin next row with p2tog. Continue working Chart pattern around leg until 9 pattern bands are complete, counting from toe to cuff.

*Decrease wedge, Row 1* (RS) K3, RT dec (sl 2 sts to cn and hold to back, k1, k2tog from cn)—5 stitches. *Row 2 & all WS rows* Purl. *Row 3* K2, 1/1 RT, k1. *Row 5* K1, 1/1 RT, k2. *Row 7* RT dec, k2—4 stitches. *Row 9* 1/1 LT, k2. *Row 11* K1, 1/1 LT, k1. *Row 13* K2, 1/1 LT. *Row 15* K1, RT dec—3 stitches. *Row 17* 1/1 LT, k1. *Row 19* K1, k2tog—2 stitches. *Row 21* 1/1 RT. *Row 23* K2tog. *Row 24* P2tog. Pull sliding loop through last stitch.

## Cuff

Change to circular needle. Pick up and k1 in each turning loop around top of sock—30 stitches. Arrange stitches for Magic Loop. *Round 1* [K1, M1, p1] around—45 stitches. *Round 2* [K2, p1] around. Continue in rib as established for 1¾". Bind off using EZ's sewn bind-off.

## SECOND SOCK

### Toe

Work same as for first sock.

### Foot

*Begin Spiral Strip* Slip next stitch with yarn in back, bring yarn forward, slip stitch back to left needle, turn work. Change to straight or double-pointed needle for right hand. *Row 1* (WS) P1, turn. *Row 2* (RS) Sl 1, k1. *Row 3* P1, p2tog. *Row 4 and all RS rows* Knit. *Row 5* P1, p3tog. *Row 7* P1, M1R, p2tog, turn. *Row 9* P2, p3tog. *Row 11* P2, p2tog. *Row 13* P2, M1R, p3tog. *Row 15* P3, p2tog. *Row 17* P3, p3tog. *Row 19* P3, M1R, p2tog. *Row 21* P4, p3tog. *Row 23* P4, p2tog. *Row 25* P4, M1R, p3tog—6 stitches. *Row 27* P5, p2tog. *Row 29* P5, p3tog. *Row 30* Begin Chart pattern. AT SAME TIME, continue joining spiral strip to toe stitches, alternating p2tog and p3tog at end of every WS row and catching turning loop at beginning of each WS row. When joining to wrapped stitch, pick up and purl wrap together with its stitch. When 30 rows of Chart are complete, all toe stitches have been worked.

Complete second sock as a mirror image of first sock, working Sliding Loop at end of every WS row and spiraling counterclockwise around leg.

## Spiral Cables

Cathy Leffingwell   Eau Claire, Wisconsin

Women's M
**A** 7½"
**B** 9"

10cm/4"

44  28

over stockinette stitch using smaller needles

 2 3 4 5 6

Super Fine weight
450 yds

2.75mm/US 2,
or size to obtain gauge,
80cm (32") or longer

2.75mm/US 2
3.25mm/US 3

**&**

Small amount smooth
waste yarn

Shown in
*AUSTERMANN* Step
in Ocean

### NOTES

**Notes 1–3** *Same as Spiral Stripes, page 127.* **4** *The cable sections at the top of the foot and the leg of the sock are worked with size 3.25mm/US 3 needles on 9 stitches. The sole of the foot is worked with size 2.75mm/US 2 needles on 6 stitches.*

## FIRST SOCK

### Toe

With circular needle, and Judy's Magic Cast-on, cast on 10 stitches each needle—20 stitches. *Round 1* Knit. *Round 2* [K1, M1L, knit to last stitch on needle, M1R, k1] 2 times. *Round 3* Knit. Repeat last 2 rounds 9 more times—60 stitches.

### Foot

*Begin Spiral Strip* Cut strand of waste yarn to mark turning loops at beginning of each RS row (see illustration, page 124). Use smaller straight or double-pointed needle in right hand. *Row 1* (RS) K1, M1L, turn. *Row 2* (WS) Sl 1, p1. *Row 3* K1, SSSK. *Row 4 & all WS rows* Purl (or knit in reverse). *Row 5* K1, SSK. *Row 7* K1, SSSK. *Row 9* K1, M1R, SSK. *Row 11* K2, SSSK. *Row 13* K2, SSK. *Row 15* K2, M1R, SSSK. *Row 17* K3, SSK. *Row 19* K3, SSSK. *Row 21* K3, M1R, SSK. *Row 23* K4, SSSK. *Row 25* K4, SSK. *Row 27* K4, SSSK. *Row 29* K4, M1R, SSK. *Row 31* K5, SSSK. *Row 33* K5, SSK. *Row 35* K5, SSSK. *Row 37* K5, SSK. *Row 39* K5, SSSK. All stitches from sole have been worked. *Row 40* Purl *Row 41* K1, M1R, k4, SSK. *Row 42* P1, M1L, p6. *Row 43* With larger needle in right hand, k3, sl3 sts to cable needle (cn) and hold in front, k1, M1R, k1, k2 from cn, SSSK (last stitch from cn with 2 sts of toe)—9 stitches on right needle. *Row 44* Purl. Work Rows 45–77 of Chart A. *Row 78* With smaller needle, p4, p2tog, p3. *Row 79* k1, k2tog, sl3 to cn hold in front, k2tog, k2 from cn, SSSK last stitch from cn with next 2 sts. All toe stitches are worked—6 stitches remain.

*Begin Sliding Loop* **Note** Join strips with Sliding Loop technique at end of every RS row throughout rest of sock unless otherwise indicated. Work 40 rows even in stockinette stitch for sole of foot, beginning with a purl row (counts as Row 80), then work Chart B for top of foot, working 4-row repeat 7 times. Repeat this 80-row sequence until 6 cable bands are complete across the top of the foot, end with Row 36 of Chart B.

### Heel opening

*End Sliding Loop* Increase 1 by picking up a stitch at next turning loop—10 stitches. Do not work sliding loop, instead work this new stitch in stockinette stitch. Work 4-row repeat of Chart B 11 times. *Begin Sliding Loop* Skip 22 turning loops and join to 23rd loop at end of next RS row. Turn, p2tog, and purl to end of row—9 stitches.

### Leg

Using larger needles only, resume working sliding loop and continue working Chart B repeat around leg and joining to previous band until 11 cable bands are complete, end with Row 32 of Chart B.

*Decrease wedge, Row 1* 3/3 RC, k3. *Row 2 & all even rows* Purl. *Row 3* K3, 3/3 LC Dec (Sl 3 to cn and hold to front, k1, k2tog; k3 from cn)—8 stitches. *Row 5* 3/2 RC (Sl 2 to cn and hold to back, k3; k2 from cn), k3. *Row 7* K3, 2/3 LC Dec (Sl 2 to cn and hold to front, k1, k2tog; k2 from cn)—7 stitches. *Row 9* 2/3 RC (Sl 3 to cn and hold to back, k2; k3 from cn), k2. *Row 11* K2, 2/3 LC Dec (Sl 2 to cn and hold to front, k1, k2tog; k2 from cn)—6 stitches. *Row 13* 2/2 RC (Sl 2 to cn and hold to back, k2; k2 from cn), k2. *Row 15* K2, 2/2 LC Dec (Sl 2 to cn and hold to front, k2tog; k2 from cn)—5 stitches. *Row 17* 1/2 RC (Sl 2 to cn and hold to back, k1; k2 from cn), k2. *Row 19* K1, 2/2 LC Dec (Sl 2 to cn and hold to front, k2tog; k2 from cn)—4 stitches. *Row 21* 1/1 RC (Sl 1 to cn and hold to back, k1; k1 from cn), k2. *Row 23* K1, 1/2 LC Dec (Sl 1 to cn and hold to front, k2tog; k1 from cn)—3 stitches. *Row 25* 1/1 RC (Sl 1 to cn and hold to back, k1; k1 from cn), k1. *Row 27* K1, SSK—2 stitches. *Row 28* SSP—1 stitch.

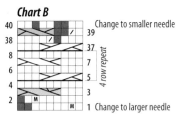

**Chart A**

Work 12 rows of chart twice, then work first 6 rows again.

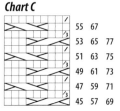

**Chart B**

Change to smaller needle

4 row repeat

Change to larger needle

**Chart C**

Work 12 rows of chart twice, then work first 10 rows again.

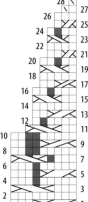

**Decrease Wedge**

**Chart Note:**
Cable symbols are not shown in stitch key; follow Decrease Wedge instructions at left.

## Stitch key

☐ Knit on RS, purl on WS
☑ K2tog on RS, p2tog on WS
☒ SSK on RS, SSP on WS
▣ P3tog
Ⓜ Make 1
▮ Stitches do not exist in these areas of chart

⬛ **2/3 LC Dec** Sl 2 to cn to front, k1; k2tog; k2 from cn
⬛ **3/3 RC** Sl 3 to cn and hold to back, k3; k3 from cn
⬛ **3/3 LC** Sl 3 to cn and hold to front, k3; k3 from cn
⬛ **3/3 LC Dec** Sl 3 to cn and hold to front, k3; k1 from cn, SSSK last stitch from cn with next 2 stitches
⬛ **3/3 LC Inc** Sl 3 to cn and hold to front, k1; M1, k1; k3 from cn
⬛ **3/3 LC Dec** Sl 3 to cn and hold to front, k1, k2tog; k3 from cn

### Cuff

Slip remaining stitch to circular needle. Pick up and k1 in each turning loop around top of sock—40 stitches. Arrange stitches for Magic Loop. *Next round* [K2, M1] 20 times—60 stitches. Work in k2, p2 rib for 2". Bind off loosely in rib.

### Heel

With circular needle, pick up and k64 around heel opening. Arrange for Magic Loop with stitches from sole on Needle 1 and stitches from leg on Needle 2. Knit 2 rounds. *Next round* [K1, SSK, knit to last 3 stitches on needle, k2tog, k1] twice. *Next round* Knit. Repeat last 2 rounds until 24 stitches remain. Graft heel.

## SECOND SOCK

### Toe

Work same as first sock.

### Foot

*Begin Spiral strip*

Slip next stitch with yarn in back, bring yarn forward, slip 1 back to left needle, turn work (counts as Row 1). Change to straight or double-pointed needle for right hand. *Row 2* (WS) P2. *Rows 3, 5 & 7* (RS) K2. *Rows 4 & 8* P1, p2tog. *Row 6* P1, p3tog. *Row 9* K1, M1L, k1. *Row 10* P2, p3tog. *Rows 11 & 13* K3. *Row 12* P2, p2tog. *Row 14* P3, p3tog. *Row 15* K1, M1L, k2. *Row 16* P3, p2tog. *Rows 17 & 19* K4. *Row 18* P3, p3tog. *Row 20* P3, p2tog. *Row 21* K1, M1L, k3. *Row 22* P4, p3tog. *Rows 23, 25, 27* K5. *Row 24* P4, p2tog. *Row 26* P4, p3tog. *Row 28* P4, p2tog. *Row 29* K1, M1L, k4. *Row 30* P5, p3tog. *Row 31, 33, 35, 37 & 39* K6. *Rows 32 & 36* P5, p2tog. *Rows 34 & 38* P5, p3tog. *Row 40* P5, p2tog. All stitches from sole have been worked. *Row 41* K5, M1R, k1. *Row 42* P1, M1L, p5, p3tog. *Row 43* With larger needle in right hand, k3, sl 3 stitches to cn and hold in front, k1, M1R, k1, k3 from cn. *Row 44* P8, p2tog. Work Rows 45–77 of Chart C. *Row 78* With smaller needle, p3, p2tog, p2, p3tog. *Row 79* Sl 2 to cn, hold in back, k3, k2tog from cn, k2tog, k1. *Row 80* P5, p2tog. All toe stitches are worked.

### Heel opening, leg, cuff, heel

Complete second sock as a mirror of first sock working sliding loop at end of every WS row, spiraling counterclockwise around leg.

### Knit in reverse (or knit back backwards)

To produce stockinette stitch fabric without turning the work or purling, alternate a row of knit (worked from right to left) with a row of knit in reverse (worked from left to right). This method is perfect for small areas (bobbles, entrelac) and ambidextrous knitters. Some left-handed knitters may choose to always knit in reverse and purl in reverse.

**1** With yarn in back of work, insert left needle from front to back into stitch on right needle and move left needle behind right needle.

**2** Bring yarn over left needle tip from back to front.

**3** While lifting right needle tip, bring yarn through stitch and onto left needle to form new stitch. Pull stitch off right needle.

Adult S
**A** 7"
**B** 8"

10cm/4"

48 

32

over stockinette stitch
using smaller needles

10cm/4"

48

26

over garter stitch
using larger needles

1 **2** 3 4 5 6

Fine weight
350 yds

3mm/US 2½,
or size to obtain gauge

Four 3mm/US 2½
Four 2.25mm/US 1

Shown in
*TWISTED FIBER ART*
Playful in Minstrel

# Perpendicular

*Anne Campbell*    Mason, Michigan

## Leg and top of foot

Work strips in number order.

**Strip 1** With larger needles, cast on 6 stitches. Work in garter stitch until piece measures 7", or desired length from bottom of heel to top of leg, excluding cuff. Bind off 5 stitches; last stitch is first stitch of Strip 2.

**Strip 2** With WS facing, pick up and p1 for every ridge along side of previous strip. Knit 5 rows. Purl 1 row.

**Strip 3** Cast on 6 stitches. *Row 1* K5, SSK (last stitch with a stitch from previous strip). *Row 2* Knit. Repeat last 2 rows until all stitches from previous strip have been worked. *Next row (WS)* Bind off 5 stitches.

## Gusset

**Strip 4** With WS facing, pick up and p1 for every ridge along side of previous strip. *Rows 1 & 2* Knit. *Row 3* K18, turn. *Row 4 & all even-numbered rows (WS)* Yo, knit to end. *Row 5* K14, turn. *Row 7* K10, turn. *Row 9* K6, turn. *Row 11* K2, turn. *Row 13* K4, knitting yo together with following stitch, turn. *Row 15* Continue knitting yo's together with following stitch as you complete gusset, k8, turn. *Row 17* K12, turn. *Row 19* K16, turn. *Rows 21 & 22* Knit. Cable cast on 23 stitches. Knit 1 row. Purl 1 row.

**Strips 5, 7, 9, 11** Work same as Strip 3.
**Strips 6, 8** Work same as Strip 2.

## Gusset

**Strip 10** With WS facing, pick up and p1 for every ridge along side of Strip 9. *Row 1* Bind off

### Construction Diagram

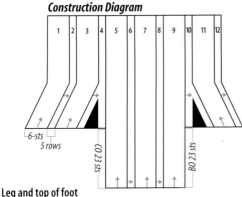

**Leg and top of foot**
Shaded area is short-row gusset; arrows indicate direction of work.

23, knit to end. *Row 2* Knit. *Rows 3–20* Work same as corresponding rows in Strip 4. Knit 3 rows. Purl 1 row.

**Strip 12** With WS facing, pick up and p1 for every ridge along side of Strip 11. Knit 5 rows. Bind off purlwise and sew bound-off edge to side of Strip 1. Or, do not bind off and graft stitches to side of Strip 1.

### Sole

Using smaller double-pointed needles (dpn), with RS facing and starting at corner between Strips 9 & 10, pick up and k16 at end of each gusset, 6 in each wide strip, and 3 in each narrow strip, end at corner between Strips 4 and 5—56 stitches.

*Sew Strip 12
to Strip 1*

## NOTES

*1 See page 168 for any unfamiliar techniques. 2 Sock begins at back of leg. Strips of garter stitch are worked with changes of direction and length to form leg, gussets, and top of foot in one piece. Stitches are picked up along side of piece for sole and toe of sock. Stitches are picked up along other side for cuff.*

## Heel

Work back and forth in short rows to form heel. *Row 1* (WS) P29, p2tog, p1, turn. *Row 2* Sl 1, k**3**, SSK, k1, turn. *Row 3* Sl 1, p**4**, p2tog, p1, turn. *Row 4* Sl 1, k**5**, SSK, k1, turn. *Row 5* Sl 1, p**6**, p2tog, p1, turn. Continue to work 1 more stitch before decrease on every row until *Row 26* Sl 1, k**27**, SSK, k1, turn—30 stitches. *Row 27* P29, sl 1, pick up a stitch from bound-off edge of Strip 10, purl this stitch together with slipped stitch. *Row 28* K29, sl 1 knitwise, pick up a stitch from bound-off edge of Strip 4, SSK this stitch together with slipped stitch. Repeat last 2 rows until you reach ends of Strips 4 & 10, picking up approximately 3 stitches for every 4 rows along bound-off edges. Turn.

 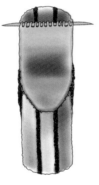

*Work short-row heel*     *Complete sole*

## Toe

Divide 30 sole stitches equally on 2 dpns. With another dpn, pick up and k24 along the edge of Strips 5–9, 6 stitches in each wide strip, and 3 stitches in each narrow strip. Join to work in the round—54 stitches. *Next round* K6, [k2tog, k6] 3 times, k2tog, k20, k2tog—49 stitches. Knit 3 rounds. *Next round* [K5, k2tog] to end—42 stitches. Knit 3 rounds even. *Next round* [K4, k2tog] to end—35 stitches. Knit 2 rounds even. *Next round* [K3, k2tog] to end—27 stitches. Knit 2 rounds even. *Next round* [K2, k2tog] to end—21 stitches. Knit 1 round even. *Next round* [K1, k2tog] to end—14 stitches. Knit 1 round even. *Next round* [K2tog] 7 times. Cut yarn. Draw through remaining 7 stitches, pull tight and fasten off.

*Work toe*

*Add cuff*

## Cuff

Using larger dpn, pick up and k6 at end of each wide strip and 3 stitches at end of each narrow strip—54 stitches. Divide evenly on 3 needles and join to work in the round—[knit 1 round, purl 1 round] twice. Knit 2 rounds. Cast on 4 stitches and work attached garter stitch I-cord as follows: *Row 1* K3, SSK last cord stitch with first stitch of cuff. Slip 4 stitches back to left needle. *Row 2* P3, p2tog (last cord stitch with next stitch of cuff). Slip 4 stitches back to left needle. *Row 3* Knit 4. Do not join this row to cuff. Slip 4 stitches back to left needle. *Row 4* Repeat Row 2. Repeat these 4 rows until all cuff stitches are worked. Graft remaining 4 stitches to cast-on edge of cord.

*intermediate*

Adult S
**A** 7"
**B** 8"

10cm/4"

36
30
over stockinette stitch

1 2 **3** 4 5 6

Light weight
300 yds

Two 2.75mm/US 2,
or size to obtain gauge

**&**

Cable needle
Beading needle

52 buttons
6mm (¼") diameter

Shown in
*MOUNTAIN COLORS*
Bearfoot in Winter Sky

# Convertible A Go-Go

*Terri D. Gogolin*     *Milan, Michigan*

## Detachable cuff
String 26 buttons on yarn, using a beading needle and passing yarn through one hole of button from back to front, then through other hole from front to back. Move each button into place as it is needed. Cast on 36 stitches. Work Chart pattern 5 times, placing a button at each side on Row 4, then every 6th row. Bind off. Sew bound-off edge to cast-on edge.

## Leg
Cast 26 stitches onto each of 2 circular needles—52 stitches. Join to work in the round. *All rounds* [P1, k3] around. Work until piece measures 2½".

## Heel flap
Work back and forth on 26 stitches on Needle 1 for heel; Needle 2 holds 26 instep stitches. *Row 1* [Sl 1, k1] to end. *Row 2* Sl 1, purl to end. Repeat last 2 rounds 13 more times.

## Turn heel
*Row 1* (RS) K15, SSK, k1, turn. *Row 2* Sl 1, p5, p2tog, p1, turn. *Row 3* Sl 1, k6, SSK, k1, turn. *Row 4* Sl 1, p7, p2tog, p1, turn. *Row 5* Sl 1, k8, SSK, k1, turn. Continue to work 1 more stitch before decrease every row, until *Row 10* Sl 1, p13, p2tog, p1—16 stitches. *Row 11* Knit.

## Gussets
Continuing with heel needle, pick up and k14 along left side of heel flap. With other needle, knit instep stitches. With heel needle, pick up and k14 along right side of heel flap, knit to end of heel needle—70 stitches: instep stitches now on Needle 1, heel stitches on Needle 2. *Next round* **Needle 1** Knit; **Needle 2** k1, SSK, knit to last 3 stitches, k2tog, k1. *Next round* Knit. Repeat last 2 rounds 8 more times—26 stitches on each needle.

## Foot
Work in stockinette stitch until foot measures 6½" from back of heel, or 1½" less than desired length.

## Toe
*Round 1* [K1, SSK, knit to last 3 stitches on needle, k2tog, k1] 2 times. *Round 2* Knit. Repeat last 2 rounds 6 more times, then work Round 1 four times—8 stitches remain. Cut yarn and draw through remaining stitches. Pull tight and fasten off.

## NOTES
*1 See page 168 for any unfamiliar techniques. 2 Sock is worked cuff down on 2 circular needles. 3 To place button: With yarn in front, slide button close to needle, slip next stitch purlwise, move yarn to back and pull snug before working next stitch. 4 Wear cuff buttoned into top of sock as shown, or just pull it on over sock.*

### Chart

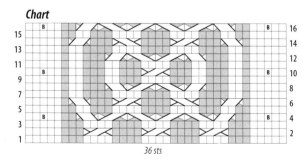

36 sts

### Stitch key

| | |
|---|---|
| ☐ | Knit on RS, purl on WS |
| ▨ | Purl on RS, knit on WS |
| ◸◹ | **4/4 RC** *Sl 2 to cn and hold to back, k2; k2 from cn* |
| ◺◿ | **4/4 LC** *Sl 2 to cn and hold to front, k2; k2 from cn* |
| ◸◹ | **4/4 RPC** *Sl 2 to cn and hold to back, k2; p2 from cn* |
| ◺◿ | **4/4 LPC** *Sl 2 to cn and hold to front, p2; k2 from cn* |
| ◸◹ | **3/3 RPC** *Sl 1 to cn and hold to back, k2; p1 from cn* |
| ◺◿ | **3/3 LPC** *Sl 2 to cn and hold to front, p1; k2 from cn* |
| B | Button position is for first repeat of chart only: place button on 4th row, then every 6th row. |

Adult M
**A** 7½"
**B** 9½"

10cm/4"

50

34

over stockinette stitch

 2 3 4 5 6

Super Fine weight

**MC** 375 yds
**CC** 150 yds each cuff

Optional: 2mm/US 0, 60cm
(24") for Ruffled cuff

Four 2mm/US 0
or size to obtain gauge

2.75mm/US C-2

**&**

Optional: spool of Wooly
Nylon to match MC
Stitch markers
180 size 8/0 black seed
beads for Beaded Cuffs
Beading needle

Eight 6mm (¼") ball
buttons for each pair of cuffs

Shown in
*ONLINE* Supersocke Silk in
Black (MC), *LORNA'S LACES*
Shepherd Sock in China Blue
(CC for Striped Cuff), *KNIT ONE
CROCHET TOO* Ty-Dy Socks in
Panama (CC for Variegated Cuff),
and *CHERRY TREE HILL* Supersock
in Cherry (CC for Beaded Cuff)

# Off the Cuff

*Eda Lee Haas*    *Bellevue, Washington*

## Sock cuff options

**Welted Cuff** With MC, cast on 64 stitches. Arrange on 3 double-pointed needles and join to work in the round. [Purl 4 rounds. Knit 4 rounds.] 2 times. Purl 4 rounds. Change to k1, p1 rib and work 4". Knit 1 round. Purl 4 rounds.

**Ruffled Cuff** With MC and circular needle, cast on 256 stitches. Do not join; work back and forth in rows. *Row 1* Purl. *Row 2* [K2tog] to end—128 stitches. *Row 3* Purl. *Row 4* [K2tog] to end—64 stitches. *Row 5* Purl. Arrange stitches on 3 double-pointed needles and join to work in the round. Work 1" in stockinette stitch. Change to k1, p1 rib and work 4". Use tail from cast-on to sew ends of ruffle together.

## Ankle
Work 12 rounds stockinette stitch.

## Heel flap
*Next row* K32, turn work. Work back and forth on these 32 stitches for heel. Place remaining 32 stitches on hold for instep. *Next row* (WS) Sl 1, purl to end. *Next row* (RS) [Sl 1, k1] to end. Repeat last 2 rows 14 more times.

## Turn heel
*Row 1* (WS) Sl 1, p16, p2tog, p1, turn. *Row 2* Sl 1, k**3**, SSK, k1, turn. *Row 3* Sl 1, p**4**, p2tog, p1, turn. *Row 4* Sl 1, k**5**, SSK, k1, turn. *Row 5* Sl 1, p**6**, p2tog, p1, turn. Continue working 1 more stitch before decrease each row until *Row 14* Sl 1, k**15**, SSK, k1, turn—18 stitches.

## Gussets
Pick up and k15 along left side of heel flap. With another needle, knit 32 instep stitches. With another needle, pick up and k15 along right side of heel flap, then knit 9 heel stitches—80 stitches. Slip remaining 9 heel stitches to next needle; beginning of round is at center of heel. *Next round* **Needle 1** Knit to last 3 stitches, k2tog, k1; **Needle 2** knit; **Needle 3** k1, SSK, knit to end. *Next round* Knit. Repeat last 2 rounds 7 more times—64 stitches.

## NOTES
*1 See page 168 for any unfamiliar techniques. 2 Sock is worked cuff down on double-pointed needles. 3 Optional: work strand of Wooly Nylon together with MC to reinforce heel and toe. 4 Choose Welted or Ruffled cuff option for socks and make as many detachable cuffs as desired.*

## Foot

*Next round* K2, left lifted increase (L inc), k4, place marker (pm), SSK, knit to last 8 stitches, k2tog, pm, k4, right lifted increase (R inc), k2. *Next round* K2, L inc, knit to marker, SSK, knit to 2 stitches before next marker, k2tog, knit to last 2 stitches, R inc, k2. Repeat last round 23 more times. Work even in stockinette stitch until foot measures 7½" from back of heel, or about 2" less than desired length.

## Toe

There are 16 stitches on Needle 1, 32 on Needle 2, and 16 on Needle 3. *Round 1* **Needle 1** Knit to last 3 stitches, k2tog, k1; **Needle 2** k1, SSK, knit to last 3 stitches, k2tog, k1; **Needle 3** k1, SSK, knit to end— 60 stitches. *Round 2* Knit. Repeat last 2 rounds 11 more times—16 stitches. Graft toe.

## DETACHABLE CUFFS

### Striped cuff

With MC, cast on 30 stitches, leaving a tail 36" long. *Rows 1 & 2* With MC, sl 1, knit to end. *Rows 3 & 4* With CC, sl 1, knit to end. Repeat these 4 rows 34 more times. Attach buttons while binding off as follows: Using crochet hook in place of right needle, bind off 3 stitches. *With a stitch on hook, insert hook through shank of button, then into next stitch. Draw a loop through next stitch, button, and stitch on hook. Bind off 7 stitches. Repeat from* twice. Attach final button and bind off remaining 2 stitches. Using cast-on tail and crochet hook, work button loops along cast-on edge as follows: slip stitch 1, *chain 4, skip 4, slip stitch 4; repeat from* twice, chain 4, skip 4, slip stitch 1. Fasten off.

### Variegated cuff

With CC, cast on 30 stitches, leaving a tail 36" long. *Row 1* Sl 1, knit to end. Repeat this row until 70 garter ridges are complete. Bind off with buttons and work button loops as for Striped Cuff.

### Beaded cuff

String 90 beads (87 required by chart, plus a few extra just in case) on CC. Slide beads into position as needed. Cast on 30 stitches, leaving a tail 36" long. Knit 16 rows (8 ridges). *Begin working bead pattern from chart,* Row 1 (RS) Knit. Row 2 (WS) Following chart, knit to first shaded square, slide bead up to needle and knit next stitch, continue across row, placing bead where shown on chart. Repeat last 2 rows to end of chart. Knit 7 more ridges. Bind off with buttons and work button loops as for Striped Cuff.

**Bead Chart**

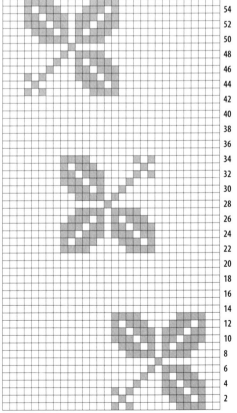

54
52
50
48
46
44
42
40
38
36
34
32
30
28
26
24
22
20
18
16
14
12
10
8
6
4
2

30 sts

■ *Place bead before this stitch on WS row.*

*Each row of Chart represents
1 garter ridge or 2 knit rows.*

# Sanquhar Socks

**Candace Eisner Strick**   *Mansfield Centre, Connecticut*

Adult M
**A** 8"
**B** 9"

10cm/4"

38
34
over Salt & Pepper pattern

 2 3 4 5 6
Super Fine weight

**A** 250 yds
**B** 220 yds

Four 2mm/US 0,
or size to obtain gauge

Shown in
*AUSTERMANN* Step Classic
in Black (A), *ZITRON* Trekking
XXL in color 107 (B)

## NOTES
*1 See page 168 for any
unfamiliar techniques.*
*2 Sock is worked cuff down
on double-pointed needles.*

### Salt & Pepper Pattern

*Round 1* [Knit 1 with A (K1A), knit 1 with B (k1B)] to end. *Round 2* [K1B, k1A] to end. Repeat Rounds 1 and 2 for pattern.

## RIGHT SOCK

### Cuff

With A, cast on 64 stitches. Arrange on 3 needles, place marker (pm) for beginning of round and join to work in the round. Work in k2, p2 rib for 11 rounds. *Next round* Knit, increasing 14 stitches evenly around—78 stitches.

### Leg

Work 7 rounds in Salt & Pepper pattern. Work Chart A, Chart B, Chart C and Chart D.

### Heel

With A, k39; place these stitches on hold for instep. Work back and forth on remaining 39 stitches for heel. *Row 1* (RS) K38, wrap next stitch and turn (W&T). *Row 2* (WS) P37, W&T. *Row 3* Sl 1, knit to 1 stitch before wrap, W&T. *Row 4* Sl 1, purl to 1 stitch before wrap, W&T. Continue working 1 fewer stitch before turn each row until 15 stitches are between wrapped stitches. *Row 25* Knit to first wrap, hide wrap, W&T. *Row 26* Purl to first wrap, hide wrap, W&T. *Row 27* Knit to double wraps, hide wraps, W&T. *Row 28* Purl to wraps, hide wraps, W&T. Repeat Rows 27 and 28 until all heel stitches have been worked.

### Foot

Resume working in the round. Work Chart E across 39 instep stitches; work Salt & Pepper on 39 sole stitches. Continue through Row 42 of Chart E.

### Big Toe

*Round 1, Instep* Work Round 43 of Chart E over 26 stitches, place on hold; work over 13. *Sole Stitches* K1A, work 11 Salt & Pepper, k1A; place remaining 26 stitches on hold; cast on 13 stitches as follows: 1A, 11 stitches Salt & Pepper, 1A—

39 stitches for big toe. *Next round* Work Chart F, k1A, 11 Salt & Pepper, k2A, 11 Salt & Pepper, k1A. Continue as established, decreasing on second and third section of toe same as for Chart F—3 stitches. Cut yarn, draw through remaining stitches and fasten off.

### Toes

Replace held stitches onto needles. Join yarn at side of foot opposite big toe. *Round 1* Work 26 stitches of Chart G, pick up and k13 along cast-on edge of big toe as follows: 1A, 11 Salt & Pepper, 1A. On sole stitches, k1A, work 24 in Salt & Pepper, k1A—65 stitches. *Round 2* Maintaining patterns, shape toe as follows: k1, SSK, knit to last 3 stitches, k2tog, k1. *Next round* Work even. Repeat last 2 rounds 9 more times. AT SAME TIME, beginning on Round 2, work double decrease in center of 13 picked-up stitches every row. When 1 stitch remains in center section, knit it together with adjacent stitch on sole. When Chart G is complete, graft toes.

## LEFT SOCK

### Cuff, Heel, Foot

Work as for Right Sock.

### Leg

Work 7 rounds in Salt & Pepper. Work Chart H, Chart I, Chart D, and Chart B.

### Big Toe & Toes

Work as for Right Sock, working Chart F for Big Toe and Chart J for Toes and reversing shaping.

**Chart J**

22
20

10

1

26 sts

**Chart F**

28

20

10

1

13 sts

**Chart E**

43

40

30

20

10

1

13-st repeat

Start at this end for right foot ←

Start at this end for left foot →

**Chart B**

13

10

1

26-st repeat

**Chart C**

13

10

1

26-st repeat

**Chart D**

13

10

1

26-st repeat

**Chart I**

13

10

1

26-st repeat

**Chart G**

22
20

10

1

26 sts

### Color key
- ☐ A
- ▨ B

### Stitch key
- ▨ ☐ Knit on RS, purl on WS
- ▨ ╱ K2tog
- ▨ ╲ SSK
- ▨ ⅄ K1, k2tog, pass k over

**Chart H**

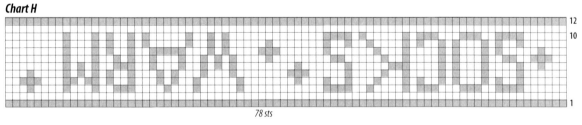

12
10

1

78 sts

**Chart A**

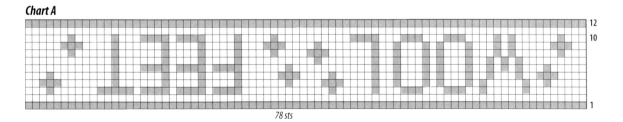

12
10

1

78 sts

**Adult S**
**A** 7"
**B** 8"

10cm/4"

48

32

over stockinette stitch

 2 3 4 5 6

Super Fine weight

**MC** 240 yds

**CC** 30 yds

Five 2.5mm/US 1½,
or size to obtain gauge

2.25mm/US B-1

**&**

Small amount smooth waste
yarn

Shown in
*REGIA* Silk in color 0001 (MC)
and 0035 (CC)

# SakuraNo Tabi Slippers

*Natalia Vasilieva    Moscow, Russia*

## SEED STITCH

*Row 1* [K1, p1] to end of row.
*Row 2* Knit the purl stitches and purl the knit stitches.
Repeat last 2 rows for pattern.

## RIGHT SLIPPER

### Heel

With waste yarn and a temporary cast-on, cast on 21 stitches. Join MC. Working back and forth, work 38 rows Seed Stitch. Bind off until 1 stitch remains; do not cut yarn. Pick up and k18 down left edge of piece. Remove waste yarn and recover 20 stitches from cast-on edge; place on a spare needle and work in Seed Stitch. Pick up and k19 along right edge of piece—58 stitches.

### Foot

Working back and forth, work 70 rows Seed Stitch, end with WS row. *Next row* Work in Seed Stitch to last stitch. Join to work in the round by knitting together first and last stitch of row. *Next round* Arrange stitches as follows: **Needle 1** K15; **Needle 2 & 3** Work Seed Stitch over 14 each; **Needle 4** k13, knit together last stitch with first stitch from Needle 1—56 stitches. Work 32 rounds, or length to toe division, keeping Needles 1 & 4 in stockinette stitch and Needles 2 & 3 in Seed Stitch.

### Big toe

*Set-up* K14 on **Needle 1**; work 8 stitches from **Needle 2** in Seed Stitch; place remaining 34 stitches plus first 6 stitches of next round on hold; cast on 5 stitches to bridge the gap; divide the 21 stitches evenly on 3 needles; beginning of round is between 3rd and 4th cast-on stitch. *Next round* K10, Seed Stitch 9, k2; repeat last round 14 times more, or until toe is ½" shorter than desired length. Rearrange stitches: 10 stockinette stitches are on Needle 1, and 11 Seed stitches are divided between Needles 2 & 3. *Next round, decrease round* **Needle 1** K1, SSK, knit to last 3 stitches, k2tog, k1; **Needle 2** k1, SSK, work in Seed Stitch to end; **Needle 3** work in Seed Stitch to last 3 stitches, k2tog, k1—17 stitches. *Next round* Work in stockinette stitch and Seed Stitch as established. *Next 2 rounds* Repeat decrease round—9 stitches. Cut yarn, draw through remaining stitches, pull tight, and fasten off.

### Toes

*Set-up* Move held stitches to 4 needles; beginning at center of cast-on edge at base of big toe, join yarn and arrange stitches as follows: **Needle 1** pick up and k2 from cast-on edge, then work 9 stitches in Seed Stitch; **Needle 2** work 11 in Seed Stitch; **Needle 3** k11;

## NOTES

*1 See page 168 for any unfamiliar techniques. 2 Worked heel to toe on double-pointed needles.*

**Needle 4** k9, then pick up and k2 from cast-on edge—44 stitches. *Next round, decrease round* **Needle 1** K2, work in Seed Stitch to end; **Needle 2** work in Seed Stitch to last 3 stitches, k2tog, k1; **Needle 3** k1, SSK, knit to end; **Needle 4** knit. Maintaining stockinette and Seed Stitch as established, repeat decrease round every other round twice, then every round 7 times—24 stitches. Rearrange stitches so 12 stitches on bottom of toes are on Needle 1 and 12 stitches on top of toes are divided on Needles 2 and 3. *Next 4 rounds* **Needle 1** K2, work in Seed Stitch to last 5 stitches, k2tog twice, k1; **Needle 2** k1, SSK twice, knit to end; **Needle 3** knit—8 stitches. Cut yarn, draw through remaining stitches, pull tight, and fasten off.

## LEFT SLIPPER

### Heel and Foot
Work same as Right Slipper.

### Toes
*Set-up* Work 34 stitches in patterns as established, place next 16 stitches on hold, cast on 4 stitches to bridge the gap, knit to end of round. Rearrange 44 stitches as follows: **Needle 1** K9; **Needle 2** k11; **Needle 3** work 11 in Seed Stitch; **Needle 4** work 9 in Seed Stitch, k2; move remaining 2 stitches to beginning of Needle 1; this is new beginning of round. Complete to match Right Slipper, working decreases at end of Needle 2 and beginning of Needle 3.

### Big Toe
*Set-up* Move held stitches to 2 needles. Beginning at center of cast-on edge at base of toes, join yarn and arrange stitches as follows: **Needle 1** Pick up and k2 from cast-on edge, work 5 stitches in Seed Stitch; **Needle 2** work 4 in Seed Stitch, k3; **Needle 3** K4, pick up and k3 from cast-on edge—21 stitches. Complete to match Right Slipper.

### Finishing

#### Flowers
*Foundation Round* With CC and crochet hook, chain (ch) 5 and join with slip stitch (sl st) to form a ring. *Round 1* Ch 1 (counts as 1 single crochet), single crochet (sc) 14 into ring, join with sl st into first ch. *Round 2* Ch 1, *[sc 1, ch 4, 2 triple crochet (trc)] into next stitch, [2 trc, ch 4, sc] into next stitch, sc, repeat from* 4 more times, join to first sc with sl st; *do not cut yarn.* Join flower to instep of sock by working a ring of sl sts through both flower and slipper at base of petals. Continuing with CC, work 1 round sc around ankle opening. Work 1 round reverse sc. Repeat for other slipper.

**intermediate**

Adult M
**A** 8"
**B** 7½"

10cm/4"

48

32

over stockinette stitch

 **1** 2 3 4 5 6

Super Fine weight
375 yds

Two sets of five 2.25mm/US 1,
or size to obtain gauge

**&**

1 pair inexpensive
store-bought socks

Polyester fiberfill to
stuff socks

Unsweetened Kool-Aid
2 packets each Orange,
Lemon, and Black Cherry

White vinegar

Cotton swabs

Microwave-safe dish

Microwave oven

Shown in
*ZITRON* Trekking Pro
Natura undyed

# Pedicure Polka

*Charles D. Gandy*     *Clayton, Georgia*

## Cuff

Cast on 256 stitches. Divide evenly on 4 needles and join to work in the round. *Round 1* Knit. *Rounds 2 & 3* [K2tog] to end of round—64 stitches. *Rounds 4–10* Knit. Cut yarn. Set aside. Using second set of needles, cast on and repeat Rounds 1–3. Place longer ruffle inside shorter ruffle, with WS of shorter ruffle against RS of longer ruffle. *Join ruffles* [Knit first stitch from shorter ruffle together with first stitch from longer ruffle] until all stitches are joined—64 stitches.

## Leg

Work in stockinette stitch until piece measures 6".

## Heel flap

K32 from Needles 1 & 2 onto a single needle. Work back and forth on these stitches for heel. Needles 3 & 4 hold 32 stitches for instep. *Row 1* (WS) Sl 1, purl to end. *Row 2* [Sl 1, k1] to end. Repeat last 2 rows 12 more times, then Row 1 once.

## Turn heel

*Row 1* (RS) K18, SSK, k1, turn. *Row 2* Sl 1, p5, p2tog, p1, turn. *Row 3* Sl 1, k6, SSK, k1, turn. *Row 4* Sl 1, p7, p2tog, p1, turn. *Row 5* Sl 1, k8, SSK, k1, turn. Continue to work 1 more stitch before decrease every row until *Row 13* Sl 1, k16, SSK, k1, turn. *Row 14* Sl 1, p16, p2tog, turn. *Row 15* Sl 1, k17—18 stitches.

## Gussets

Continuing with heel needle, pick up and k17 along left side of heel flap. With another needle, k16 on Needle 2. With another needle, k16 on Needle 3. With another needle, pick up and k17 along right side of heel flap, then k9—84 stitches; beginning of round is at center of heel. Arrange 26 stitches each on Needles 1 & 4 and 16 stitches each on Needles 2 & 3. *Round 1* **Needle 1** Knit to last 3 stitches, k2tog, k1; **Needles 2 & 3** knit; **Needle 4** k1, SSK, knit to end of round. *Round 2* Knit. Repeat last 2 rounds 9 more times—64 stitches.

## Foot

Work in stockinette stitch until foot measures 7", or to base of big toe.

## NOTES
*1 See page 168 for any unfamiliar techniques. **2** Sock is worked cuff down on double-pointed needles.*

## Dyeing

Mix ¼ cup vinegar into a sink full of lukewarm water. Place socks in and leave to soak. Mix each color of Kool-Aid separately in a small dish with 2–3 tablespoons of vinegar.

Stuff store-bought socks with polyester fiberfill. Squeeze excess water from handknit socks, then slide them over the stuffed socks. This will prevent the dye bleeding through.

Using cotton swabs as dye applicators, paint edges of inner ruffle with Black Cherry. Paint edge of outer ruffle with Black Cherry, then apply bands of Orange and Lemon so the color fades as it moves away from the edge. Repeat with rolled edges at toes. Apply dots of Black Cherry at random on legs of socks and dots of Orange on feet.

Place wet, dyed socks in a microwave-safe dish and microwave on High for 2–3 minutes to set the dye. Rinse in cold water.

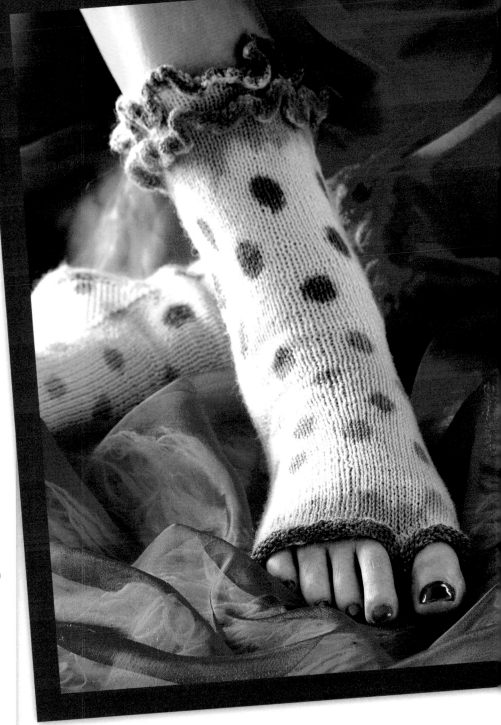

## Toe

*Left (right) sock: Next round* K6 (38), place next 20 stitches on hold for big toe, cast on 6 stitches to bridge the gap, knit to end of round—50 stitches. Work in stockinette stitch for 1". Bind off. Return held stitches to needles; pick up and k6 along cast-on edge of toes—26 stitches. Join to work in the round. Work in stockinette stitch for 1". Bind off. Sew rolled edges of toes to right side.

*intermediate*

Adult S
**A** 7"
**B** 6½"

10cm/4"

44 [chart] 

32

over stockinette stitch

**1** 2 3 4 5 6

Super Fine weight

**MC** 200 yds
**CC1, CC2** 15 yds each
**CC3** 10 yds

Five 2.75mm/US 2,
or size to obtain gauge

Shown in
*UNIVERSAL YARNS* Pace in
Olive (MC) and Yellow (CC3)
and Pace Step in Purple
(CC1) and Pink (CC2)

# Flowers on Lattice

Sarah L. Yost     *Berlin, Maryland*

## Leg
With MC, cast on 52 stitches. Divide evenly on 4 needles and join to work in the round. *Round 1* Knit. *Begin Chart* Work Rounds 1–4 until piece measures approximately 5" from beginning, end with Round 4 of Chart.

## Heel flap
Slip 13 stitches from Needle 2 to Needle 1. Needles 3 & 4 hold 13 stitches each for instep. Work back and forth over 26 stitches on Needle 1 in Chart pattern until flap measures 2", end with a RS row.

## Turn heel
*Row 1* (WS) P17, p2tog, p1, turn. *Row 2* Sl 1, k**9**, SSK, k1, turn. *Row 3* Sl 1, p**10**, p2tog, p1, turn. *Row 4* Sl 1, k**11**, SSK, k1, turn. *Row 5* Sl 1, p**12**, p2tog, p1, turn. *Row 6* Sl 1, k**13**, SSK, k1, turn. *Row 7* Sl 1, p**14**, p2tog, p1, turn. *Row 8* Sl 1, k**15**, SSK, k1—18 stitches.

## Gussets
Continuing with heel needle, pick up and k13 along left side of heel flap. With another needle, continue Chart pattern as established over 26 instep stitches. With another needle, pick up and k13 along right side of heel flap, then k9 to center of heel—70 stitches; beginning of round is at center of heel. Rearrange with 22 stitches each on Needles 1 & 4 and 13 stitches each on Needles 2 & 3. *Round 1* **Needle 1** Knit; **Needles 2 & 3** continue Chart pattern; **Needle 4** knit. *Round 2* **Needle 1** Knit to last 3 stitches, SSK, k1; **Needles 2 & 3** continue Chart pattern; **Needle 4** k1, k2tog, knit to end. Repeat last 2 rounds 8 more times—52 stitches.

## Foot
Work in stockinette stitch on Needles 1 & 4 and Chart pattern on Needles 2 & 3 until foot measures 6", or ½" less than desired length. Work in k1, p1 rib for 4 rounds. Bind off loosely.

## Flowers
With CC 1 or CC2, cast on 25 stitches. [Sl 1, bind off 4] to end—5 stitches. Change to CC3 and k5. Bind off. Sew ends of piece together to form flower. Make 6 flowers with CC1 and 6 with CC2.

## Finishing
Sew flowers to socks as shown in photo, or as desired.

### Chart
[chart with 13-st repeat, rows 1–4]
*13-st repeat*

### Stitch key
☐ Knit
⊙ Yarn over (yo)
╱ K2tog

### NOTES
*1 See page 168 for any unfamiliar techniques. 2 Sock is knit from cuff down on double-pointed needles.*

**144**

*intermediate +*

Adult S
**A** 7"
**B** 9"

10cm/4"

40 [grid] 

24

with 2 strands held together
over Garter Ridge pattern

1 **2** 3 4 5 6

Fine weight
**A–E**
150 yds each

Two 3.5mm/US 4, 40cm
(16") or longer,
or size to obtain gauge

**&**

Stitch markers

About 400 size 6/0 iridescent
seed beads in a mix of colors
that coordinate with yarn

Beading needle

Shown in
*ROWAN* Kidsilk Haze in
Hurricane (A), Trance (B),
Jelly (C), Heavenly (D) and
Dewberry (E),

# Mermaid's Tail

*Beverly Roberts*    *Hockessin, Delaware*

## Garter Ridge
*Rounds 1–3* Knit. *Round 4* Purl.

## P1 with Bead
With yarn in front, slide bead up to right needle, purl next stitch, gently tug yarn so bead is securely held between 2 stitches.

## Cuff
String 96 beads on one ball of A. With beaded strand and a second strand of A held together (A+A), cast on 96 stitches. Divide on 2 circular needles, place marker, and join to work in the round. *Round 1* [P1 with bead, p1] to end of round. *Begin Chart* Work Chart pattern, changing color as indicated and repeating Rounds 19–22 six times. At beginning of Round 5, string 72 beads onto B. At beginning of Round 14, string 24 beads onto C.

## Ankle
*Next round* With A+A, [k2, p1, p2tog, k2, p2tog, p1, k2, p2, k1, k2tog, p2, k2tog, k1, p2] 2 times—40 stitches. Work 3 rounds k2, p2 rib. Continuing in rib, work 4 rounds A+B, 4 rounds B+B, and 4 rounds B+C.

## Heel flap
With C+C, work back and forth on 20 stitches only for heel flap. *Row 1* (WS) K2, purl to last 2 stitches, k2. *Row 2* K2, [sl 1, k1] to last 2 stitches, k2. *Row 3* Repeat Row 1. *Row 4* K2, [k1, sl 1] to last 2 stitches, k2. Repeat last 4 rows 5 more times.

## Turn heel
*Row 1* (WS) Sl 1, p10, p2tog, p1, turn. *Row 2* Sl 1, k**3**, SSK, k1, turn. *Row 3* Sl 1, p**4**, p2tog, p1, turn. *Row 4* Sl 1, k**5**, SSK, k1, turn. *Row 5* Sl 1, p**6**, p2tog, p1, turn. *Row 6* Sl 1, k**7**, SSK, k1, turn. *Row 7* Sl 1, p**8**, p2tog, p1, turn. *Row 8* Sl 1, k**9**, SSK, k1—12 stitches.

## Gussets
Continuing with heel needle, pick up and k12 along side of heel flap and 2 stitches in corner between needles. With instep needle, k4, M1, k3, M1, k7, M1, k3, M1, k3. With heel needle, pick up and k2 in corner between needles, then 12 stitches along side of heel flap. K6 to center of heel and place marker for beginning of round—64 stitches. The round just completed is Round 1 of Garter Ridge Pattern on heel needle and Round 19 of Chart pattern on instep needle. Change colors in established sequence. *Next round, decrease round* On heel needle, knit to last 2 stitches, k2tog; on instep needle, knit all

## NOTES
*1 See page 168 for any unfamiliar techniques. 2 Sock is worked cuff down on 2 circular needles.
3 Socks are worked with 2 strands of yarn held together throughout. 'A+A' means work with 2 strands of color A. B+C means work with 1 strand each of colors B and C. Wind each skein of yarn into 2 separate balls before beginning. 4 Work slipped stitches as if to knit.*

stitches; on heel needle, SSK, knit to end of round. *Next round* Continue in patterns, working decrease round every other round 9 more times—44 stitches.

**Foot**
Work even until foot measures 7½" from back of heel, or approximately 1½" less than desired length, end with Round 21 of chart. *Next round* On heel needle, purl; on instep needle, p3, p2tog, p2, p2tog, p6, p2tog, p2, p2tog, p3; on heel needle, purl—40 stitches.

**Toe**
Remove beginning of round marker and k10 to end of heel needle. Work toe with next color combination in sequence. *Round 1* [K8, k2tog, place marker (pm), k8, k2tog] 2 times. *Round 2* Knit. *Round 3* [Knit to 2 stitches before marker, k2tog, knit to last 2 stitches on needle, k2tog] 2 times. Repeat last 2 rounds 3 more times, then work Round 3 three times—8 stitches remain. Graft toe.

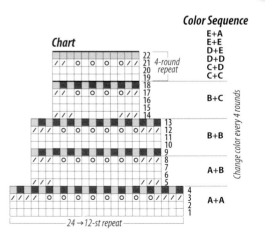

**Chart**

**Color Sequence**

E+A
E+E
D+E
D+D
C+D
C+C

4-round repeat

B+C

B+B

A+B

A+A

Change color every 4 rounds

22
21
20
19
18
17
16
15
14
13
12
11
10
9
8
7
6
5
4
3
2
1

24 → 12-st repeat

**Stitch key**

☐ Knit
▨ Purl
▨ K2tog
◉ Yarn over (yo)
■ Purl 1 with bead

**Child's S**
**A** 5½"
**B** 4"

10cm/4"

48

32

over stockinette stitch

**1** 2 3 4 5 6

Super Fine weight

**A** 200 yds
**B** 40 yds

Five 2.25mm/US 1,
or size to obtain gauge

3.25mm/ D

4 black and clear eye
buttons ½"/12mm diameter

Shown in
*COLINETTE* JitterBug
in Lapis (A) and
Magenta (B)

# Socktopus

*Pamela J Whyte*    *Beaverton, Oregon*

## Diagonal Openwork
*Round 1* [K2tog] to end. *Round 2* [M1 Open, k1] to end. Repeat these 2 rounds for pattern.

## Cuff
With A, cast on 48 stitches. Arrange stitches evenly on 4 dpn and join to work in the round. Work in k5, p1 rib for 1".

## Leg
Work in Diagonal Openwork Pattern until piece measures 2" from cast-on, end with Round 2.

## Heel flap
K24. Work back and forth on these stitches only for heel flap, leaving remaining 24 stitches on hold for instep. *Row 1* (WS) Sl 1, purl to end of row. *Row 2* [Sl 1, k1] to end. Repeat these 2 rows 11 more times.

## Heel Turn
*Row 1* (WS) Sl 1, p14, p2tog, p1, turn. *Row 2* Sl 1, k**7**, SSK, k1, turn. *Row 3* Sl 1, p8, p2tog, p1, turn. *Row 4* Sl 1, k**9**, SSK, k1, turn. *Row 5* Sl 1, p**10**, p2tog, p1, turn. *Row 6* Sl 1, k**11**, SSK, k1, turn. *Row 7* Sl 1, p**12**, p2tog, p1, turn. *Row 8* Sl 1, k**13**, SSK, k1 — **16** stitches remain.

## Gussets
Continuing with the same needle, pick up and k12 down side of heel flap. With a free needle, work Round 1 of Diagonal Openwork across first **12** instep stitches, then use another needle to continue pattern across remaining **12** instep stitches. Use a free needle to pick up and k12 up side of heel flap and k8 from heel turn — 64 stitches. Beginning of round is at center of heel. *Round 1* **Needle 1** Knit to last 3 stitches, k2tog, k1; **Needles 2 & 3** work pattern; **Needle 4** k1, SSK, knit to end of round. *Round 2* **Needle 1** Knit; **Needles 2 & 3** work pattern as established; **Needle 4** knit. Repeat these 2 rounds 7 times more — 48 stitches.

## NOTES
*1 See page 168 for any unfamiliar techniques. **2** Sock is worked top down on double-pointed needles.*

## Foot

Continue in stockinette stitch on Needles 1 & 4 and pattern on Needles 2 & 3 until foot measures 3" from back of heel, or 1" less than desired length.

## Toe

Continue with A for one sock (boy), change to B for the other sock (girl). *Round 1* **Needle 1** Knit to last 3 stitches, k2tog, k1; **Needle 2** k1, SSK, knit to end of needle; **Needle 3** knit to last 3 stitches, k2tog, k1; **Needle 4** k1, SSK, knit to end of round. *Round 2* Knit. Repeat last 2 rounds 5 more times, then repeat Round 1 twice—16 stitches remain. Knit stitches on Needle 1. Cut yarn, leaving an 18" tail. Graft toe.

## Socktopus legs (make 16)

Using crochet hook and A, chain 30. Double crochet (dc) 3 in 3rd chain from hook, then dc 3 in each remaining chain stitch. Turn and work 1 slip stitch in each dc. For 8 legs of girl socktopus, work final slip-stitch row with color B. Sew 8 legs to cuff of each sock, positioning legs at purl stitches in rib.

## Eyes

Sew 2 buttons to top of toe of each sock, about ½" from end. For girl, use A to embroider straight stitches above each eye for lashes.

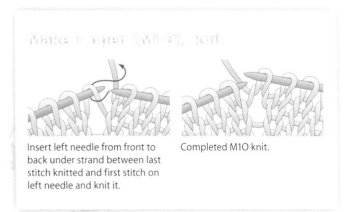

Make Loopet (M1O), knit

Insert left needle from front to back under strand between last stitch knitted and first stitch on left needle and knit it.

Completed M1O knit.

*intermediate*

Child's S
**A** 5½"
**B** 5¾"

10cm/4"
40
28
over stockinette stitch

1 **2** 3 4 5 6
Fine weight
**A** 200 yds
**B** 50 yds

Five 2.25mm/US 1
or size to obtain gauge

3.25mm/US D-3

**&**

Small amount smooth waste yarn
Cable needle (cn)

Shown in
*COLINETTE* JitterBug in
Whirley Fig (A) and
Velvet Leaf (B)

# Caterpillar Lace

*Diane Wells-Nowell*   *Pebble Beach, California*

## RIB PATTERN
*Row 1* (RS) K1, [k1, p2, k2, p2, k1] to end.
*Row 2* (WS) [P1, k2, p2, k2, p1] to last stitch, p1. Repeat Rows 1–2 for Rib Pattern.

## CABLES
*1/1 LPC* Slip stitch to cn and hold to front, p1; p1 from cn
*1/1 RPC* Slip stitch to cn and hold to back, p1; p1 from cn
*1/1 LC* Slip stitch to cn and hold to front, k1; k1 from cn
*1/1 RC* Slip stitch to cn and hold to back, k1; k1 from cn

### Cuff
Use crochet hook, waste yarn, and a temporary cast-on to cast on 48 stitches. Arrange 12 stitches each on 4 needles and join to work in the round. *Round 1* With A, [k2, p4] to end. Repeat Round 1 until piece measures 1". *Next round* [K2, 1/1 LPC, 1/1 RPC] to end. *Next round* [P2, 1/1 LC, 1/1 RC] to end.

### Leg
Work Chart A until piece measures 3½" from beginning, end with Row 1. *Next round* [P2, 1/1 LC, 1/1 RC] 4 times, work Chart pattern to end.

**Chart A**

2
1
└ 6-st repeat ┘

**Stitch key**
☐ Knit
▨ Purl
⟋ K2tog
⟍ SSK
⊙ Yarn over (yo)
⅄ SK2P

### Heel
*Row 1* (RS) P1, k**23**, wrap next stitch and turn work (W&T). Slip purled stitch at beginning of row to adjacent instep needle. Work heel back and forth on these 24 stitches only. *Row 2* P**22**, W&T. *Row 3* K**21**, W&T. *Row 4* P**20**, W&T. Continue as established, working one fewer stitch each row until *Row 18* P**6**, W&T. *Row 19* K**6**, pick up wrap and knit it together with its stitch, W&T. *Row 20* P**7**, pick up wrap and purl it together with its stitch, W&T. *Row 21* Knit to stitch with double wrap, knit both wraps together with stitch, W&T. *Row 22* Purl to stitch with double wrap, purl both wraps together with stitch, W&T. Repeat last 2 rows until all wrapped stitches have been worked. Turn to resume working in the round.

## NOTES
*1 See page 168 for any unfamiliar techniques. 2 Sock is worked cuff down on double-pointed needles.*

150

## Foot

*Next round* **Needles 1 & 2** Knit;
**Needles 3 & 4** continue in Chart A.
Continue working stockinette stitch on
sole and Chart pattern on instep until
foot measures 4" from back of heel or
approximately 2" from desired length.
*Next round* **Needles 1 & 2** Knit; **Needles
3 & 4** [p1, 1/1 LC, 1/1 RC, p1] 4 times.

## Toe

*Round 1* **Needle 1** K1, SSK, knit to end;
**Needle 2** knit to last 3 stitches, k2tog,
k1; **Needle 3** k1, SSK, knit to end;
**Needle 4** knit to last 3 stitches, k2tog,
k1. *Round 2* Knit. Repeat last 2 rounds 8
times—12 stitches. Graft toe.

## Finishing
### Leaves

With WS of sock facing,*pick up 3
stitches from temporary cast-on. Join
B and work 3 rows of I-cord. Work leaf
from Chart B. Fasten off. Pick up next 3
stitches from cast-on. Join B and work 6
rows of I-cord. Work Chart B. Fasten off.
Repeat from* 7 more times, alternating
long and short I-cord stems.

### Chart B

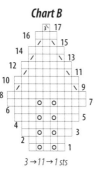

3 →11 →1 sts

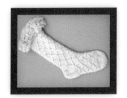

**experienced**

**A** 8"
**B** 9"
Leg length from fold
of cuff to top of heel 11"

10cm/4"

32 ▦

26

over stockinette stitch

1 2 **3** 4 5 6

Light weight
**A** 300 yds
**B** 40 yds

1 **2** 3 4 5 6

Fine weight
**C** 30 yds

Four 3.5mm/US 4,
or size to obtain gauge

4mm/US G-6

**&**

Cable needle (cn)
Tapestry needle
14 silver jingle bells 1/3"
(9mm) diameter
1 yd satin fabric for lining
Sewing thread to match
fabric

Shown in
*ARTYARNS* Regal Silk in color
250 (A) and Beaded Silk and
Sequins in color 250S (B);
*PLYMOUTH YARNS* Gold Rush
in Silver (C)

# Silver Bells

*Karin Kussman*     *Cincinnati, Ohio*

**Double Loop Stitch** Insert right needle into next stitch knitwise, wind yarn over right needle and left index finger twice, then over right needle again, draw all 3 loops through the stitch and place on left needle, insert right needle through back of these loops and original stitch and knit together through back loops.

## Cuff
With B, cast on 72 stitches. Arrange 24 stitches on each of 3 needles and join to work in the round. *Round 1* Knit. *Round 2* [Double Loop Stitch, k1] to end. Loops will fall to WS of work. *Round 3* Knit. *Round 4* [K1, Double Loop Stitch] to end. Repeat last 4 rounds 3 more times.

## Leg
Change to A and knit 1 round. Work Chart Rows 1–12 six times, then Rows 1–5 once more.

## Heel flap
*Next row* K32; turn work. Work back and forth on these stitches for heel flap. Place remaining 40 stitches on hold for instep. Slipping first stitch of every row, work stockinette stitch for 13 rows, end with a purl row.

## Turn heel
*Row 1* (RS) K20, SSK, turn. *Row 2* Sl 1, p8, p2tog, turn. *Row 3* Sl 1, k8, SSK, turn. *Row 4* Sl 1, p8, p2tog, turn. Repeat last 2 rows 9 more times—10 stitches.

## Foot
Knit 10 heel stitches. Pick up and k11 sts along left side of heel. Work across instep stitches in pattern as established (Row 6 of Chart). With another needle, pick up and k11 sts along right side of heel—72 stitches. Knit 1; place marker (pm) for new beginning of round. Working chart pattern on all stitches, work Rows 7–12, then Rows 1–12 twice, then Rows 1–3. *Next round* Knit, decreasing 2 stitches evenly around—70 stitches.

## Toe
*Round 1* [K10, pm] to end. *Round 2* [Knit to 2 stitches before marker, k2tog] to end. *Round 3* Knit. Repeat last 2 rounds 8 more times—7 stitches. Cut yarn, draw through remaining stitches, pull tight, and fasten off.

## NOTES
**1** *See page 168 for any unfamiliar techniques.* **2** *Sock is worked cuff down on double-pointed needles.*

**Chart**

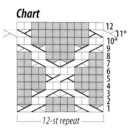

*12-st repeat*

**Stitch key**

☐ Knit on RS, purl on WS

▨ Purl on RS, knit on WS

 **2/2 RC** Sl 2 to cn and hold to back, k2; k2 from cn

**2/2 LC** Sl 2 to cn and hold to front, k2; k2 from cn

**2/2 RPC** Sl 2 to cn and hold to back, k2; p2 from cn

**2/2 LPC** Sl 2 to cn and hold to front, p2; k2 from cn

\* End last repeat of Row 10 two stitches before end,
incorporate those stitches in first 2/2 LC.
End Row 11 with k2 instead of 2/2 LC.

**Finishing**

*Smocking* Thread a double strand of C on a tapestry needle
and stitch horizontally across each cable crossing as shown
in photo.

*Cuff* With A, sew jingle bells randomly among loops on cuff.
Fold cuff over so loops show on RS. Tack in place.

*Lining* Fold satin fabric in half. Lay stocking on doubled
fabric and trace outline of stocking. Cut 2 pieces and sew
around edges by hand or machine, right sides together,
leaving top of lining open.

*Facing* With A, pick up and knit 72 stitches around top
of stocking at fold line. Join to work in the round. Work in
stockinette stitch for 1". Bind off.
Insert lining into sock. Fold facing down to cover top edge of
lining and use sewing thread to stitch it in place.

*Loop* With 1 strand of B and 2 strands of C held together,
make a crochet chain 4" long. Sew to fold of cuff.

# And the winners are...

*What exactly do you look for in a sock?*

*Lucy:*
It's got to fill the function. No matter how exquisite, if it doesn't fit the foot, if it isn't comfortable to wear, then it's not really a sock...

*Cat:*
It's a piece of art...

*Sandi:*
Workmanship is an important issue for all socks.

*Above: Contest judges Sandi Rosner, Lucy Neatby, and Cat Bordhi. Below, left: Voting for Knitter's Choice took place online and live at STITCHES West.*

**South West Trading Company**

**SOX Forever**
Yamuna Weiner
*page 164*

**Unleash the Creativity**
Charles D. Gandy
*page 166*

**Addi Turbo by Skacel**

**The Pros**
Cindy Craig
*page 48*

*Cindy's socks were chosen from 36 entries from the US, Canada, and Australia. She was in the audience at the STITCHES Student Banquet and received her award onstage.*

**Skacel**

**It's good to get Hosed**
Vanessa Malone
*page 52*

**Socks to Dye For**
Betty Salpekar
*page 156*

**Step into the Future**
Arden Okazaki
*page 115*

**Regia**

**Best Foot Forward**
Charles D. Gandy
*page 166*

**Toe Tapping**
Janice Talkington
*page 86*

**Twist & Shout**
Natalia Vasilieva
*page 55*

**Mountain Colors**

**Cuff Down**
Terri D. Gogolin
*page 132*

**Not Cuff Down**
Nancy Hazen
*page 109*

**Cherry Tree Hill Yarn**

**Most Colorful Socks**
Linda McGibbon
*page 88*

## $500 Third Prize
### Leslie Comstock
*page 82*

Ten-year-old Elizabeth was our youngest entrant with these, her first socks.

Wendy was in the audience at the STITCHES Student Banquet and received her award onstage.

Cathy's inspiration came from the Sliding Loop technique in issue 63, page 29. There were 40 entries in this category.

## $1500 Second Prize
### Kirsten Hall
*page 106*

You'll find all the photos of the winning *Think Outside the Sox Contest* socks, winner comments, and videos on the Web: KnittingUniverse.com/SOX

Betty was in the audience at the STITCHES Student Banquet where she received a $6000 check from XRX Publisher Alexis Xenakis and a standing ovation from the audience. Leopard Spots also won $500 in the Skacel-sponsored category, "Socks to Dye For."

156

## $6000
### GRAND Prize
Betty Salpekar

# A

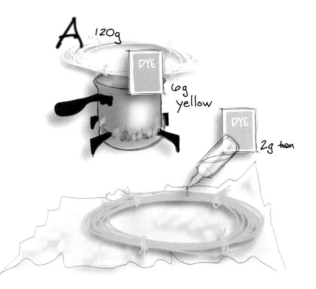

120g

6g yellow

2g tan

## Dyeing

Wind yarn in hanks and tie loosely to prevent tangling.

Dye with yellow using package directions for stovetop method.

Lay out on plastic.
Apply dots and lines, then
turn hanks over and repeat.
Let set for 0:30 minutes.

Steam over boiling water.
0:30 minutes.

Rinse and
hang to dry.

# C

65g

4.6g

Dye with Cocoa Brown
on stovetop.
Lay out on plastic.
Work as before.

2.3g

Knit your socks according to chart.

## Spot Dyeing

Trace and cut out plastic liner in shape of sock.
Place inside sock to prevent bleedthrough.

Mix tan and orange dye.
With an eyedropper, dampen just the center
of each spot with warm water.
Drop dye on centers of spots.

1.7g each

Cover with plastic and
let set for 1:00 hour.

Remove liner and
microwave for
0:01 minute
Rinse and block.

Since Rit® dyes are not food safe, use pots and utensils dedicated to dyeing, not those you use for cooking.

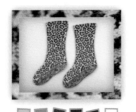

**experienced**

Women's M

**A** 8"
**B** 9"

10cm/4"

42
40

over Chart pattern with A

10cm/4"

42
32

over stockinette stitch
with A and B held together

 **1** 2 3 4 5 6

Super Fine weight
**A** 550 yds
**C** 300 yds
**D** 50 yds

1 **2** 3 4 5 6

Fine weight
**B** 75 yds

2.25mm/US 1, 120cm (47") long
or size to obtain gauge

**&**

8 stitch markers in 4 different colors

Dye supplies
Rit® Dye powder in 42 Golden
Yellow, 16 Tan, 20 Cocoa Brown,
25 Dark Brown, and 42 Sunshine
Orange

2 gallon size heavy weight
plastic freezer bags

3 small squirt bottles

eyedropper

plastic wrap

Shown in
*ZITRON* Trekking Pro Natura
Undyed (A, C & D) and *ROWAN*
Kidsilk Haze in Cocoa (B)

# Leopard Spots

*Betty Salpekar*    Woodstock, Georgia

## INCREASE 2 (Inc 2)

M1, k1, M1.

## Sole

*Note 1* Hide short row wraps when you encounter them.

*Note 2* Make sure to catch stranded yarn not in use when making turns in leopard pattern of foot.

With A and B held together and using Judy's Magic Cast-on, cast 44 stitches onto each needle—88 stitches.

*Set-up round* **Needle 1** Loop cast on 1 stitch (center toe stitch), k2, place toe marker (TM), k40, place heel marker (HM), k2; **Needle 2** Loop cast on 1 (center heel stitch), k2, place heel marker (HM), k40, mark for beginning of round—90 stitches. *Round 1* [K1, M1] 4 times, k1, knit to **HM**, [k1, M1] 4 times, k1, knit to end—98 stitches. *Round 2 and all even-number rounds* Knit. *Round 3* [K1, M1] 3 times, k3, [M1, k1] 3 times, knit to **HM**, k1, M1, k3, inc 2, k3, M1, knit to end—108 stitches. *Round 5* K4, Inc 2, k5, Inc 2, k10, wrap next stitch and turn work (W&T), p31, W&T, k11, Inc 2, k7, Inc 2, knit to **HM**, k1, M1, k5, Inc 2, k5, M1, knit to end—120 stitches. *Round 7* K1, M1, k9, [M1, k1] 3 times, M1, k9, M1, knit to **HM**, k1, M1, k7, Inc 2, k7, M1, knit to end—130 stitches. *Round 9* K12, Inc 2, k3, Inc 2, knit to **HM**, k6, Inc 2, k3, Inc 2, k3, Inc 2, knit to end—140 stitches. *Round 11* K13, Inc 2, k5, Inc 2, k25, W&T, p61, W&T, k13, M1, k13, Inc 2, k7, Inc 2, k13, M1, knit to **HM**, k7, Inc 2, k5, Inc 2, k5, Inc 2, knit to end—156 stitches *Round 13* K16, Inc 2, k9, Inc 2, knit to **HM**, k8, Inc 2, k7, Inc 2, k7, Inc 2, knit to end—166 stitches. *Round 15* [K4, M1] repeat to first **HM**, knit to second **HM**, [k4, M1] to end—189 stitches. Cut both yarns.

## Foot

Arrange stitches for Magic Loop, with WS of sole facing. Join A and C ready to work center 21 stitches of toe. Work back and forth in rows,

## NOTES

**1** *See page 168 for any unfamiliar techniques.* **2** *Sole is worked from sole up with 1 circular needle using Magic Loop method.*

158

**Chart A**

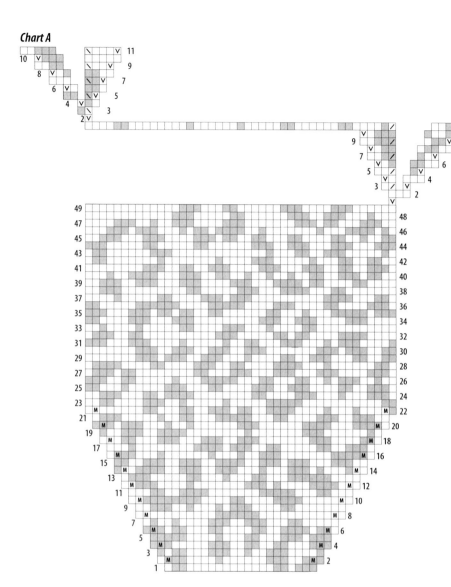

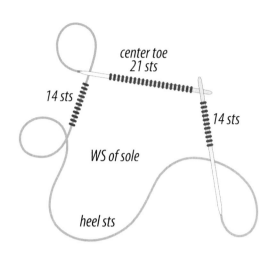

center toe
21 sts

14 sts

14 sts

WS of sole

heel sts

**Color key**
☐ A
▨ C
▨ D

**Stitch key**
☐ Knit
▨ Purl
⧄ K2tog on RS, p2tog on WS
⧅ SSK on RS, SSP on WS
Ⓜ M Make 1 in appropriate color
Ⅴ Sl1 purlwise with yarn at WS of work

joining to sole stitches at the beginning and end of each row. *Begin Chart A, Row 1* (WS) P1, place marker (pm), p19 according to Chart, pm, p1, sl 1 from sole, turn. *Row 2* (RS) K2tog (sole stitch with first stitch), M1, knit to marker, M1, SSK (last stitch with next sole stitch), sl 1 from sole, turn. *Row 3* SSP, purl to marker, p2tog, sl 1 from sole, turn. Repeat last 2 rows through Row 23 of Chart. *Next row* K2tog, knit to second marker, SSK, sl 1 from sole. *Next row* SSP, purl to marker, p2tog, sl 1 from sole. Repeat last 2 rows through Row 48 of Chart. *Row 49* Return slipped stitch from Row 48, work across to marker, k1, wrapping next stitch and turn work (W&T).

**Triangle Insert**
*Row 1* Sl 1, W&T. *Row 2* P3, hiding wraps, W&T. Continue triangle inserts from chart, hiding wraps as you encounter them, ending each row with W&T. When chart is complete, cut both yarns.

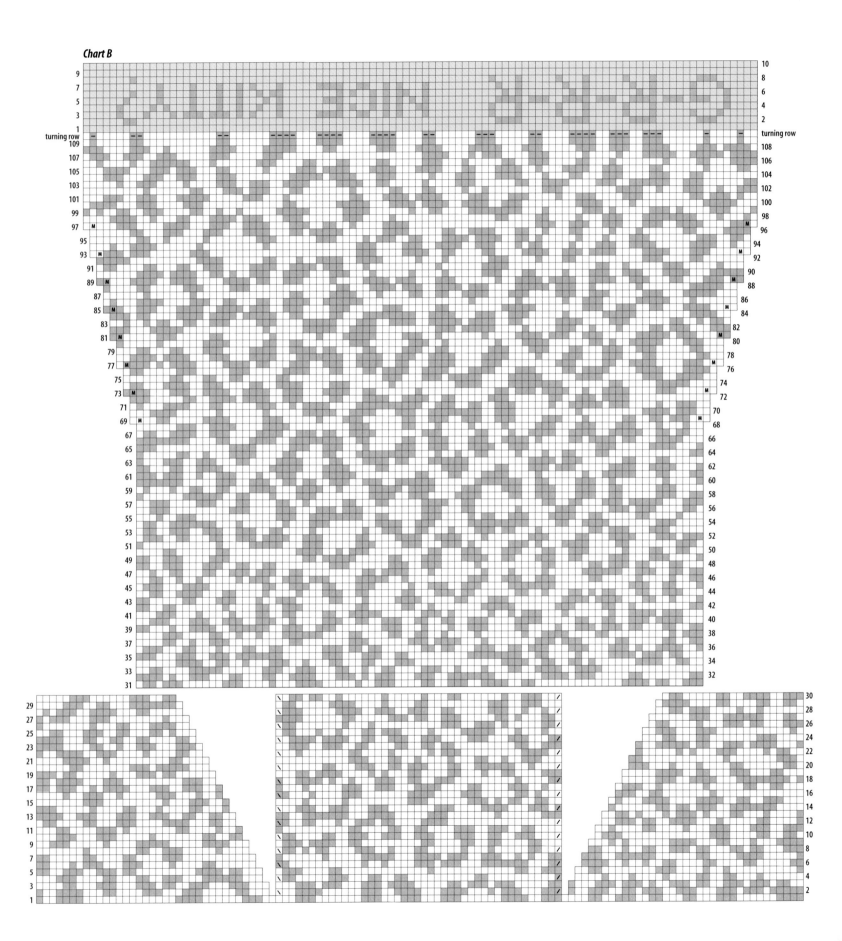

Chart B

## Leg

Rearrange stitches so beginning of round is at center of heel. Join yarns with RS facing to work in the round. Work Chart B through Round 110 of Chart (turning round).

## Cuff

Change to color D and smaller needle, and work Rounds 1–10 of facing. Bind off loosely. Fold facing to inside of sock at turning round and sew down.

# Gallery

**Impressionist Sea Socks** *(left page)*
Yamuna Weiner

**Franklin's Art Socks** *(center)*
Franklin D Hyry

**Basket Weavers Socks** *(middle right)*
Aleta Van Kampen

**Raspberries & Cream** *(lower right)*
Geraldine Claire McCulloch

***Dreadsox*** *(left page)*
***Snake in the Grass*** *(center)*
Charles D Gandy

***Jaws*** *(top right)*
Lucille Reilly

***Elizabeth's Garden*** *(lower right)*
Elizabeth Brook Shelor

***Houndstooth Socks*** *(top left)*
Franklin D Hyry

***Year of the Dragon*** *(middle left)*
Chris Shearer

***Wire Socks*** *(lower left)*
Nomeda Grumada

***Boot Socks*** *(center)*
***Budapest Roof Tiles*** *(top right)*
Betty Salpekar

# Techniques

## BASICS

### YARN OVER (YO)

**Between knit stitches**
Bring yarn under the needle to the front, take it over the needle to the back and knit the next stitch.

**Between purl stitches**
With yarn in front of needle, bring it over the needle to the back and to the front again; purl next stitch.

**After a knit, before a purl**
Bring yarn under the needle to the front, over the needle to the back, then under the needle to the front; purl next stitch.

**After a purl, before a knit**
With yarn in front of the needle, bring it over the needle to the back; knit next stitch.

**On next row**
Knit or purl into front of yarn-over unless instructed otherwise. The yarn-over makes a hole and adds a stitch.

**Yarn over twice (yo2)**
After bringing yarn over the needle (first yarn-over), wrap yarn completely around needle a second time. On next row, work into double yarn-over as instructed.

**TIPS**
• A yarn-over's location—between knits, between purls, between a knit and purl or a purl and knit—determines how the yarn-over is made.
• Often the stitch before or after a yarn over is not a knit or a purl, but a decrease. If it is a knit decrease (k2tog, SSK, etc), treat it as a knit; if it is a purl decrease (p2tog, SSP, etc), treat it as a purl. On the next row, work into the yarn-over as if it is a regular stitch.

*TO BEGIN AND END ROWS WITH YARN OVERS, SEE PAGE 65.*

### SLIP WITH YARN IN FRONT (WYIF)

Move the yarn to the **front** on a right-side row before slipping the stitch.

### SLIP PURLWISE (sl 1 p-wise)

*1* Insert right needle into next stitch on left needle from back to front (as if to purl).

*2* Slide stitch from left to right needle. Stitch orientation does not change (right leg of stitch loop is at front of needle).

### SLIP KNITWISE (sl 1 k-wise)

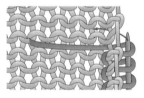

*1* Insert right needle into next stitch on left needle from front to back (as if to knit).

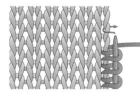

*2* Slide stitch from left to right needle. Stitch orientation changes (right leg of stitch loop is at back of needle).

### PICK UP AND PURL —— PICK UP AND KNIT ——

With wrong side facing and yarn in front, insert needle from back to front between first and second stitches, catch yarn, and purl.

Insert **into** center of first stitch, catch yarn and knit a stitch. For a firmer edge, insert needle in space **between** first and 2nd stitches.

### PICKING UP LOOPS FROM A TEMPORARY CAST-ON

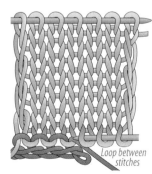

*Loop between stitches*

Temporary cast-ons use waste yarn to hold the loops that form between stitches under the needle. When this waste yarn is removed, these loops can be placed on a needle and worked into.
**Note** There is always one fewer loop than cast-on stitches. Adjust for this by casting on one more stitch, then decreasing one in first row; or by simply decreasing in the last row. The instructions in this book include that adjustment.

# TEMPORARY CAST-ONS

## INVISIBLE CAST-ON

**1** Knot working yarn to contrasting waste yarn. Hold needle and knot in right hand. Tension both strands in left hand; separate strands so waste yarn is over index finger, working yarn over thumb. Bring needle between strands and under thumb yarn so working yarn forms a yarn-over in front of waste yarn.

**2** Holding both yarns taut, pivot hand toward you, bringing working yarn under and behind waste yarn. Bring needle behind and under working yarn so working yarn forms a yarn-over behind waste yarn.

**3** Pivot hand away from you, bringing working yarn under and in front of waste yarn. Bring needle between strands and under working yarn, forming a yarn-over in front of waste yarn. Each yarn-over forms a stitch.
Repeat Steps 2–3 for required number of stitches. For an even number, twist working yarn around waste strand before knitting the first row.

## PICKING UP STITCHES IN CHAIN

**1** With crochet hook and waste yarn, loosely chain the number of stitches needed, plus a few extra chains. Cut yarn.
**2** With needle and main yarn, pick up and knit 1 stitch into the back 'purl bump' of the first chain. Continue, knitting 1 stitch into each chain until you have the required number of stitches. Do not work into remaining chains.

# CAST-ONS

## LONG-TAIL CAST-ON, KNIT

Make a slipknot for the initial stitch, at a distance from the end of the yarn, allowing about 1½" for each stitch to be cast on.
**1** Bring yarn between fingers of left hand and wrap around little finger as shown.

**2** Bring left thumb and index finger between strands, arranging so tail is on thumb side, ball strand on finger side. Open thumb and finger so strands form a diamond.

**3** Bring needle down, forming a loop around thumb.
**4** Bring needle **under** front strand of **thumb loop**…

**5** …up **over index finger yarn**, catching it…

**6** …and bringing it **under** the front of **thumb loop**.

**7** Slip thumb out of its loop, and use thumb to adjust tension on the new stitch. One knit stitch cast on.

Repeat Steps 3–7 for each additional stitch.

## LONG-TAIL CAST-ON, PURL

**1–3** Work as Steps 1–3 of long-tail cast-on, knit.
**4** Bring needle **behind yarn** around index finger, **behind** front strand of **thumb loop**…

**5** …up **over index finger yarn**, catching it…

 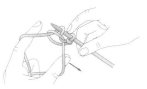

**6** …and bringing it **in front** of **thumb loop**…then backing it out **under thumb loop** and **index finger yarn**.

**7** Slip thumb out of its loop, and use thumb to adjust tension on the new stitch. One purl stitch cast on.

Repeat Steps 3–7 for each additional stitch.

## CAST-ON IN PATTERN

*K2, p2 rib cast on in k2, p2 pattern*

*K2, p2 rib cast on in knit*

## LOOP CAST-ON (ALSO CALLED E-WRAP CAST-ON)

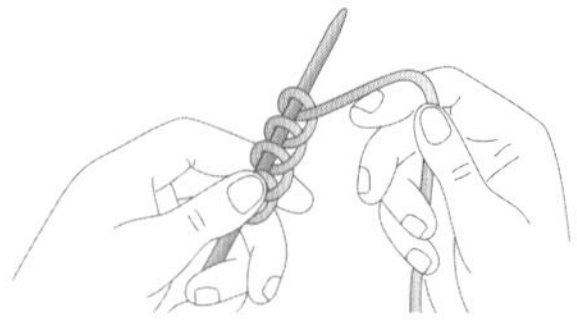

**1** Hold needle and tail in left hand.
**2** Bring right index finger under yarn, pointing toward you.

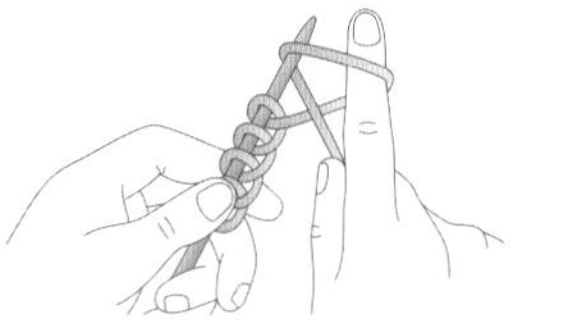

**3** Turn index finger to point away from you.
**4** Insert tip of needle under yarn on index finger (see above); remove finger and draw yarn snug, forming a stitch.
Repeat Steps 2–4 until all stitches are on needle.

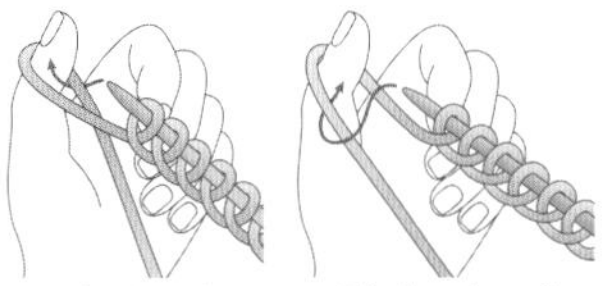

***Left-slanting*** ***Right-slanting***

Loops can be formed over index or thumb and can slant to the left or to the right. On the next row, work through back loop of right-slanting loops

## CABLE CAST-ON

**1–2** Work as for Steps 1 and 2 of Knit Cast-on (see below).
**3** Insert left needle in loop and slip loop off right needle. One additional stitch cast on.

**4** Insert right needle **between** the last 2 stitches. From this position, knit a stitch and slip it to the left needle as in Step 3.
Repeat Step 4 for each additional stitch.

## TWISTED LONG-TAIL CAST-ON

Make a slipknot for the initial stitch, leaving a long tail (allowing about 1" for each cast-on stitch.
**1** Bring yarn between fingers of left hand and wrap around little finger as shown.

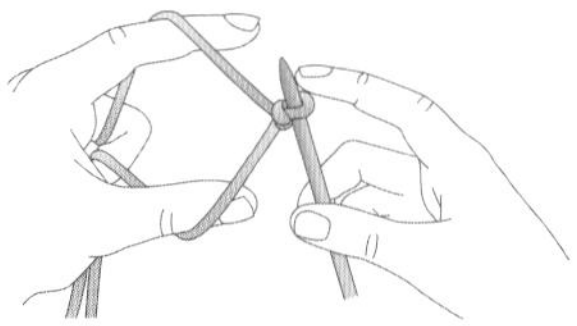

**2** Bring left thumb and index finger between strands, arranging so tail is on thumb side, ball strand on finger side. Open thumb and finger so strands form a diamond.

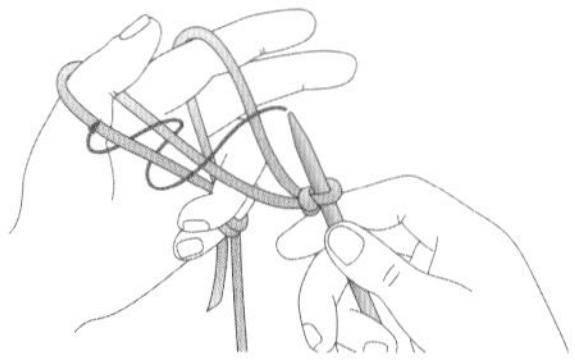

**3** Bring needle down, forming a loop around thumb.
**4** Bring needle in **front** of front strand of **thumb loop**, back **under both** strands of thumb loop, catching **back strand** and bringing it in **front** of front strand…

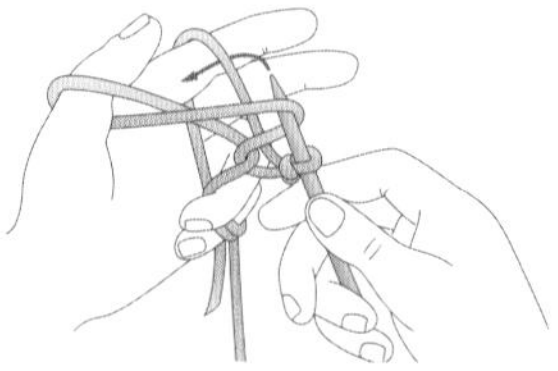

**5**…up **over index finger yarn**, catching it…

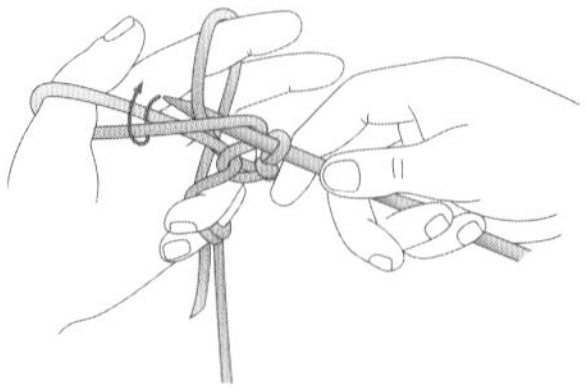

**6**…and bringing it **over** the front strand and **under** the back strand of **thumb loop**.

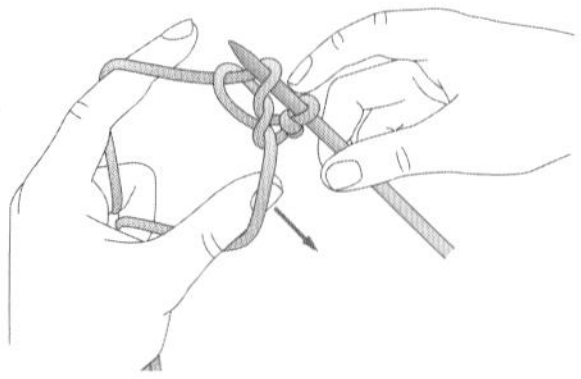

**7** Slip thumb out of its loop, and use thumb to adjust tension on the new stitch. One knit stitch cast on.

Repeat Steps 3–7 for each additional stitch.

## KNIT CAST-ON

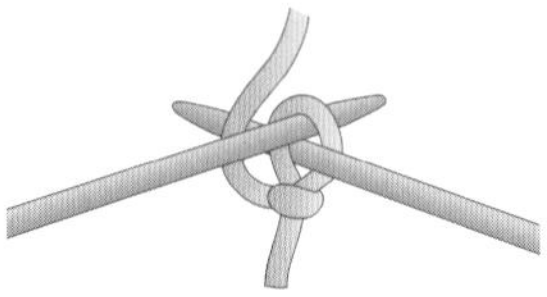

**1** Start with a slipknot on left needle (first cast-on stitch). Insert right needle into slipknot from front. Wrap yarn over right needle as if to knit.

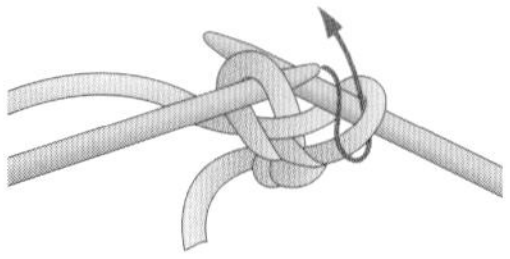

**2** Bring yarn through slipknot, forming a loop on right needle.
**3** Insert left needle **under loop** and slip loop off right needle. One additional stitch cast on.

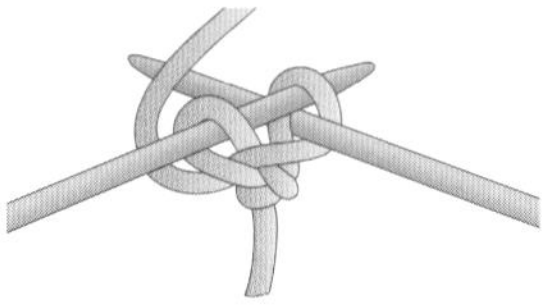

**4** Insert right needle into the last stitch on left needle as if to knit. Knit a stitch and transfer it to the left needle as in Step 3.
Repeat Step 4 for each additional stitch.

## 2-COLOR CAST-ON

With 1 strand each A and B held tog, make a slip knot on needle (this does not count as a stitch—it will be dropped).
**1** Arrange the yarn so that color A goes around the index finger and color B goes around the thumb. The yarn is held snuggly in the palm with the other 3 fingers.

**2** Bring the tip of the needle under the yarn that runs in front of the thumb.

**3** Bring a loop of the yarn from the index finger…

**4** …through the loop you just made of the thumb yarn.

**5** Release the loop from the thumb and snug it up to the needle.

**6** Bring color A yarn from the index finger under color B yarn and wrap it around the thumb; color B yarn will wrap around the index finger. Repeat Steps 2–5 once.

**7** Bring color A yarn from the thumb under color B yarn and wrap it around the index finger; color B yarn will wrap around the thumb. Repeat Steps 2–5 once.

**8** Repeat Steps 6 and 7 until the desired number of stitches is cast on (not including the slip knot). Undo the slip knot at end of first pattern row.

## TUBULAR CAST-ON

**1** Leaving a tail approximately 4 times the width of the cast-on, fold the yarn over a needle 3–4 sizes smaller than main needle (1–2 sizes smaller than ribbing needle). Bring yarn between fingers of left hand and wrap around little finger as shown. Secure loop on needle with right index finger throughout.

**2** Bring left thumb and index finger between strands, arranging so tail is on thumb side. Open thumb and finger so strands form a diamond. Take needle **over and behind index yarn.**

**4** Bring needle toward you, **in front of both yarns, under thumb yarn,** and up between the two yarns.

**6** Take needle over and behind index yarn. Repeat Steps 3–6.

**3** Bring needle **behind and under thumb yarn** then **under index yarn,** forming a purl stitch on needle.

**5** Bring needle **over** the **index yarn**. Bring index yarn **under thumb yarn,** forming a knit stitch on the needle.

**7** End with Step 3. Note that knit stitches alternate with purl stitches.

# CIRCULAR CAST-ONS

## JUDY'S MAGIC CAST-ON

**1** Hold yarn between 2 needles. Bring working yarn over top of ndl 2 to back. Bring tail yarn behind working yarn. (This will count as the first st on ndl 2.)

**2** Hold the yarn tail over the index finger and the working yarn over the thumb as shown.

**3** Bring ndl 1 over the yarn on finger,…

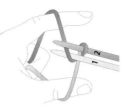

…around and under to make a loop on ndl 1. Pull the loop snug, but not tight. Each ndl has a st.

**4** To make a 2nd st on ndl 2, bring ndl 1 in front of the thumb yarn,…

…then bring ndl 2 under thumb yarn, catching it…

… and making a loop around ndl 2. Pull to snug.

**5** Repeat Steps 3 and 4 until you have the desired number of stitches cast on. You will end after Step 3, with an equal number on each ndl.

**6** Bring tail yarn down and around to the front of working yarn to secure it.

**Rnd 1 a.** Rotate the needles clockwise so that ndl 1 is on top,…

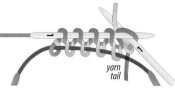

…slide stitches from ndl 2 to its cable; knit across stitches on ndl 1 using working yarn and other end of ndl 1…

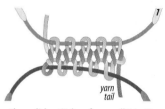

…then slide stitches from ndl 1 to its cable.

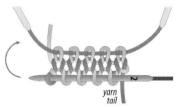

**b.** Slide sts from ndl 2 cable back to ndl. Rotate the needles clockwise again so that ndl 2 is on top and…

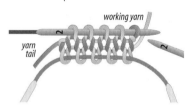

…knit across with other end of ndl 2 to complete rnd. Repeat *a* and *b* for each rnd.

## STRAIGHT WRAP CAST-ON

*Easiest on 2 circular needles or Magic Loop.*

**1** With tail coming to front between needles, wrap around both needles in counterclockwise direction, ending with ball yarn coming out to front between the needles.

**2** Slide bottom needle out to right leaving bottom stitches on cable setting up for ML. Work across the top sts. Take tail yarn down and around working yarn to secure last stitch.

**3** Rotate needles, slide sts from cable to needle tip and work across. Stitches on both needles are in a standard mount.

## CIRCLE CAST-ON

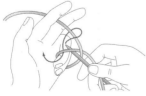

Use to cast on a few stitches at center of a flat circle.
**1** Holding tail in right hand and yarn in left hand, make a circle.
**2** Insert double-pointed needle in circle and draw yarn through, forming a stitch on needle. Do not remove fingers from loop.

**3** Bring needle under and then over the yarn, forming a yarn-over on needle.

**4** Repeat Steps 2 and 3, ending with Step 2. To cast on an even number, yarn over before beginning the first round.
**5** Arrange stitches on 3 or 4 double-pointed needles, pull tail slightly, then begin knitting around, working into the back loops of yarn-overs on the first round. Work several more rounds, then pull tail to close center.

# CROCHET

## SINGLE CROCHET (SC) —————

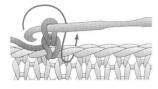

**1** Insert hook into a stitch, catch yarn, and pull up a loop. Catch yarn and pull through the loop on the hook.
**2** Insert hook into next stitch to the left.

**3** Catch yarn and pull through the stitch; 2 loops on hook.

**4** Catch yarn and pull through both loops on hook; 1 single crochet completed. Repeat Steps 2–4.

## BACKWARD SINGLE CROCHET, CRAB STITCH —————

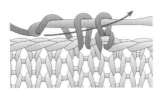

**1** Insert hook into a stitch, catch yarn, and pull up a loop. Catch yarn and pull a loop through the loop on the hook.
**2** Insert hook into next stitch to right.

**3** Catch yarn and pull through stitch only (as shown). As soon as hook clears the stitch, flip your wrist (and the hook). There are 2 loops on the hook, and the just-made loop is to the front of the hook (left of the old loop).

## DOUBLE CROCHET (DC) —————

**1** Insert hook into a stitch, catch yarn, and pull up a loop. Chain 3 (counts as first double crochet).
**2** Yarn over, insert hook into next stitch to the left (as shown). Catch yarn and pull through stitch only; 3 loops on hook.

**3** Catch yarn and pull through 2 loops on hook.

**4** Catch yarn and pull through remaining 2 loops on hook. Repeat Steps 2–4.

**4** Catch yarn and pull through both loops on hook; 1 backward single crochet completed.

**5** Continue working to the right, repeating Steps 2–4.

## CHAIN STITCH (CH ST, CH) —————

**1** Make a slipknot to begin.
**2** Catch yarn and draw through loop on hook.

First chain made. Repeat Step 2.

# TWISTS

## 1/1 RIGHT TWIST (1/1 RT) —————

**1** Bring right needle **in front of** first stitch on left needle. Knit second stitch but **do not remove** it from left needle.

**2** Knit first stitch.

**3** Pull both stitches off left needle. Completed 1/1 RT: 1 stitch crosses over 1 stitch and to the right. When worked with a cable needle, this is called a 1/1 Right Cross (1/1 RC).

## SLIP STITCH (SL ST) —————

**1** Insert the hook into a stitch, catch yarn, and pull up a loop.

**2** Insert hook into the next stitch to the left, catch yarn and pull through both the stitch and the loop on the hook; 1 loop on the hook. Repeat Step 2.

## 1/1 LEFT TWIST (1/1 LT) —————

**1** Bring right needle **behind** first stitch on left needle, and **to front between** first and second stitches. Knit second stitch, but **do not remove** it from left needle.

**2** Bring right needle to right and in front of first stitch and knit first stitch.

**3** Pull both stitches off left needle. Completed 1/1 LT: 1 stitch crosses over 1 stitch and to the left. When worked with a cable needle, this is called a 1/1 Left Cross (1/1 LC).

# DECREASES

## K2TOG

**1** Insert right needle into first 2 stitches on left needle, beginning with second stitch from end of left needle.

**2** Knit these 2 stitches together as if they were 1.
The result is a right-slanting decrease.

## P2TOG

**1** Insert right needle into first 2 stitches on left needle.

**2** Purl these 2 stitches together as if they were 1.
The result is a right-slanting decrease.

## K3TOG

**1** Insert right needle into first 3 stitches on left needle, beginning with third stitch from tip.
**2** Knit all 3 stitches together, as if they were 1.
The result is a right-slanting double decrease.

## SKP, SL 1-K1-PSSO

**1** Slip 1 stitch knitwise from left needle onto right.
**2** Knit 1 as usual.

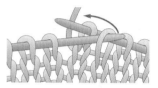

**3** Pass slipped stitch over knit stitch: 2 stitches become 1.

The result is a left-slanting decrease.

## SK2P, SL 1-K2TOG-PSSO

**1** Slip 1 stitch knitwise.
**2** Knit next 2 stitches together.
**3** Pass the slipped stitch over the k2tog: 3 stitches become 1; the right stitch is on top.
The result is a left-slanting double decrease.

## SSSK

Work same as **SSK** EXCEPT:
**1** Slip **3** stitches….
**2** Slip left needle into these 3 stitches… 3 stitches become 1.
The result is a left-slanting double decrease.

## SSK

**1** Slip 2 stitches **separately** to right needle as if to knit.

**2** Slip left needle into these 2 stitches from left to right and knit them together: 2 stitches become 1.

The result is a left-slanting decrease.

## SSP

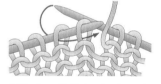

*Use instead of p2tog-tbl to avoid twisting the stitches.*

**1** Slip 2 stitches **separately** to right needle as if to knit.

**2** Slip these 2 stitches back onto left needle. Insert right needle through their 'back loops,' into the second stitch and then the first.

**3** Purl them together: 2 stitches become 1.

The result is a left-slanting decrease.

## SSSP

Work same as **SSP** EXCEPT:
**1** Slip **3** stitches….
**2** Slip these 3 stitches… into third stitch, then second, and then first.
**3**… 3 stitches become 1.
The result is a left-slanting double decrease.

## S2KP2, SL 2-K1-P2SSO

**1** Slip 2 stitches **together** to right needle as if to knit.

**2** Knit next stitch.

**3** Pass 2 slipped stitches over knit stitch and off right needle: 3 stitches become 1; the center stitch is on top.

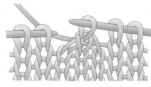

The result is a centered double decrease.

174

# INCREASES

## KNIT INTO FRONT AND BACK (KF&B)

**1** Knit into the front of next stitch on left needle, but do not pull the stitch off the needle.
**2** Take right needle to back, then knit through the back of the same stitch.

**3** Pull stitch off left needle. Completed increase: 2 stitches from 1 stitch. This increase results in a purl bump after the knit stitch.

## PURL INTO FRONT AND BACK (PF&B)

**1** Purl into front of next stitch, but do not pull stitch off needle.
**2** Take right needle to back, then through back of same stitch, from left to right…

**3** … and purl.

**4** Pull stitch off left needle. Completed increase: 2 stitches from 1 stitch. This increase results in a purl bump before the stitch on the right side.

## MAKE 1 RIGHT (M1R), KNIT

Insert left needle from back to front under strand between last stitch knitted and first stitch on left needle. Knit, twisting the strand by working into loop at front of the needle.

Completed M1R knit: a right-slanting increase.

## MAKE 1 LEFT (M1L), KNIT

Insert left needle from front to back under strand between last stitch knitted and first stitch on left needle. Knit, twisting strand by working into loop at back of needle.

Completed M1L knit: a left-slanting increase.

## MAKE 1 OPEN (M1O), KNIT

Insert left needle from front to back under strand between last stitch knitted and first stitch on left needle and knit it.

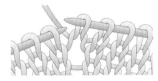

Completed M1O knit.

## MAKE 1 RIGHT (M1R), PURL

Work as for Make 1 Right, Knit, EXCEPT **purl.**

Completed M1R purl: a right-slanting increase.

## MAKE 1 LEFT (M1L), PURL

Insert left needle from front to back under strand between last stitch worked and first stitch on left needle. **Purl**, twisting strand by working into loop at back of needle from left to right.

Completed M1L purl: a left-slanting increase.

## MAKE 1 OPEN (M1O), PURL

Insert left needle from front to back under strand between last stitch worked and first stitch on left needle and purl it.

Completed M1O purl.

## LIFTED INCREASE, KNIT OR PURL

*Right lifted inc*

**Work increase before stitch**
Knit or purl into right loop of stitch in row below next stitch on left needle (1), then knit or purl into stitch on needle (2).

*Left lifted inc*

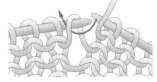

**Work increase after stitch**
Knit or purl next stitch on left needle, then knit or purl into left loop of stitch in row below this stitch (3).

# BIND-OFFS

## TUBULAR BIND-OFF FOR K1, P1 RIB (OR DOUBLE KNITS)

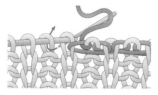  

Leave a long end of yarn, thread it in a blunt sewing needle. Assuming the first stitch is a knit stitch, bring yarn through it **as if to purl**, leave stitch on knitting needle.
**1** Take blunt needle **behind knit stitch**, between first 2 stitches, and

through purl stitch **as if to knit**. Leave stitches on knitting needle.
**2** Bring yarn around to front and through knit stitch **as if to knit**; pull stitch off knitting needle.

**3** Take blunt needle in front of purl stitch and through knit stitch **as if to purl**. Leave stitches on knitting needle.

**4** Bring yarn through purl stitch **as if to purl**; pull stitch off knitting needle.
**5** Repeat Steps 1–4. Adjust tension.

**Alternative method**
Divide the stitches onto 2 double-pointed needles: the knits on the front needle, the purls on the back needle.

## BIND OFF IN PATTERN

*k2, p2 rib bound off in pattern*     *k2, p2 rib bound off knitwise*

As you work the bind-off row for fabrics other than stockinette and garter stitch, knit or purl the stitches as the pattern requires. The bind-off (above left) is more attractive and flexible than in all-knit (above right).

## BIND OFF KNITWISE

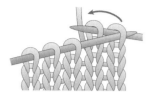 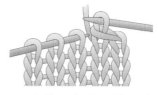

**1** Knit 2 stitches as usual.
**2** With left needle, pass first stitch on right needle over second stitch …

… and off needle: 1 stitch bound off (see above).
**3** Knit 1 more stitch.
**4** Pass first stitch over second. Repeat Steps 3–4.

*TIP*
• *Usually the bind-off should be as elastic as the rest of the knitting. To avoid binding off too tightly, bind off with a larger needle or use Suspended Bind-off.*

**FOR AN ELASTIC BIND-OFF, SEE PAGE 71.**

## EZ'S SEWN BIND-OFF

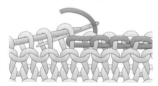 

Leave a long end of yarn and thread it in a blunt sewing needle.
**1** Insert blunt needle into next 2 stitches **as if to purl** and pull through, leaving stitches on knitting needle.

**2** Insert blunt needle into first stitch **as if to knit** and pull stitch off knitting needle.
Repeat Steps 1–2.

## BIND OFF PURLWISE

Work Steps 1–4 of **Bind off Knitwise** EXCEPT, **purl** the stitches instead of knitting them.

## SUSPENDED BIND-OFF

This method makes it very difficult to bind off too tightly.
**1** Work (knit or purl) 2 stitches.
**2** With left needle, pass first stitch on right needle over second stitch, but leave on left needle.

**3** Work next stitch (shown above).
**4** Slip both stitches from left needle. Repeat Steps 2–4.

## FASTEN OFF

Work bind-off until only 1 stitch remains on right needle. If this is the last stitch of a row, cut yarn and fasten off stitch as shown above. Otherwise, this is the first stitch of the next section of knitting.

## 3-NEEDLE BIND-OFF

***Bind-off ridge on wrong side***
**1** With stitches on 2 needles, place **right sides together**. * Knit 2 stitches together (1 from front needle and 1 from back needle, as shown); repeat from * once more.
**2** With left needle, pass first stitch on right needle over second stitch and off right needle.

**3** Knit next 2 stitches together.
**4** Repeat Steps 2 and 3, end by drawing yarn through last stitch.

***Bind-off ridge on right side***
Work as for ridge on wrong side, EXCEPT, with **wrong sides together**.

# MISC

## REFINED SHORT ROWS WRAP & TURN (W&T)

Each short row adds 2 rows of knitting across a section of the work. Since the work is turned before completing a row, stitches must be wrapped at the turn to prevent holes. Wrap and turn as follows:

### Knit side

**1** With yarn in back, slip next stitch as if to purl. Bring yarn to front of work and slip stitch back to left needle (as shown). Turn work.
**2** With yarn in front, slip next stitch as if to purl. Work to end.

**3** When you come to the wrap on a following knit row, hide the wrap by knitting it together with the stitch it wraps.

### Purl side

**1** With yarn in front, slip next stitch as if to purl. Bring yarn to back of work and slip stitch back to left needle (as shown). Turn work.
**2** With yarn in back, slip next stitch as if to purl. Work to end.

**3** When you come to the wrap on a following purl row, hide the wrap by purling it together with the stitch it wraps.

## SHAPING SHORT-ROW SOCK HEELS

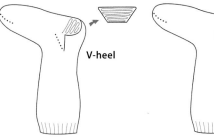

**V-heel**

**Hourglass heel**

Short rows begin at end of heel flap and lengthen to full width of heel.

Rows shorten from full width of heel then lengthen to full width of heel.

## KNITTING-IN BEADS OR SEQUINS

Using a loop of thread or fine wire, string required number of beads (or sequins) on yarn.

Slip bead up to back of work. As you knit the stitch, bring bead through to front of work and between stitches.

## DRAWING-ON A BEAD OR SEQUIN

**1** Knit the stitch you want to carry the bead. Insert a small crochet hook through the bead. (The bead's hole has to be big enough and the hook small enough.)

**2** With the hook, pull the stitch off the needle and through the hole of the bead.

**3** Replace the stitch on the needle, being careful not to twist it.

**4** Tighten the yarn and continue.

Sequins and paillettes can be added in the same way.

## WEAVING THE CARRIES

The carried yarn is woven alternately above and below the working yarn on the purl side of the work. Weaving the carries results in a firmer fabric than stranding does.

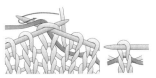

### From the knit side

To weave the carry above a knit stitch: Insert needle into stitch and under woven yarn, then knit the stitch as usual.

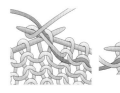

To weave the carry below a knit stitch: Insert needle into stitch and over woven yarn, then knit the stitch as usual.

### From the purl side

To weave the carry above a purl stitch: Insert needle into stitch and under woven yarn, then purl the stitch as usual.

To weave the carry below a purl stitch: Insert needle into stitch and over woven yarn, then purl the stitch as usual.

## TWISTED CORD

*1* Cut strands 6 times the length of cord needed. Fold in half and knot cut ends together.
*2* Place knotted end over a door knob or hook and right index finger in folded end, then twist cord tightly.

*3* Fold cord in half, smoothing as it twists on itself. Pull knot through original fold to secure.

## GRAFT IN STOCKINETTE

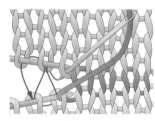

## ON THE NEEDLES

*1* Arrange stitches on 2 needles as shown.
*2* Thread a blunt needle with matching yarn (approximately 1" per stitch).
*3* Working from right to left, with right sides facing you, begin with Steps 3a and 3b:
*3a Front needle:* bring yarn through first stitch **as if to purl**, leave stitch **on needle.**
*3b Back needle:* bring yarn through first stitch **as if to knit**, leave stitch **on needle.**
*4a Front needle:* bring yarn through first stitch **as if to knit**, **slip off** needle; through next stitch **as if to purl**, leave stitch **on needle**.

*4b Back needle:* bring yarn through first stitch **as if to purl**, **slip off** needle; through next stitch **as if to knit**, leave stitch **on needle**.
Repeat Steps 4a and 4b until 1 stitch remains on each needle.
*5a Front needle:* bring yarn through stitch **as if to knit**, slip **off needle**.
*5b Back needle:* bring yarn through stitch **as if to purl**, slip **off needle**.
*6* Adjust tension to match rest of knitting.

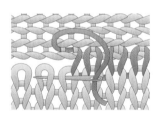

*Graft live stitches to rows*
Compensate for different stitch and row gauges by occasionally picking up 2 bars (as shown above), instead of 1.

*GRAFTING*
*An invisible method of joining live stitches. Useful at sock toes; also called Kitchener stitch.*

## INSERTING ZIPPER

Sewing a zipper into a knit can seem daunting to the uninitiated. Although the knitted fabric has stretch, the zipper does not, and the two must be joined as neatly as possible to prevent ripples. Follow these steps for a smooth installation.

*1* Measure the length of the opening. Select a zipper the length of the opening in the color of your choice. If you can't find that exact length, choose one that is a bit longer.
*2* Pre-shrink your zipper in the method you will use to clean the garment. Wash and dry it or carefully steam it (you don't want to melt the teeth if they are plastic or nylon).
*3* Place the zipper in opening, aligning each side. Allow extra length to extend beyond neck.
*4* Pin in place. Be generous with the pins, and take all the time you need. Extra care taken here makes the next steps easier.
*5* Baste in place. When you are satisfied with the placement, remove the pins.
*6* Sew in the zipper, making neat, even stitches that are firm enough to withstand use.
*7* Sew a stop at end of zipper and clip excess off if necessary.
*8* If the zipper extends beyond the opening, trim extra length.

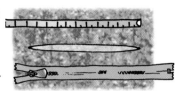

Measure

Pin

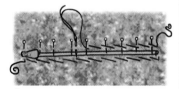

Baste

Sew In

*CC* contrasting color
*cn* cable needle
*cm* centimeter(s)
*dec* decreas(e)(ed)(es)(ing)
*dpn* double-pointed needle(s)
*g* gram(s)
*"* inch(es)
*inc* increas(e)(ed)(es)(ing)
*k* knit(ting)(s)(ted)
*LH* left-hand
*M1* Make one stitch (increase)
*m* meter(s)
*mm* millimeter(s)
*MC* main color
*oz* ounce(s)
*p* purl(ed)(ing)(s) or page
*pm* place marker
*psso* pass slipped stitch(es) over
*RH* right-hand
*RS* right side(s)
*sc* single crochet
*sl* slip(ped)(ping)
*SKP* slip, knit, psso
*SSK* slip, slip, knit these 2 sts tog
*SSP* slip, slip, purl these 2 sts tog
*st(s)* stitch(es)
*tbl* through back of loop(s)
*tog* together
*WS* wrong side(s)
*wyib* with yarn in back
*wyif* with yarn in front
*x* times
*yd(s)* yard(s)
*yo* yarn over

## WORKING FROM CHARTS

**Charts** are graphs or grids of squares that represent the right side of knitted fabric. They illustrate every stitch and the relationship between the rows of stitches.
**Squares** contain knitting symbols.
**The key** defines each symbol as an operation to make a stitch or stitches.

**The pattern** provides any special instructions for using the chart(s) or the key.
**The numbers** along the sides of charts indicate the rows. A number on the right side marks a right-side row that is worked leftward from the number. A number on the left marks a wrong-side row that is worked rightward. Since

many stitches are worked differently on wrong-side rows, the key will indicate that. If the pattern is worked circularly, all rows are right-side rows and worked from right to left.
**Bold lines** within the graph represent repeats. These set off a group of stitches that are repeated across a row. You begin at the edge of a row or

where the pattern indicates for the required size, work across to the second line, then repeat the stitches between the repeat lines as many times as directed, and finish the row.

# Specifications: At a Glance

**easy +**

**A** 8"
**B** 9"

10cm/4"

26  32

over stockinette stitch

1 2 **3** 4 5 6

Light weight
**A** 200 yds
**B** 40 yds

Double pointed needles
Four 3.5mm/US 4
or size to obtain gauge

**&**

cable needle
stitch holder

Shown in
*ARTYARNS* Regal Silk
in color 250 (A),
Beaded Silk and Sequins
in color 250S (B)

**Skill level**
*We add a plus sign and an extra colored box if the project uses a technique that may be unfamiliar.*

**Size**
*Sock measurements*

**Gauge**
*The number of stitches and rows you need in 10 cm or 4", worked as specified.*

**Yarn weight**
*And amount in yards.*

**Type of needles**
*Straight, unless circular or double-pointed are recommended.*

**Any extras**

**Original yarn**

## SIZING

Measure around the ball of your foot to find your size, our **A** measurement. Work foot to your **B** measurement.

| Children | Infant | S | M | L |
|---|---|---|---|---|
| Shoe Size | 0 to 4 | 4 to 7 | 7 to 10 | 10 to 2 |
| **A** Foot Circumference | 4½ | 5½ | 6 | 6½ |
| **B** Foot Length | 4 | 5 | 6 | 7½ |

| Women's | S | M | L |
|---|---|---|---|
| Shoe Size | 3 to 6 | 6 to 9 | 9 to 12 |
| **A** Foot Circumference | 7 | 8 | 9 |
| **B** Foot Length | 9 | 10 | 11 |

| Men's | S | M | L |
|---|---|---|---|
| Shoe Size | 6 to 8 | 8½ to 10 | 10½ to 12 |
| **A** Foot Circumference | 7 | 8 | 9 |
| **B** Foot Length | 9½ | 10½ | 11 |

## YARN WEIGHT

|  1 | 2 | 3 | 4 | 5 | 6 |
|---|---|---|---|---|---|
| **Super Fine** | **Fine** | **Light** | **Medium** | **Bulky** | **Super Bulky** |

**Also called**

| Sock Fingering Baby | Sport Baby | DK Light-Worsted | Worsted Afghan Aran | Chunky Craft Rug | Bulky Roving |
|---|---|---|---|---|---|

**Stockinette Stitch Gauge Range 10cm/4 inches**

| 27 sts to 32 sts | 23 sts to 26 sts | 21 sts to 24 sts | 16 sts to 20 sts | 12 sts to 15 sts | 6 sts to 11 sts |
|---|---|---|---|---|---|

**Recommended needle (metric)**

| 2.25 mm to 3.25 mm | 3.25 mm to 3.75 mm | 3.75 mm to 4.5 mm | 4.5 mm to 5.5 mm | 5.5 mm to 8 mm | 8 mm and larger |
|---|---|---|---|---|---|

**Recommended needle (US)**

| 1 to 3 | 3 to 5 | 5 to 7 | 7 to 9 | 9 to 11 | 11 and larger |
|---|---|---|---|---|---|

Locate the Yarn Weight and Stockinette Stitch Gauge Range over 10cm to 4" on the chart. Compare that range with the information on the yarn label to find an appropriate yarn. These are guidelines only for commonly used gauges and needle sizes in specific yarn categories.

## NEEDLE & HOOK SIZES

| US | MM | HOOK |
|---|---|---|
| 0 | 2 | A |
| 1 | 2.25 | B |
| 1½ | 2.5 | |
| 2 | 2.75 | C |
| 2½ | 3 | |
| 3 | 3.25 | D |
| 4 | 3.5 | E |
| 5 | 3.75 | F |
| 6 | 4 | G |
| 7 | 4.5 | 7 |
| 8 | 5 | H |
| 9 | 5.5 | I |
| 10 | 6 | J |
| 10½ | 6.5 | K |
| 11 | 8 | L |
| 13 | 9 | M |
| 15 | 10 | N |
| 17 | 12.75 | |

## WEIGHT CONVERSIONS

| ¾ oz | 20 g |
|---|---|
| 1 oz | 28 g |
| 1½ oz | 40 g |
| 1¾ oz | 50 g |
| 2 oz | 60 g |
| 3½ oz | 100 g |

## MEASUREMENT CONVERSIONS

| | **X** | | **=** | |
|---|---|---|---|---|
| centimeters | | 0.394 | | inches |
| grams | | 0.035 | | ounces |
| inches | | 2.54 | | centimeters |
| ounces | | 28.6 | | grams |
| meters | | 1.1 | | yards |
| yards | | .91 | | meters |

# contributors